Post-Conflict Tajikistan

Post-Soviet, post-conflict Tajikistan is an under-studied and poorly understood case in conflict studies literature. Since 2000 this Central Asian state has seen major political violence end, countrywide order emerge and the peace agreement between the parties of the 1990s civil war hold. Superficially, Tajikistan appears to be a case of successful international intervention for liberal peacebuilding, yet the Tajik peace is characterised by authoritarian governance.

Via discourse analysis and extensive fieldwork, including participant observation with international organisations, the author examines how peacebuilding is understood and practised in Tajikistan. The book challenges received wisdom that peacebuilding is a process of democratisation or institutionalisation, showing how interventions have inadvertently served to facilitate an increasingly authoritarian peace and fostered popular accommodation and avoidance strategies. Chapters investigate assistance to political parties and elections, the security sector and community development, and illustrate how transformative aims are thwarted whilst 'success' is simulated for an audience of international donors. At the same time the book charts the emergence of a legitimate order with properties of authority, sovereignty and livelihoods.

Providing a challenge to the theoretical literature on peacebuilding and a first-ever research monograph of post-conflict peacebuilding in this under-studied case, this book will be of interest to academics working on Peace Studies, International Relations and Central Asian Studies.

John Heathershaw is Lecturer in International Relations at the University of Exeter. His research interests include the politics of aid, development, peacebuilding and security assistance, with a focus on Central Asia.

Central Asian studies series

Post-Conflict Tajikistan

The politics of peacebuilding and the emergence of legitimate order

John Heathershaw

Routledge
Taylor & Francis Group

LONDON AND NEW YORK

First published 2009
by Routledge
2 Park Square, Milton Park, Abingdon, Oxon OX14 4RN

Simultaneously published in the USA and Canada
by Routledge
270 Madison Ave, New York, NY 10016

Routledge is an imprint of the Taylor & Francis Group, an informa business

© 2009 John Heathershaw

Typeset in Times by Wearset Ltd, Boldon, Tyne and Wear

British Library Cataloguing in Publication Data
A catalogue record for this book is available from the British Library

Library of Congress Cataloging in Publication Data
A catalog record for this book has been requested

ISBN10: 0-415-48403-0 (hbk)
ISBN10: 0-203-87921-X (ebk)

ISBN13: 978-0-415-48403-9 (hbk)
ISBN13: 978-0-203-87921-4 (ebk)

Contents

Preface

'Well, I'm not sure a bad election is good for peacebuilding.' This was the remark of a senior officer of the OSCE election observation mission on discovering the topic of my research. It was 1 March 2005, two days after Tajikistan's parliamentary elections, the second since the general peace agreement of 1997. I was listening to the perspectives of fellow observers on what had been peaceful but decidedly uncompetitive elections. What did this acute fusion of the non-violent and the non-democratic mean for post-conflict Tajikistan? The initial report of the observation team had praised the lack of violence and had couched concerns about official interference in typically formulaic and diplomatic language. Behind closed doors, many were more sanguine. The somewhat defensive tone and explicit scepticism which coloured these remarks struck me as significant. They seemed significant not for their half-hearted defence of the public protestations of the international community that Tajikistan must choose democracy, but for their uncertainty that this was even the right question to be asking. I too was *not sure*, and remain so, about what should or would be the future for post-conflict Tajikistan. Moreover, I felt that in our ambivalence, the election monitors and I were accompanied by most if not all of those in the international community, in Tajikistan's political elite, and in the population. What, I was led to ask, are the implications of this disaffection towards our description and prescription of peacebuilding and our understanding of peace as a value, ideal and state of affairs.

There are many who have assisted, advised and otherwise helped since I began researching Tajikistan in 2001. Mark Hoffman provided consistent encouragement and support for my ideas throughout my dissertation research. At the LSE, I was fortunate to be among a peer group of extremely able PhD students including Antoine Bousquet, Douglas Bulloch, Stacy Closson and Steffi Ortmann. I received helpful comments from scholars of peace studies at the Kroc Institute, Notre Dame, where I conducted post-doctoral work. Particularly insightful have been remarks from Scott Appleby, Jennie Burnet, John Darby, David Montgomery, Svetlana Peshkova and Peter Wallensteen.

I am profoundly in debt to the American University–Central Asia (AUCA) in Bishkek, Kyrgyzstan, where I taught from 2001 to 2003. Countless colleagues and students provided invaluable comments, questions and responses, including

Gulnara Aitpaeva, Askat Dukenbaev, Emilbek Juraev, Timerlan Moldogaziev and Burul Usmonilieva. My knowledge of Tajikistan was enriched by participants in my directed reading classes of 2001 and 2002, in particular Davlatsulton Dorgabekova, Shodi Abdulvasiev, Bakhtiyor Naimov, Boris Pilipenko, Muzaffar Suleymanov and Zamira Yusufjonova. I was also privileged to supervise or read in their formative stages the studies of several honours students including those of Said Yakhoyev, Abdujalil Abdurasulov, Lena Rotoklya, Tolgonai Berdikiyeva, Anara Karugolova and Nodira Inoyatova.

Across the region I was reminded of the extent of Central Asia's diversity. I witnessed violence, looting and gunshots whilst on fieldwork, but not in Tajikistan. I experienced the events of the 'Tulip Revolution' of March 2005 when Kyrgyzstani friends battled to preserve human life and dignity whilst others battled for power. On 13 May 2005, I was privileged to receive the hospitality and protection of the staff of Mercy Corps in Ferghana, Uzbekistan, as many less fortunate souls died at the hands of fellow citizens and their own government in the neighbouring town of Andijon. These events endowed me with a sense of the dramatic immeasurability of events, an awareness of the privileges and powerlessness of the foreigner, and a realisation that we are all students of Central Asia. I am in debt to numerous colleagues who have affirmed that genuine expertise demands a willingness to listen to the voices of others. These include, amongst others, Christine Bichsel, Tim Epkenhans, Matteo Fumagalli, Michael Hall, Alisher Ilkhamov, Morgan Liu, Anna Matveeva, Nick Megoran, Madeleine Reeves, Daniel Stevens, Chad Thompson, Stina Torjesen, Tomasso Trevisiani, Gert Jan Veldwisch and Gunda Weigman.

My fieldwork in Tajikistan received supplementary financial support from the ESRC and the Cambridge Committee for Central and Inner Asia. I was invaluably supported by working, discussing and living with numerous colleagues and friends in Tajikistan. In 2005, research assistance was skillfully provided by Alexander Sadikov, Otabek Sindarov and Bakhtiyor Naimov. In 2007, I conducted research alongside Parviz Mullojanov, an insightful and talented colleague. The staff of Mercy Corps were a pleasure to work with, especially Adrian, Amanda, Colin, Faiz, Faizali, Iveta, Jeff, Justin, Kevin, Mohira, Rustam and Zebo. The staff members of international agencies and institutions were unfailingly generous. In particular I must thank Rahmonali Bobokhonov, Davlatyor Jumakhonov, Mirza Jahani, Suhrob Kaharov, Zainiddin Karaev, Jan Malekzade, Daniel Passon and Suhrob Shoyev. Together these relationships with international workers gave me a greater understanding of the particular ways in which the discursive practices of international peacebuilding depart from the formal discourses of donors. I furthermore benefited tremendously from the insights of many Tajikistani experts including Rashid Abdullo, Jumahon Alimi, Turko Dikayev, Muzaffar Olimov, Saodat Olimova, Ibrohim Usmonov and Mukhibullo Zubaidulloev.

Special mention must go to numerous residents of Tajikistan who brought to my attention the richness of social life in the country. The hospitality proffered by Cully and Julie, Jeff and Kate, Heather and David, and Ed and Ruth was so generous as to be almost Tajiki. Bunafsha taught Tajik language and much more besides to my wife and me. Rustam's 'culture shock' in the Rasht Valley reminded me that one doesn't have to be a foreign citizen to feel on the 'outside' of a community or nation, and of the profound differences between urban and rural life in Central Asia. Khairullo and the residents of Kizil Ketmen gave me hope that international assistance could 'work' in some respects if it was sufficiently reliant on local knowledge and experiences. Khurshed, Zarina and Parvina in Kulob welcomed my wife and me into their family and in doing so taught us some of the complexities of Tajik home-life. The residents of Dombrachi affirmed that poverty begets generosity. The voters of the Rasht valley's routine enactment of 'democratic participation' provided me with the most vivid example of how little elections actually matter to the course of everyday life in Tajikistan. These relationships and experiences enhanced this book and reminded me of its limitations as a product of my own limited knowledge.

Finally, my close family and friends provided welcome reminders that there's more to life than research. My mum and dad, Pam and Dave, have been unstinting in their love, support and desire to understand what on earth I'm doing. My sister, Helen, and daughter, Grace, remind me of the importance of not taking everything seriously. My wife, Julia, has compensated for my failings in so many ways other than merely being a keen editor and critic of my work. Her readiness to travel with me on my fieldwork made my experiences richer and more reflective.

It is to my family, in the many meanings of the word, that this book is dedicated.

Notes on sources and transliteration

Data were collected in five languages – English, Russian, Tajik, and, on a small number of occasions, Uzbek and Kyrgyz (the latter three largely through translation). I transliterate textual examples from Tajik and Russian using the Library of Congress system or transliteration. For place and person names I have tried to adopt versions most commonly used and/or recognisable in English. In addition, I mark foreign text in *italics*. In cases of commonly used words I do not use italics. All are included in a glossary.

Transcribed interviews are referenced in the text and included in the bibliography. Other interviews, group interviews and survey data are referenced in endnotes. Some informant names have been changed; this is done sometimes at the request of the informant, sometimes at my discretion (on occasions when I feel the way I am using the text – e.g. to indicate dissenting comment – might compromise an informant in their community). Such cases are clearly indicated in the endnote, e.g. 'Interview with international official, Dushanbe, May 2005'.

Unless otherwise indicated, all quotations are verbatim. Transcripts and audio recordings of these interviews in their original language are held by the author for reference purposes. Other quotes are taken from documentary sheets, questionnaires or handwritten notes of interviews. These were used when data were gathered as part of an international programme evaluation, where tape-recording was refused by the informant or was impossible due to technical problems or excessive background noise. Press sources are cited with abbreviated references. A list of sources and abbreviations thereof can be found in the appendix.

1   Introduction

Just as political science is about two problems – the use of power and the legitimation of the use of power – violence studies are about two problems: the use of
violence and the legitimation of that use.

(Galtung 1990: 291)

Every established order tends to produce (to very different degrees and with very
different means) *the naturalisation of its own arbitrariness.*

(Bourdieu 1977: 164)

In Tajikistan there is some kind of peace. More ambiguously still, the environment
is said to be 'post-conflict'. Although its war, which began in 1992, formally ended
with a general peace agreement of 1997, significant political violence continued
until 2001. Since then the last armed groups and independent commanders have
been eradicated or expelled. The incumbent regime faces no substantive opposition, neither military nor political. Social and economic life, whilst remaining des-
perately poor, improved considerably in the early part of the 2000s. Tajikistan's
history since independence has been dominated by war-making, peace-making and
peacebuilding. How this conflict was transformed is one of the great stories of
post-Soviet Central Asia. In this study I investigate how peace came to Tajikistan,
and particularly how external actors have contributed to that process through their
approach of international peacebuilding. In doing so, I pursue a political analysis
of the emergence of legitimate order in Tajikistan's international, national and
local spaces in the years since 2000. That is, I examine the contending discourses
and practices of building peace in post-conflict Tajikistan.

Post-conflict Tajikistan

Today no one seems to be able to explain with any great conviction or credibility
either the why (what caused) or the how (what constitutes) of peace in Tajikistan.
There is no single authoritative account of the civil war; there are no open academic or political debates over the whys and wherefores. Most of the military
battles, human costs, and social and political implications are partially known or

overlooked. Ordinary Tajikistanis are loath to dwell on the events of conflict. Their leaders merely repeat the mantras of peace and stability. Both leaders and citizens often reduce 'peace' to the June 1997 peace agreement between the government, under President Rahmon[1], and the opposition, under Said Abdullo Nuri. Building peace here becomes the process of achieving and adhering to a formal agreement between leaders. Even those more sanguine about the bargains struck behind the scenes are prone to focus on the elite-level process for compromise (Barnes and Abdullaev 2001). As I was told by one Tajikistani political scientist, 'John, it's all about elites!' This extremely thin description is nevertheless posited by many scholars, policy-makers, and representatives of the parties as an example which the world can learn from (contributions in Seifert and Kraikemayer 2003). However, one must ask: what is the world to learn? Are we to assume that a common interest, between elites and their followers, was attained and maintained throughout? Are we to imagine that a single idea or conception of peace is followed, or at least tolerated, by all? Are Tajiks of all regional groups, genders and ages bound to a single elite pact which shapes their consent to the authority of the state? The implicit and at times explicit answer to these questions by Tajikistan's political leaders is in the affirmative – that Tajikistan is united, it has overcome, it is sovereign. Such accounts have a tautological quality: we have peace because we have peace.

It is hardly surprising that this explanation is unconvincing to practitioners and analysts of international peacebuilding who have been sceptical about the durability of Tajikistan's peace (Schoeberlein 2002; Lynch 2001; Hall 2002; Collins 2003; ICG 2001a). However, sceptics have few resources with which to explore the nature of peace when this peace does not conform to the ideal of the 'liberal peace' (Paris 1997). International, English-language analyses have consistently seen peace (in Tajikistan) in terms of a dichotomy where the peril of further conflict can only be avoided through the promise of democratisation (Bertram 1995; Sisk 2001; OSI 1999: 84). Yet Tajikistan's experience with peacebuilding refuses to abide by this peril/promise dichotomy as its peace has proved durable while its government has become increasingly authoritarian. It remains a case which is not explained by the literature on peacebuilding (Heathershaw 2005a; Nakaya 2008: 1).

Analysts have proposed various partial explanations for this puzzle or paradox. 'War weariness' (Schoeberlein 2002), the effects of labour migration (Olimova and Bosc 2003) and cultural passivity (Olimova and Bowyer 2002) are all suggested as reasons why Tajikistan remains without violence yet authoritarian. Others have suggested that warlord politics continues to characterise Tajikistan (Dadmehr 2003; Nourzhanov 2005). More recently scholars have begun to examine international assistance as a possible factor behind Tajikistan's move to post-conflict authoritarianism, emphasising the role of Russia and regional powers (Jonson 2006), or failures in international financial and development assistance which fostered a new oligarchy (Nakaya 2008).

There is some truth to each of these aspects, yet they are incomplete. These factors in themselves do not explain how or why Tajikistan's peace has held despite the fact that international assistance has failed to bring about a liberal peace. Moreover, the success of Tajikistan in avoiding further war is more than a historical anomaly or a temporary reprieve, and the lack of progress in democratisation more than a matter of impatience with an inevitably long-term process of transition. The paradigms used by internationals, leaders and citizens to capture the character of Tajikistan's peace are all, to varying degrees, partial and potentially deceptive. The approach I offer below is also not without flaws. However, popular and elite representations cannot merely be cast aside by the social scientist in favour of better explanations based perhaps on economic networks or informal political institutions. Rather, a better explanation must take account of the work that these discourses do – their reductions, oversights, affirmations and negations – in producing and reproducing social realities of peace. It is this peace which internationals, elites and subordinates together make and remake. This raises questions of peace which go beyond the case of Tajikistan.

The politics of peacebuilding

Students of peacebuilding have become increasingly aware of how actually existing peace departs from the ideal posited in international discourse. Models of third-party international peacebuilding in themselves tell us little about how peacebuilding is practised, by what means it holds, and by what means it fails under conflict and the resumption of widespread violence.[2] In many cases conflict between elites is merely frozen until some point in the future – as in other post-Soviet cases such as Transdniestr, Nagorno-Karabakh, Abkhazia and South Ossetia (Lynch 2004). Even in places such as Tajikistan where conflict is *transformed* – in the sense that a return to war over similar issues and amongst similar actors is unthinkable for the foreseeable future – the liberal peace provides a misleading frame. It is descriptively unconvincing, conceptually unenlightening and normatively uninspiring.

Both Paris (1997, 2001) and Doyle and Sambanis (2000) began with a critical perspective on international peacebuilding before offering major reformist reworkings of the liberal peace. Paris (2004) offered a revised version which emphasises institution-building before transition to a market economy and liberal polity which he labels Institutionalisation Before Liberalisation (IBL). Doyle and Sambanis (2006) similarly, yet in a defence of the practice of UN peacebuilding, argued for the selection of ecologies of transitional authority based upon a calculation of three variables: hostility, local capacities and international capacities. Both of these works have been widely received as major steps forward in the conceptualisation of peacebuilding, particularly from the policy community. However, such enthusiastic responses merely seem to indicate the weakness of the field of inquiry. Paris, for example, offers an extremely thin and formalistic reading of institutions in IBL, which are equated to the laws and organs of state (2004: 205–207). No attempt is made to understand the informal institutional structures which, whilst largely impenetratable to international actors, may determine who reaps and rules in practice. In Doyle and Sambanis, the UN is assumed to have authority and legitimacy simply by virtue of its status as the global organisation (2006: 13, 347). In both texts assumptions are made about the normative or 'soft' power and agency of international actors (conceived as 'third-parties') to generate fundamental political, economic and social change in the conflicting others. These assumptions are entirely consistent with two axioms which have limited the study of peacebuilding since its inception. First, it is taken for granted that building peace is about building broadly liberal-democratic institutions, at the level of state and/or civil society, *within* the post-conflict society in question. Here a clear boundary between national and international politics is established. Second, it is commonly accepted that the external role is one of a benign *third party*. These two axioms characterise the discourse of international peacebuilding of which Paris and Doyle and Sambanis offer merely graduated versions of a (neo-)liberal peace (Richmond 2005; Heathershaw 2008a: 616–618).

My interest here is not in the degree of international peacebuilding's impact on national parties but the nature of peacebuilding as a political process involving multiple parties, discourses and practices. In this I am inspired by an emerging critical literature on peace operations which has largely developed in Europe over the last decade. There are two distinct critiques which are relevant here. A first set of scholars has undertaken political economy analyses to expose the looting, resource capture and less conspicuous forms of larceny (e.g. faulty privatisation) that exist in the onset, continuation and aftermath of war. The Collier–Hoeffler (C–H) model of civil war onset (Collier *et al.* 2003; Collier and Sambanis 2005) is the most influential and comprehensive effort to theorise 'Greed'. According to the C–H model, insurgents can be considered criminals – indistinguishable from bandits and pirates. War here is, to innovate on Clausewitz, the continuation of economics by other means (Keen 2000b: 27). This rather reductive argument for greed over grievance has been heavily criticised, from both quantitative analysts (Sambanis 2005) and those who favour more qualitative approaches (Berdal 2005). Kalyvas labels the greed contention 'tautological' in that 'violence is used because "it pays"', noting that general, macro-level explanations are 'pitched at too high a level of generality' (2006: 388). Not withstanding these concerns, political economy approaches have been important in highlighting the importance of shadow economic relationships in the constitution of both war and peace. In Tajikistan, we see these with respect to spurious privatisation and land reforms which characterise the new order.

Writers influenced by post-structuralism have sought to address a different question, one concerned with the politico-symbolic significance of international intervention and peace operations (Weber 1995; Debrix 1999; Hansen 2006). Debrix regards UN peacekeeping practice as simulation where the world body presents a façade of 'riot control' (1999: 5). Peacekeeping is not hegemonic in that it achieves or represents its ostensible goals. Rather, it is hegemonic because it is able to simulate them. In this sense Debrix argues,

> Peacekeeping does not represent (disciplinary) liberal ideology. Once again, it simulates it. Peacekeeping depicts a fantasy space or dream land of inter-

national affairs (where peacekeeping operations are successful, governance is realised, etc.) inside which claims to neoliberalism on a global scale can be made.

(Debrix 1999: 216)

The work of Debrix in particular illustrates that while international peacebuilding may fail in its transformative goals, this is not to say that it does not serve a purpose for its producers. In this performative discourse, UN peacekeeping claims legitimate authority for international intervention and oversight. They thus produce a fantasy alternative to the liberal-democratic peace, a 'virtual liberal peace' (Richmond and Franks 2007: 30). In Tajikistan we see this in the simulation of opposition political parties, border management and community self-government under international peacebuilding.

A small collection of scholars has begun to bridge the divide between analyses of the political economy of peace and those of the virtual world of international peace operations (Duffield 2002; Pugh 2003; Richmond 2005). Some have taken an anthropological approach in order to explore the micro-politics of international peacebuilding and development assistance and the economies of exploitation which they sustain or challenge (Nordstrom 2004; Richards 2005). This requires a broadening of the anthropological lens beyond the particular relationships and practices of a given community to those of the production of policy and practice by the international community. As Duffield notes, the global South, becomes 'a mirror which reflects policy decisions and aid fashions that have been formulated elsewhere' (2002: 264). In this sense it involves 'political rivalry and alliance not only within institutions but between them as well' (ibid.). This study provides glimpses of the politics of peacebuilding which Duffield is alluding to in order to answer the two puzzles of this study: how peacebuilding, despite its deceptions, lives on; and, second, how peace holds. But these questions are not really separable. In order to understand the role of international peacebuilding we need to inform our analysis of it in terms of some theoretical reflection on peace.

Peace as legitimate order

The concept of peace has a much longer history. While peacebuilding, including the UN's 'post-conflict peacebuilding' (Boutros-Ghali 1992), only entered policymaking and academic discourse following the end of the Cold War, there is a much greater heritage to the concept of peace. Peace, like peacebuilding, is essentially both normative and descriptive. In these terms, Boulding (1964) and Galtung (1969) have made a profound and lasting if problematic contribution to the study of peace with the distinction between 'negative' and 'positive' peace. While negative peace marks the end of physical violence, it is positive peace which signifies the end of structural violence (Galtung 1969: 183). This conceptual dualism in peace studies remains the standard, accepted by most scholars in the field. For example, Doyle and Sambanis' study restates the dichotomy in terms of sovereign and participatory peace (2006: 18). Critical analysts have shunned Galtung's positivist methods yet retained the radical impulse of his definitions of positive peace and extend it to include, for example, the emancipation of humanity from 'interpretative violence against *otherness*' (Patomäki 2001: 723–737), or the practising of 'communicative action' which transcends power relations (Jabri 1996). However, perhaps few democratic polities, let alone post-conflict settings, would meet these criteria for positive peace. Galtung's work itself is replete with demonstrations as to how places where physical violence is limited are beset by structural and cultural violence (esp. 1975). Yet if all actually existing examples of peace take various forms of negative peace, whilst positive peace remains something that exists only in ideal-type form, then one has to question the descriptive utility of this dichotomy and in particular the notion of a transition between these two poles in a process of peacebuilding.

Conceptions of positive peace seem far removed from the lived experience of 'peace' in post-conflict places such as Tajikistan. At best, this everyday experience is proximate to negative peace (Lund 2003; Paris 2004; Junne and Verkoren 2005). But these messy products of peacebuilding interventions are problematic. Whilst the division between positive and negative peace has come to constitute the last word in both analytical and normative terms, it also seems to have shifted the study of peace away from the 'positive' or productive functions of negative peace: how structural and symbolic violence emerges, is resisted and accommodated.[3] These questions remain valid. How does such 'violence' become institutionalised? How do beliefs act to justify it? How does it become legitimate? As Galtung notes in the quote cited above, legitimacy lies at the heart of the study of violence just as it lies at the heart of the study of politics (1975: 185).

Legitimacy is an over-deployed yet under-theorised concept in peace studies. It is often applied casually as a marker of liberal democracy and a descriptor used interchangeably with justice. A wide range of researchers implicitly retain a crude notion of legitimacy in their advocacy for peace (Chanaa 2002: 34; Fukuyama 2004: 99). 'In sum', Sisk, for example, argues, 'there is simply no more just or legitimate way to peacefully manage differences among contending groups than democracy, however difficult it may seem to move from violent to electoral competition' (2001: 785). Boutros-Ghali made similar judgements of the objective quality of legitimacy in his *Agenda for Democratisation*. Democracy, he argued, 'conferred' legitimacy on government by its very nature (1996: para 18, 24). But such arguments leave peacebuilding at a conceptual dead-end, unable to explain the emergence of messy alternatives to 'democracy' which actually constitute a 'peace' in the more stable post-conflict settings. As Clark notes,

> the abiding error is to treat legitimacy as a property of individual actions, and to imagine that we can set up criteria for assessing them in accordance with an independent legitimacy scale. This ignores the fact that legitimacy is a *social* property – not an attribute of action. Those norms that feed into the claims of legitimation are mediated through politics and consensus.
>
> (2005: 254)

The policy-prescriptive *objectivist* approach to legitimacy colours and weakens much of the usage of the concept with peace studies.

However, the more typical social scientific error is found in adopting a *subjectivist* approach to legitimacy (Connolly 1984). For Weber, legitimacy can be equated to acceptance of rule or, as Beetham describes, 'the *belief in legitimacy* on the part of the relevant social agents' (1991: 6), both elites and subordinates. Each system of rule thus has its own form of legitimacy. In 'Politics as a Vocation', Weber describes his three grounds for legitimacy as the authority of (i) 'custom' (traditional legitimacy), (ii) the 'gift of grace' (charismatic) and (iii) 'legal statue' (legal). He notes that actual cases exhibit 'highly complex variations, transitional forms and combinations of these pure types' (2004: 34). Following Weber, political scientists have reduced the concept to top-down attempts by governments to convince their populations that their domination is justified – a campaign of legitimation (Beetham 1991: 10), or what might today be considered a campaign of nation-building.[4] Yet this subjectivist approach is almost entirely ineffective at plotting the emergence or deterioration of an order of legitimacy. Clark notes that such an understanding entails, 'a restatement of an extant consensus (as long as it lasts), with no additional insight into why that consensus existed in the first place, not any account of how it can inhibit its own demise' (2005: 248).

Despite these deficiencies, the Weberian approach has been adopted in the study of post-Soviet Central Asia (contributions in Cummings 2001a). Cummings recognises the limits of the Weberian approach noting that its claim that the legitimacy of regimes is 'possible but not verifiable' in the Central Asian context (2001b: 14). She notes that as post-colonial leaders who did not fight for independence but had self-rule thrust upon them, Central Asian leaders 'have had to work at cultivating legitimacy' (ibid.: 15). Yet equating legitimacy with acceptance leads to a familiar dead-end. Where approval is difficult to ascertain, Cummings finds instrumental grounds for legitimacy in forms of the distribution of patronage amongst the elite, and to a lesser degree, to the citizenry. 'Legitimacy' she argues,

> means something different in the context of authoritarian rule and something different in the Central Asian context. An authoritarian regime must establish its legitimacy, or acceptance of the right to rule, among those on whom it depends to retain its position (usually key elites and certain sectors of society). It must also maintain passive legitimacy among society at large. The presidents of Central Asia have opted primarily for legitimacy on instrumental rather than normative grounds.
>
> (Cummings 2001b: 16)

Yet this risks confusing legitimacy with effectiveness (Lipset 1963; Beetham 1991), as much as the objectivist approach confuses it with justice. Clearly such self-legitimating strategies of patronage are prevalent in Central Asia although it is difficult to claim that this makes the region unique. Moreover, it is simply not adequate to disregard local normative discourses and their role in generating an emergent legitimate order. Human subjects, including Central Asian ones, are, to varying degrees, ethical and faithful as much as they are instrumental and profane.

Advancements in thinking about legitimacy offer a way out of this impasse. 'Legitimacy', Beetham remarks, 'is not the icing on the cake of power, which is applied after baking is complete, and leaves the cake itself essentially unchanged. It is more like the yeast that permeates the dough, and makes the bread what it is.' It is thus 'not merely an important topic but the central issue in social and political theory' (1991: 39, 41). He offers an alternative definition of legitimacy which considers it to be the *intersubjective* constitution of political power. It has three elements.

Power can be said to be legitimate to the extent that:

1   it conforms to established *rules*;
2   the rules can be justified by reference to *beliefs* shared by both dominant and subordinate;
3   there is evidence of *consent* by the subordinate to the particular power relation.

(Beetham 1991: 15–16, emphasis added)

These three components of legitimacy are interdependent. Rules, beliefs and consent as intersubjective properties emerge in a discursive environment. But this is not say that the legitimacy is largely normative or procedural. This approach provides 'a bridge or an alliance between is and ought' (Barker 2001: 8). 'Obedience', Beetham notes, 'is therefore to be explained by a complex of reasons, moral as well as prudential, normative as well as self-interested, that legitimate power provides for those who are subject to it' (ibid.: 27).

Intersubjective legitimacy potentially provides a richer, 'positive' description of a 'peace' such as Tajikistan's than that provided by 'negative peace' or 'war weariness'. Unlike 'negative peace', legitimacy sets limits on subordinates and, to a lesser extent, elites which extend beyond simply refraining from arbitrary or unofficial violence. International stability and legitimacy, Clark notes, 'are the same state of affairs otherwise described' (2005: 248). Yet it cannot be said that legitimacy *causes* peace or order. Rather, it *constitutes* the form and content of peace in a given context. In order to explore this form and content extensively we must make legitimacy more complex: showing how it is made manifest in terms of discourse and practice, differentiated by hidden and public spaces, and how it generates emergent properties and processes.

Discourse and practice

As should be apparent from the analysis above, I adopt an interpretive, post-positivist approach to the study of Tajikistan's emergent and legitimate order and its attendant politics of peacebuilding. My starting assumptions, ontological positions and conceptual categories are taken in light of this epistemological turn. Without rehashing the bridging debates of the social sciences it is worth briefly stating what a post-positivist approach does and does not do. First and foremost such an approach avoids causal analysis of objectively determined independent and dependent variables in favour of a constitutive analysis of inter-dependent and intersubjective powers, properties and processes. An interpretive approach requires a study of intersubjective dynamics. Methodologically, as will be discussed below, it is difficult to see how these dynamics can be identified without substantial fieldwork and without the language skills and prior experi-ence of an area studies specialist. Ontologically and analytically, investigating the theoretical terrain of the post-conflict via the concept of legitimacy involves the application of the categories of discourse and practice.

Discourses have intertextual power in engendering subject roles for leaders, followers and resistors of the peace. Practices are the actions and sets of actions we habitually take in our everyday social and political lives. Post-conflict sub-jects are directly affected by their discursive environments and the common practices and habits of these environments. They, like everyone, are socially and mimetically constructed subjects whose agency emerges in context. Their and our political ideas and interests are shaped in an environment which cannot simply be transformed into or supplanted by a better political order, model of economic exchange or cultural milieu according to the designs of international peacebuilders. Thus, neither an abstract nor an entirely subjective (intrasubjec-tive) sentiment has power. Rather, power is found in the discourses and practices which emerge from an economic model (e.g. those of Marxism), political order (e.g. 'the Khan') or sentiment (e.g. 'trust').

At this point it is worth considering one of the principal objections to this kind of analysis that might be offered (privately, of course) by Tajikistanis them-selves. This is nicely summarised in the quote below from former presidential advisor and government minister, Ibrohim Usmonov.

> Heads of state and other leading figures (*drugie glavnye litsa*) [...] want to show that they want [democracy]. They never announce that 'I come in order to rob from my people. I came in order to wage war. I came in order to bring hunger.' No one ever made such an announcement. The worst tsar, the worst king, never announced that, and neither do they now. In actual fact it is their actions which should show what they want. What they say is not what they do.
>
> (2005a: 11)

This quote illustrates a number of apparent challenges to the productive power of elite discourse. First, and most fundamentally, this is a denial of the idea that legitimacy is accrued normatively, either through norm transfer from interna-tional organisations to elites through international peacebuilding's seminars and workshops, or through grand national narratives. Second, it is a challenge to dis-course analysts who see nothing beyond the verbal symbolic. Words, especially written words, are not the totality of action. Representations can be undermined by unspoken or unwritten acts of political manipulation and personal enrichment. While they are profoundly important conveyers of meaning and shapers of expectation, public discourses are inconsistently productive and can be 'thin simplifications' of reality. However, in some contrast to Usmonov, I would argue that politically what they say is a very significant part of what they do; *textual* representation (including verbal and oral communication) is the primary means by which human subjects negotiate their positions, possessions and relationships in both public and hidden spaces. Even when the worst tsar breaks his word he does so with yet more words, to different audiences, at different times.

The understanding of discourse adopted here is much more holistic than that assumed by most critics. I understand discourse broadly in terms of Foucault's 'discursive formation' – an order or 'system of dispersion between objects, types of statement, concepts or thematic choices' (1974: 38). I seek to grasp the *larger intersubjective context* where, 'meaning and practice arise out of interaction', and 'within which moves of one kind or another would be seen to be reasonable and therefore justifiable' (Fierke and Jørgensen 2001: 117, 125). This requires a study of the mimetic processes, whereby 'the individual assimilates himself or herself' to the symbolic world (Gebauer and Wulf 1995: 2–3), through the creation and practising of texts in everyday experiences. I consequently attempt to balance my discourse analysis with participant observation of practice. Yet discourse and practice are no more clearly demarcated or opposed than are political research and political practice. 'Thick' discourse takes a practical (actual, habitual) form and discourse analysis, when it is combined with ethnography (ideally to a greater extent than has been possible in this study), can shed light on these productive dimensions. Equally, practice is made meaningful in discourse and communicated in discursive representation. This is not to say that there are not extra-practical and extra-representational forms of political life in the form of the sublime, of emotion and other forms of affect. Nor that discourse and practice are not contingent on the uncertain playing out of events, of chance, providence or (mis)fortune. Rather it is to argue that these things are difficult to conceptualise beyond the recognition of their basic form, and that all such theorisations involve exclusions.

Public and hidden

One of the basic exclusions which I adopt in this study is the conceptual dualism of James C. Scott's public and hidden *aspects* of discourse. For Scott, 'public transcripts' of conformity and unity offer 'an indifferent guide to the opinion of subordinates' (1990: 3). Thus he widens the scope of discourse analysis, adding an ethnographic dimension and introducing the idea of the 'hidden transcript' which is 'beyond direct observation by powerholders' (ibid.: 4). Scott's approach to discourse demands ethnographic explorations of wider private or hidden, often oral, practices. A hidden, alternative reality – 'an extensive offstage social existence' – is sustained by what Scott calls 'the infrapolitics of subordinate groups' (1990: 21). His later work (1998) highlights how a large array of attempts to impose 'high-modernist' ideologies – from Soviet collectivism to Brazilian city-planning – onto various societies which have been defeated by the *mētis* ('cunning' and 'practical knowledge') of locals who are able to subvert their masters' grand designs. This argument may be extended to peacebuilding which, whilst lacking the explicit authoritarianism of many of Scott's examples, nevertheless exhibits many of the features of high-modernism.

The public–hidden duality has two important ramifications for the study of peacebuilding processes. First, Scott's approach shows the limited yet significant powers of public discourse and practice. He acknowledges that public transcripts are not simply incitements to dissonance but can limit that dissonance to the private, and exclude it from the public. They are themselves productive of 'peace' (legitimate order). Thus practices of 'symbolic display' which extend beyond what Scott calls the 'command performance of consent' become central to constructing 'a *show of discursive affirmation from below*' (1990: 17, 20, 58). The dominant can, 'accommodate a reasonably high level of practical resistance so long as that resistance is not publicly and unambiguously acknowledged' (ibid.: 57). An unanswered or unambiguous act of resistance would give confidence to others to be insubordinate and before long authority breaks down. When sincere consent is absent, the dominant demand 'at least the simulacrum of sincere obedience' (ibid.: 58). Such public acts from elites are also functional in the reproduction of their 'we' group. They must act towards subordinates according to a public transcript of (racial, physical, moral and/or intellectual) superiority and via practices of mutual affirmation, concealment of incompetence, the euphemistic representation of forms of violence, the stigmatisation of subordinates, and public shows of unanimity and togetherness. 'At every occasion', Scott notes, 'on which the official euphemism is allowed to prevail over other, dissonant versions, the dominant monopoly over public knowledge is publicly conceded by subordinates' (ibid.: 45–53).

Second, Scott's work reveals the relationship between discourse and practice in the process of emergence. Scott claims that public and hidden transcripts are dialectically related: 'the practice of domination, then, creates the hidden transcript' (ibid.: 27). Moreover, he notes,

> power relations are not, alas, so straightforward that we can call what is said in power-laden contexts false and what is said offstage true. Nor can we simplistically describe the former as a realm of necessity and the latter as a realm of freedom. What is certainly the case, however, is that the hidden transcript is produced for a different audience and under different constraints of power than the public transcript. By assessing the discrepancy *between* the hidden transcript and the public transcript we may begin to judge the impact of domination on public discourse.
>
> (Scott 1990: 5)

This formulation of the relationship between transcripts is controversial in sociological literature in its binary spatialising of political discourse and practice.

Tilly (1991) has noted that Scott's work takes the hermeneutic tack in insisting on four transcripts, rather than the three supposed in Gramscian hegemony, while in practice seeming to replicate the three transcript model. This tension arises from the nature of Scott's model where both the elite–subordinate and public–hidden divisions are dialectical under conditions of hegemony. In theory then they could be collapsed to a single transcript study (surely an unhelpful route), or equally expanded to include a proliferation of transcripts. As Tilly asks, who is to say how many there should be. 'Why not', he asks, 'as many discourses as subordinates?' (ibid.: 598). Ultimately the answer here can only be justified in terms of the empirical study of a given context. In Chapters 3 and 4, I argue for a starting point of a minimum of six transcripts in the study of peacebuilding in Tajikistan. Assessing dissonance and ambivalence amongst the elite, both national and international, and resignation and disquiet amongst subordinates, helps us better understand the form and substance that peace and peacebuilding take.

Properties and processes

Whilst discourse and practice are the powers by which conflict polities can be analysed, authority, sovereignty and livelihoods are the *properties* by which these polities can be assessed. However, as emergent properties they are contingent upon *processes* of creation and re-creation – of (re-/de-)centring, (di)simulating, and (re-/de-)territorialising.

The search for better criteria or properties and processes of peacebuilding is ongoing and this work is but one intervention in that debate. In a recent special issue of *Security Dialogue* the editors identified three elements of post-conflict order: representation, welfare and security (Schwarz 2005: 444). Yet peacebuilding here remains a problem-solving process – something that *we* directly do to *them*. The focus remains on public goods which can be provided to, or facilitated for, the people, by local political authorities, themselves aided by international organisations. Such an approach inscribes to the participants in this process of 'post-conflict peacebuilding' many of the desires, rights and responsibilities of a functioning liberal- or social-democratic state. However, as Rubenstein notes in the same volume 'intervention involves claims about legitimacy, standing and authority that are socially constructed and culturally constituted' (2005: 528). Any new approach which attempts to objectify the a priori nature of peace has misunderstood the political and relational character of peacebuilding.

Here I pursue a more critical approach by bringing in post-positivist ontologies and methodologies to the study of peacebuilding. I do not explore *either* international 'peacebuilding' initiatives *or* the practices of local politics, but the relationship between the two. Chapters 5 to 7 emphasise the consequences of international interventions in terms of how normative stances and material allocations are reinterpreted and reappropriated in context. Similar to Schwarz (2005) and his contributors, I consider the building of peace in terms of three elements. However, I identify these as the emergent properties of authority, livelihoods and sovereignty. These properties do not have fixed ethical, temporal and spatial parameters but their form and substance shift grounds according to global and local dynamics. In considering the particular case of Tajikistan, I implicate international assistance in the 'negative' as well as 'positive' consequences of peacebuilding, including state violence and corruption.

Research design and methodology

As noted above, peace is differentiated across scales or levels. The challenges of designing a research process significantly comprehensive to assess multiple discourses and spaces of a complex political order necessitated investigation of multiple formations of identity-based community manifest in numerous locations across Tajikistan. In order to grasp the communities at play in a context of international peacebuilding I explored and adapted Hansen's (2006) approach to discursive 'selves' in international intervention, following a semi-structured interpretative analysis of the temporal, ethical and spatial dimensions of texts and their dichotomies of ideal- and enemy-others – in both public and hidden aspects. Given the variety of media used, in several different languages, it would have been extremely difficult, if not impossible, to conduct a comprehensive and standard content analysis using electronic devices or manual techniques. I gathered my sources during fieldwork rather than remotely where I would have been limited to archive and web-based material. I particularly sought out documents and reports which were mentioned to me by my interviewees, interlocutors and colleagues.[5] I observed (and sometimes participated in) the use and abuse of some of these texts in context.

Intermittent fieldwork over several years allowed me to spend a significant amount of time comparing and contrasting the data which emanate from these different spaces. Primary research took place in several stages between 2003 and 2007 with a total of about ten months of that time spent in Tajikistan. Research was divided between the capital city, Dushanbe, and the regions. Working in many different sites, from INGO offices to specific *mahalla*, I felt I was often sacrificing depth in favour of breadth. However, this concern was mitigated by a number of factors. First, I was able to visit most of these sites many times over many months and began to become familiar with local characters and leaders. Second, as I spread my time across the country I began to appreciate some of the similarities and differences across regions. On the one hand, I may have missed some of this diversity had I not observed differences in lived experience of war and peace between, for example, the Uzbek areas of the West, or the Kulobi districts of the South. On the other hand, I may have been less confident of the common threads of issues such as labour migration and community governance had I not been able to see these diverse parts. Third, I consoled myself that it is the task of the student of International Relations, much to the chagrin of our more ethnographic colleagues, to consider breadth over depth – to be ethnographic at the 'international level' of foreign diplomats and aid workers, as well as gaining some insight into the 'local level' of villagers.

My participant observation included formal employment with international organisations working in Tajikistan. International agencies and donors often provided my entry point to the field, but also opportunities for an ethnographic analysis of the international community. As a consultant, I was effectively a full-time member of staff for Mercy Corps for over three months, leading a four- to six-person research team in a formal evaluation of a major international programme. My experience as an election observer with the OSCE was another extremely rich participatory opportunity. Being given significant autonomy to design research processes in several cases, I felt I was able to discern both the affects and effects of international discourses and find the autonomy to undertake my own independent studies. Formal periods of participant-observation with these organisations are detailed in Table 1.1. Other data collection – in the form of elite interviews, newspaper surveys, observations and photography, and living with and getting to know individuals – took place independently of these organisations.

My dual role – as international employee and academic researcher – provided access and experience, as well as ethical concerns. I was clear to explain to interviewees my status and the purpose of both avenues of my research. I gained permission to use the data collected for the organisation. In one case this was written into my contract, in other cases I gained permission formally or informally from a senior person within the organisation. However, there is a larger and insurmountable issue raised by this kind of fieldwork. As my research interventions were concomitant with the international interventions I purported to study this exacerbated the barriers between myself and the people and practices I was studying. In such circumstances, the goal of absolute objectivity was all the more untenable and my own subject position was laid bare. As Robben and Nordstrom comment,

> We depart for the field bowing under the weight of our own culture, propped up and propelled by Western assumptions we seldom question, shielded from the blaze of complex cultural diversity by a carefully crafted lens of cultural belief that determines as much as clarifies what we see. When we purport to speak for others, we carry the Western enterprise into the mouths of other people. No matter our dedication, we cannot escape the legacy of our culture.
>
> (1995: 11)

In this light I do not claim that I was able to transcend my own cultural baggage, but rather that what knowledge I gained was the product of my situation and collaboration with other internationals, elites and subordinates, many of whom I came to count as friends. I have sought to represent the voices of others and put them in context; but they remain my representations.

Overview of the book

This book is in two halves. The historical background and basic discourses and practices of post-conflict Tajikistan are explored and interpreted in Chapters 2 to

Table 1.1 Work with international organisations

Dates	Organisation	Activity	Theme [Chapter]	Regional location
June–July 2003	International Alert/DfID	Research on small arms issues and policy vis-à-vis international agreements	Security sector [6]	Dushanbe
February 2005	OSCE (ODIHR)	Election observation – Tajikistan parliamentary	Political parties and elections [5]	Rasht valley
April–June 2005	Mercy Corps	Final Evaluation of Mercy Corps Community Action Investment Programme (CAIP)	Community development [7]	Khatlon; Rasht valley
June–July 2005	Mercy Corps	Internal Evaluation of Mercy Corps Peaceful Communities Initiative (PCI)	Community development [7]	Sughd
July–August 2005	AKDN/GTZ	Assessment of Water Usage Associations	Community development [7]	Rasht valley
June–September 2007	DfID	'Drivers of Change' study	All [5, 6, 7]	Dushanbe; Khatlon; Rasht valley; Sughd

4. The beginnings of an analysis of any given post-conflict context must be found in a thorough understanding of the basic history and complex historiographies of that conflict and peace process. Chapter 2 embarks on this process with a thumbnail sketch of Tajikistan over the last twenty years, showing how legitimate order was dismantled as the governing idea, key relationships and dominant institutions of the Soviet Union broke down. It opens up the contingent nature of events and alludes to their varying interpretations. These communities of imagination and interpretation – global, elite and local – are then explored in the two subsequent chapters in terms of their public and hidden discourses.

Chapter 3 examines global discourses and practices in the so-called 'international community' in Tajikistan – the subject positions of international agencies, embassies, non-governmental and intergovernmental organisations. I show how the major discursive conflicts of peacebuilding in global terms come to dominate how Tajikistan is understood and objectified for intervention. Moreover, I investigate hidden dissonance in the international community in the form of scepticism, cynicism and pessimism towards the public programmes and protestations of peacebuilding. I find that peacebuilding is ambivalently practised and it is this very uncertainty, I suggest, which is productive of shifting practices of international peacebuilding in Tajikistan.

Chapter 4 explores two vital discourses of the Tajik[6] peace: elite and subordinate. Elite and subordinate subject positions are highly intersubjective; they are constituted and bounded primarily in their representations and imaginations of each other. At the same time neither elites nor subordinates constitute a single community of practice as they are divided by boundaries of identity: gender, regional solidarity, social class and the urban–rural divide. I raise some of these tensions here for them to be considered in more depth in the second part. Despite (or because of) this extant fragmentation, my analysis suggests that it is vital to understand the spatio-hierarchical divide of elite and subordinate in order to understand the politics of peacebuilding and the emergence of legitimate order. I explore this divide in terms of its genealogical routes in the Soviet and pre-Soviet periods and in its contemporary public and hidden aspects. Elite professions of national 'authority' and 'stability' are negated in practice by semi-concealed acts of corruption and regional networks of solidarity and patronage. Popular denials of politics and testimonies to community harmony are undermined by moments of dissent where protestations and lamentations of injustice break through the public veneer. However, the primary dynamic of elite-subordinate relations in Tajikistan is found in how domination is not openly resisted but publicly accommodated and (less publicly) avoided by the poor.

In the second half, the politics of peacebuilding and the emergence of legitimate order are considered in terms of the powers, processes and properties of authority (Chapter 5), sovereignty (Chapter 6) and livelihoods (Chapter 7). In addition to the framework which I have constructed for this analysis, I also make reference to peacebuilding's key pillars, in terms of three core themes: democracy, including the development of political parties and free and fair elections (Chapter 5); security, including the reintegration of former combatants and the management of borders (Chapter 6); and, finally, development, including the rehabilitation of local economies through community-based organisations (Chapter 7). In each of the three chapters, the centring of power and resources to the elite representing 'the state' dialectically produces hidden practices of popular avoidance and elite corruption.

Chapter 5 considers the processes and property of authority in light of international intervention for democratisation. It examines programmes in support of political parties and elections and explores the way international initiatives have been thwarted and reconstituted by the processes of the re-/de-centring of political *authority* in Tajikistan's post-conflict space. International peacebuilders' positions in the momentary in-between spaces of international intervention make such strategies ineffective at producing normative change in context. The principal triumph of 'peacebuilding' for the Tajikistani elite has been its ability to re-centre the legitimate terrain of political authority with the recaptured state and thus become states-people. In this process certain individuals have fallen by the wayside due to their unwillingness to accept the terms of this 'statecraft' and the 'authority' of the ruling clique around Rahmon. In this sense, 'the state' (state-idea) is the mythical solidarity group around which political power is organised. The re-centring of the patriarchal state is, however, accompanied by the decentring practices of patronage and clientelistic networks.

Chapter 6 explores how the ostensible objectives of security sector reform are stymied whilst the discourses and practices of intervention have contributed to the simulation of Tajikistani *sovereignty* (singular). International, regional and national securities are not properties themselves but securitisation discourses which inscribe certain internal and external threats. Sovereignties, similarly, are emergent properties of post-conflict order in Tajikistan, but diverge between contending authoritative actors at the Tajik–Afghan border. Sovereignty (supreme political authority) is thus 'divided' across multiple domestic and international players who are able to impersonate the state (Reeves 2006). The state-idea remains strong whilst the state-system (as a single order) is weak. This paradox is resolved in terms of simulation and dissimulation. Simulacra of sovereignty and the multiple representations of the state-idea are publicly dominant and productive of international recognition of Tajikistan, regionally and globally. However, these simulacra barely conceal the inconsistencies and violent injustices perpetrated by the state and the dependency of the ruling regime on the continued avoidance measures of its impoverished population and the complicity of international partners. As sovereignty is simulated it is, concomitantly, dissimulated.

Chapter 7 turns back to the everyday practices of peace in rural areas. These practices, more than any other considered here, destabilise the political gaze of peacebuilding and highlight the fragility of the emerging legitimate order. *Livelihoods* have been rehabilitated but also re-spatialised across local and translocal scales of, respectively, subsistence and labour migration. More specifically, space has been re-territorialised (through formal land 'reform' via local patronage networks) and de-territorialised (in parallel, illegal practices, especially migrant networks). I investigate how interventions for community development are in fact co-opted via informal political–economy networks which dominate Tajikistan's rural communities. These networks have their origins in the Soviet-era kolkhoz system yet have evolved under the new migration–subsistence political economy. While the local elite control the best land, the poorest are forced to rely on remittances from migrant family members to survive. The functionality of this highly unequal economic structure for peace is examined in light of the dispersal of a huge proportion of men of fighting age beyond the borders of the state. I suggest that resource capture in terms of the re-territorialisation produces the de-territorialisation of livelihoods and the translocation (re-spatialisation) of Tajikistani communities.

Finally, in Chapter 8, I draw some conclusions and implications of my analysis for our understanding of international peacebuilding and contemporary Tajikistan. I suggest that if we wish to understand peacebuilding better we must engage in in-depth studies of post-conflict, post-colonial spaces.

2   War and peace in post-Soviet Central Asia

Civil war and its consequences have dominated Tajikistan's short history of independent statehood. In 1992, not long after the dissolution of the Soviet Union, the country descended into several years of political violence. While the most intense fighting had ended by 1993, a peace agreement was not signed until 1997 and renegade commanders remained at large until 2001. The 'Kulobisation' of Tajikistan (Akiner 2001), where cadres from the southern region of Kulob came to hold most of the key positions in government, notwithstanding the power-sharing mechanism of the General Agreement, was confirmed by Emomali Rahmon's victory in fraudulent presidential elections of 1999 and 2006 and his subsequent consolidations of power. This chapter introduces the Tajik case in terms of an interpretative narrative of its historical origins and junctures. It provides an outline of the war and peace process from the Soviet period to contemporary post-conflict peacebuilding interventions. It is shown that while violence was not inevitable, these dramatic events evolved so that peace became war, and vice versa. In such a way, as peace has emerged out of war, Tajikistan has refused to follow the pathway of international peacebuilding towards a reformed and democratic political order.

There is no definitive account of the conflict: many of the details are contested or obscured by the limited or partial records of the events of the time.[1] Attributing causality here is an arduous and, potentially, deceptive task. There are nevertheless several good narratives of part or all of the Tajik war and peace process in the 1990s.[2] Rather than repeat these accounts this chapter provides a skeletal history of the period whilst paying special consideration to the role of representation in the conflict and introducing the historiographical trends which have produced the dominant accounts of the conflict internationally. The chapter utilises an academic literature on Tajikistan which, in Chatterjee's characterisation, 'is no longer scanty but scattered' (2002: 11), as well as a number of primary sources, press reports and testimonies. Dwelling on the representation and writing of war-starting and -ending brings an interpretative dimension to the fore. In this sense, war-ending is a product of historiography as it is a product of history. Certain interpretations of the war are proferred by its victors to legitimise their own power and authority. This chapter sets the scene for Chapters 3 and 4, which provide a greater historiographical dimension in focusing on how multiple political discourses – international, elite and subordinate – inform various readings of the conflict and post-conflict politics and in such a way legitimate certain practices. The first section sets out the principal terms and events of the political conflict which divided the country on regional lines during the Soviet era, and led to increasing mobilisation against the regime after independence. The second section details the major phases of the war as the regime lost all remaining legitimacy and power and the population faced turmoil before a new government established itself. The final section provides a sketch of the main features of Tajikistan's emergent peace, illustrating the limits of international intervention and the increasingly authoritarian dynamics of post-conflict politics.

The conflict

The citizens of the Republic of Tajikistan, a poverty-stricken country in Central Asia, have endured much violence and suffering since the state gained independence on 9 September 1991 (see Figure 2.1). The Soviet era had brought political boundaries and a centre of power (with the creation of the Tajik Soviet Socialist Republic on 16 October 1929), as well as a sense of political identity to a people without a history of modern statehood. Yet during the era of the Soviet Union, as the poorest republic of the USSR, Tajikistan was structurally dependent on Moscow. By 1991, the republic received a higher proportion of its revenue from the Union budget (47 per cent), and maintained a greater inter-republic trade deficit,

Figure 2.1 Basic map of Tajikistan.[1]

Note

1   Available from: University of Texas at Austin library (www.lib.utexas.edu/maps/tajikistan.html), accessed 15 October 2006. Courtesy of the University of Texas Libraries, The University of Texas at Austin.

than any of the other republics (World Bank 1992). With the demise of the Soviet Union, these relationships quickly broke down and what remained of national resources became the objects of conflict. Within months of independence this conflict led to a 'swift and seemingly inexorable descent into a brutal civil war' (Rubin 1994: 207) which led to over 50,000 deaths and more than 250,000 refugees.

Origins and interpretations of the conflict

Four modes of interpretation can be found in the literature on the causes of war in Tajikistan. Some of these explanations have gained particular prominence in the international academic literature whereas other, at certain times, have been popular amongst local scholars and journalists or in official discourse.

First, the conflict is most prominently seen as a battle of regional solidarity groups. Ethnic identities in Tajikistan are complex phenomena which have been highly politicised since the emergence of the Republic in the 1920s. Soviet-era ethnologies painted a picture of a substantial Uzbek minority in the west, Russians in the capital and regional centres, and the Tajik majority dominating the main agricultural lands of the southern, northern and central valleys. This obscures the diversity of ethnicities and regional solidarities which have emerged over the twentieth century. Much of the population in the west of the country, for example, has followed the bilingual Tajik–Uzbek tradition of ancestors who were at one time known as 'sarts'. Their emergence as 'Tajik' or 'Uzbek' was a more modern phenomenon spawned by Soviet ethnological classification. Furthermore, the 'Tajik' areas of the eastern part of the country are populated by Pamiri people professing Shi'a Ismaili Islam and speaking various eastern Iranian dialects related to, but distinct from, what today is considered to be Tajiki language.

Tajikistan's conflict was given shape not by ethno-national identity but by the modern politico-administrative dynamics of the republic. Whilst Gharmi and Kulobi factions fought together on both sides in the *basmachi* Islamist revolts of the 1920s (Roy 2000: 46–49, 95; 1998: 134–135), they battled each other in one of the key inter-regional conflicts which led to the civil war of the 1990s. The explanation for this shift clearly lies in what passed between these two conflicts. Under the Soviet system, administrative structure provided the vehicles for political advancement and, to some extent, enrichment. Inchoate local identities and communities were transformed during the Soviet era into hybrid regional solidarity groups between which posts were inequitably shared. These recomposed regional groups fought for power – a process known locally as 'regionalism' (*mestnichestvo*, *mahalgero'y*). Inter-regional rivalry was further exacerbated by a series of population movements that had the effect of crystallising the regional identities which would be the vehicles for conflict during the civil war. Among the most important of these forced migrations were the relocations of Tajiks from the central mountain ranges of Karategin (Gharm) and Darvaz to Khatlon's cotton-producing valleys between 1925 and 1940, and from the Pamirs between 1947 and 1960 (Usmon 2004). Whilst generating animosity towards the authorities, the organisation of these groups into their own *kolkhozes* also made integration of migrants and locals more difficult. Most of these migrants, particularly so-called 'Gharmis', consequently avoided integration and held firm to regional identities and loyalties; it was from these groups that the opposition drew much support during the conflict (Akiner 2002). Collective farm units (kolkhoz and sovkhoz) were 'tribalised' as 'new recompositions of solidarity groups resulting from sedentarism or population transfers' (Roy 2000: 88). Thus ethnic or 'clan' identity did not have a primordial value but were given social and political meaning by the migrations. It is in this sense that Roy labels the inter-Tajik conflict, 'the war of the kolkhoz' (ibid.: 94–96).

Public goods were distributed inequitably across this regionally based system. Although Dushanbe was the capital of the Tajik SSR, the northern province (Leninabad *oblast*, now Sughd *veloyat*, also known by its major city, Khujand), which had developed under Russian imperial power, provided the majority of the governing elite of the republic, including all the first secretaries of the communist party between 1946 and 1992. Moreover, it was economic and politico-administrative links with the southern cotton-producing region of Kulob which allowed northern elites to maintain their domination of the political life of the republic. The Tajikistan SSR went through numerous governmental reshuffles reflecting the ascendancy of the Leninabad–Kulob alliance over politically weaker regions such as Gharm and the Pamirs. However, Pamiris (especially in the Police [MVD]), Gharmis and Russians continued to hold key posts and the idea of Leninabadi domination obscured a more complex set of power relations based on patronage networks both within and between regional elites, and with power-brokers in Moscow. In such an inconsistent fashion regional identity emerged during the Soviet period and remained the key vehicle for the mobilisation of armed groups during the conflict. The divisions of the conflict between (to generalise) Hissori Uzbeks, Khujandi Tajiks and Kulobi Tajiks on the one side and (to generalise again) Gharmi Tajiks and Pamiris provides only a basic starting point in any understanding of the conflict.

A second way of viewing the conflict is as a battle of ideas and ideologies. The reforms initiated by Gorbachev following his election as General Secretary on 11 March 1985 provoked a variety of reactions within Tajikistan, ranging from hopes for greater autonomy to disappointment at the vagueness of early announcements (Hammer 1998). By the autumn of 1989 it was clear that substantive reform was in process with a new constitution on the cards that offered the possibility of a greater decentralisation of power to the republics. Around this time reformist groups with wide-ranging aims began to be established by journalists and academics. However, as across the region, reformers faced conservative party elite, detached from popular concerns and the emerging aspirations of the intelligentsia. *Yovaroni Bozsozi* ('Friends of Reconstruction and Reconciliation'), the first significant group, was established in 1988 demanding the establishment of Tajik as a state language and making vague calls for economic and political liberalisation. It was soon banned by the authorities (Jawad and Tadjbaksh 1995: 11).

Nevertheless other movements sprang up espousing agendas of democratisation, regional autonomy, national revival and political Islam (see below), including *Rastokhez* ('Renaissance'), formed in September 1989 by nationalists and anti-colonialists amongst the intelligentsia and educated elite. Whilst some were quickly quashed others managed to attract reformist cadres from the party and bureaucracy.³ A language law to promote the use of Tajik in governmental affairs was adopted in 1989 and elite criticism of Moscow, national territorial delimitation and the early Soviet period was not uncommon. Public demonstration became a technique of public education and an indication of a burgeoning and indigenous civil society. As Atkin remarks, demonstrations 'provided a school in the streets where the opposition could propound its views to people who gathered, sometimes by the thousands' (Atkin 1997: 288). The media, particularly television, also provided fora of debate between conservatives and reformers, providing a medium of popular dissemination of reformist discourses and conservative responses (Khodjibaeva 1999). However, importantly the period of demonstrations in the autumn of 1991 and spring of 1992 – labelled by Jawad and Tadjbaksh (1995) as the 'Tajik Spring' – is represented quite differently in contemporary elite and popular accounts (see Chapter 3), where they are often seen as causes for the violence and disorder which followed.

A third way of interpreting the conflict is as a battle for survival and a fight over resources. This is the political economy approach which explains war in terms of greed (of elites) and need (of their followers). Poverty was indeed hugely important in the making of the Tajik conflict. In the summer of 1992 there were numerous incidents of violence perpetrated to get food, other basic supplies, or better housing. One Kulyabi fighter in the Vakhsh valley is cited in an account of the conflict by the BBC's Monica Whitlock.

> There was no soap, no flour, nothing [...]. The only way to get food was to go on raiding parties. Families sent their sons to fight, not for the glory of Kulyab, or for power, or for Sangak [Safarov, leader of the Popular Front], but because their boys might come back with some potatoes. And then they could manage for another day.
>
> (2002: 167–168)

For many of the actual perpetrators of violence their acts may have been economically rather than politically motivated. This reinforces Lynch's point that the fall of the Soviet Union had disastrous micro-economic consequences which shaped the local-level dynamics of the conflict, where 'the struggle focused on land and resources between regionally-defined groups' (Lynch 2001: 55).

There was a structural-economic context to this fight for resources with its roots in the ecological crisis brought about by the forced migrations. These population movements brought the proportion of Tajiks living in the mountains from 70 per cent in the mid-1920s to 30 per cent in the early 1990s, even though agricultural land composed just 7 per cent of the republic's territory (Niyazi 1999: 191). Usmon (2004: 246–247) concurs that forced migrations provided huge pressure on resources and brought disagreements and violence over usage of pasture and water. He cites the case of 'Kommunizm' Kolkhoz in Kabodiyonski district of Hatlon province where in the middle of 1960s violence took place between 'the local population' of ethnic Uzbeks and settlers from the mountain regions of Karategin (Gharm). By the time of independence over half of agricultural land was used for cotton farming, putting a tremendous strain on water and food production. This was exacerbated by population growth (an average of 3.5 per cent per annum) which exceeded the rise in revenues from cotton (Niyazi 1999: 188). Niyazi argues that the Tajik civil war was '[a] struggle of the regions for survival brought forth by the rapid demographic growth, forced migration, overpopulation of valleys, and catastrophic insufficiency of water, land, energy and food production resources' (ibid.: 191). In this sense political Islam was 'the response of a traditional society to the rapid process of industrialisation', a defence of local forms of production against 'gigantomania' (ibid.: 187, 189).

Finally, the conflict is interpreted as an instrumentalist struggle amongst elites: a ruling faction confronted by opportunistic individuals seeking personal advancement in a weak institutional environment (Rubin 1998: 139–142; Akhmedov 1998). Akiner, for example, comments that over-reliance on a regionalist explanation 'obscures the fluidity and ambiguities of the situation' and 'underestimates the power of individuals to influence events' (2001: 21). The opposition eventually incorporated a wide range of ideological positions, and a coalition of different regions, which was later divided between National-democratic and Islamist blocs. The former included the Democratic Party of Tajikistan (DPT), founded in August 1990, led by elites representing a number of local areas disenfranchised or marginalised in government.[4] Added to these groups were the Pamiri organisations, foremost of which was *La'li Badakhshon* ('Ruby of Badakshon'), also created in 1990, which strove for greater Badakshoni autonomy but allied with groups from other regions in March 1992. Many of these groups found considerable support from governmental figures, thus blurring the government–opposition dichotomy. For example, during the war, the head of the Ministry of the Interior (MVD), Navzhuvanov, a Pamiri and *La'li Badakhshon* supporter, brought the main portion of MVD troops to the 'opposition' camp to fight against the government.

In the patriarchal and patrimonial social context of Tajikistan, leadership was clearly important but the notion that the conflict was entirely and instrumentally manipulated by elites is not convincing. Indeed any one of the above paradigms is in itself insufficient. Tajikistani citizens are not simply followers and their motives to commit violence were a complicated mix of solidarity, ideology, survival and loyalty. Each of these modes of interpretations of the conflict is important for understanding the extent and content of war and peace.

Prelude to war

Regionally and ideologically based movements, further complicated by family ties, intermarriage and bitter personal rivalries, embodied a once legitimate national political order whose total collapse occurred rapidly and unexpectedly. However, it was the international unravelling of the Soviet empire which provided the backdrop for the formation of conflict and the onset of war. In this sense the inter-Tajik war can be properly understood not as a civil war (narrowly defined) but a post-Soviet conflict, a complex crisis of decolonisation.

This complexity is witnessed by the case of the development of political Islam and the emergence of the most enduring opposition group, *Hizbi Nahzati Islom* (Islamic Renaissance Party, IRP). After its formation on 6 October 1990 by a number of young clerics, including Said Abdullo Nuri, the future leader of the opposition, the IRP became the most significant opposition movement. The party declared itself part of the all-Union IRP which had been formed at a conference in the Russian republic in the summer of that year. Nevertheless the party was rooted locally with its origins in both 'parallel'/unofficial and 'official'/state-sanctioned Islam as they had evolved in Tajikistan through the 1970s and 1980s.[5] By 1989, whilst there were only seventeen officially registered mosques in Tajikistan, around 2,000 were operating illegally (Atkin 1989: 47–53). Many younger members of the clergy were at this time active in underground circles. They were vocal in criticising the fees charged for clerical duties and became involved in seizing a number of mosques from the official clergy in the late 1980s. It was these people who formed and joined the IRP. Others – often older – opposed the politicisation of Islam and supported the conservative hard-liners in government. The official Muslim religious authority, the Qazi Akhbar Turajonzoda, at first straddled the two groups. His office, the Qaziyyat, was created in 1988 during perestroika. He did not join the IRP, and sometimes publicly criticised its radicalism, but nevertheless stayed in regular communication with the organisation and moved closer towards it in the face of government intransigence (Gretsky 1994: 17, 19). The IRP's agenda was largely moderate, even if many of its members eventually turned to violence. The party aimed to introduce Islamic law gradually into Tajik society rather than pursue an immediate and fundamental overhaul of the state. It drew widespread support from so-called 'Gharmi' people, particularly the migrant communities of the southern Vakhsh valley area (from migrant communities around the city of Kurghon Teppa), as well as some residual support from the Pamiri region of Darvaz and the Karategin (now Gharm) area of the Rasht valley.

The Dushanbe riots of February 1990 were the first major act of violence and whilst following a very different pattern to the demonstrations of late 1991 and early 1992 they became an important symbol for both opposition and government. The riots involved criminal gangs but also popular protests against poor living standards and were apparently triggered by rumours that Armenian migrants had received preferential access to state housing. They led to twenty-five deaths and 800 injuries and led to a state of emergency being declared and maintained until July 1991 (Auten 1996: 199–212). Whilst many of the deaths were by-passers caught in the cross-fire or killed arbitrarily by nervous security forces, at the time the authorities attempted to depict the riots as organised by *Rastokhez* and Islamic radicals, whilst in Moscow they were portrayed as ethnic riots targeted against Russians (Atkin 1997: 297; 2001: 99). At the time both these representations broke down as an official report, which eventually leaked out, blamed the republican government for the debacle. 'To advocates of reform', Atkin notes, 'the February events became a symbol of the regime's implacable resistance to change and its readiness to take the lives of its own citizens' (1997: 284–285). However, as will be explored in Chapter 4, this contemporary elite version of the origins of violence (as a natural product of democratic protest) has largely survived in the post-war period as a feature of both elite and popular discourses. Mullojanov (2001b: 224) charts the decline of the Tajik democrats from their loss of public opinion following the February 1990 riots.

The principal catalyst to conflict was the fall of the Soviet Union. It increased the perceived opportunities of the opposition to make gains whilst substantially weakening the regime. While the Tajikistani republic declared its sovereignty (on 25 August 1990) an overwhelming majority of its citizens and leaders apparently favoured the continuance of the Soviet Union as demonstrated by the March 1991 Union-wide referendum.[6] However, the political status of the republic was being dictated by events in the Slavic and Baltic republics of the USSR. In the summer of 1991, the coup against Gorbachev (20 August) took events out of the Tajik leadership's hands. Kakhar Makhamov, the First Party Secretary and President of the Republic and a hardliner, openly backed the coup and, following mass demonstrations against him in Dushanbe, was forced to step down. Amidst continuing protests against the republican government, the Supreme Soviet reluctantly declared independence on 9 September 1991 – the twelfth of fourteen former Soviet republics to do so. Presidential elections were organised for 27 October 1991 and pitted Rahmon Nabiev, a conservative former First Secretary from the Khujand region, against Davlat Khudonazarov, a joint candidate of opposition parties and well-known liberal reformer and film director from the Pamirs.[7] Amidst vote-rigging and much rancour between regional elites, Nabiev won with 57 per cent of the vote. The level of support for Khudonazarov nevertheless indicated the strength of opposition to the new regime both among Islamic and secular reformers.

At this point, with intense conflict but as yet few deaths, devastating civil war was surely not inevitable. Chatterjee characterised this period as 'the fight for legitimacy' (1995: 8), yet the role of key national elites and outside powers during this time were characterised by acts of gesture and coercion rather than the exercise of legitimate power. Conciliating agents were conspicuous by their absence. Here the role of individual acts and contingent events must be emphasised. First, both Nabiev (who had an alcohol problem and 'vacillated, making concessions to the opposition and then withdrawing them' [Akiner 2001: 36]) and Kenjayev (the speaker of Parliament, who used a televised address to attack Navjuvanov, head of the MVD, for exceeding his powers) played key roles in the descent to war. Second, the extreme turbulence of this period of history meant that many foreign policy miscalculations were made by an outside world inexperienced with the new situation and lacking embassies in the country. In February 1992, for example, US Secretary of State, James Baker, visited

Tajikistan seeking to assert American influence in the new region. He had a long private meeting with Nabiev where it is thought he offered US support if Tajikistan resisted 'fundamentalism' and Iranian influence. He refused to meet leaders of the opposition (Akiner 2001: 36). These policy choices may have precipitated the descent to violence and represent an international failure to grasp the nature of the conflict. Preventative diplomacy was conspicuous by its absence as the international community was distracted by ongoing crises in the Former Yugoslavia, Somalia, Afghanistan and Cambodia amongst other places.

The war

International support and interference was crucial to the course of the war and the political outcome. Tajikistan's civil war was never the entirely domestic struggle that is implied by many outside observers, particularly the leaders of regional powers Russia and Uzbekistan, who were themselves the main international protagonists in the conflict. The war can be divided between the intense period of war often portrayed as an internal struggle but where Russian and Uzbek support proved decisive, and a later period where intervention was both regional and Western-international.

1992: from conflict to war

The high-intensity period of the conflict itself occurred over a year of tumult, 1992–1993, and can be divided into six phases; militarisation, ignition, governmental breakdown, battle for power, government recapture and opposition fightback. The first of these, January–May 1992, was a period of *militarisation* and criminalisation. Nabiyev and Kenjayev, increasingly illegitimate, were recalcitrant against the opposition despite growing protests. A variety of issues of political and economic reform provided an umbrella for secular and Islamic wings to coalesce in opposition to the government. Yet for many of those attending the protests the immediate motivations were born in survival and the search for sustenance (Whitlock 2002: 156, 160). The opposition demonstrations, taking place in Shahidon square in Dushanbe, continued consistently for fifty straight days and coincided with the rise of the *mujahedin* and the fall of the old Soviet-backed government of Najibullah in Afghanistan. Whitlock claims this parallel was emblematic in the eyes of many opposition demonstrators who saw Ahmad Shah Mas'ud, an ethnic Tajik and the leader of the northern *mujahedin*, as a national hero (2003: 158–159). Militant and criminal figures were already forming militia and becoming stronger within both government and opposition factions. The IRP, for example, formed a militia, *Najoti Vatan* (Salvation of the Motherland) in late 1991. The increasingly anxious government made numerous pleas for calm whilst organising pro-government demonstrations at Ozodi square less than two kilometres from Shahidan. However, it was unable to present a show of force as the Russian army was under order from Moscow not to interfere whilst the police were divided between the two sides.

The moment of *ignition* occurred in early May 1992. The Ozodi demonstrators were largely Kulobi and led by Sangak Safarov, a convicted murderer,[8] who would subsequently form the pro-government *Sitodi Milli* (Popular Front of Tajikistan [PFT]) – a coalition of militias based on Kulobi and Uzbek Hissori factions that at its height numbered around 20,000 fighters (Nourzhanov 2005: 119). With many thousands on both pro- and anti-government sides, matters escalated quickly and dramatically. Thirteen criminal gangs connected with anti-government elites and operating under the collective name of Youth of Dushanbe City (YDC), who had been demonstrating on a third square, Aini, declared war on the government (Akiner 2001: 37). President Nabiev and his advisors consequently took the fateful decision on 1 May to escalate matters by distributing 2,000 Kalashnikovs in Ozodi square to Safarov's men to form a 'Presidential Guard' (Mullojanov 2001b: 241). On the very same day, the 14th session of the Supreme Soviet began with a call for the establishment of a tripartite commission composed of leaders from both sides and governmental representatives (Nazriev and Sattorov 2005: 143). In response, opposition leaders mobilised their militias, which were rapidly forming in the regions, and secured the support of MVD troops and presidential guards. On 5 May, they launched attacks to take most of the key government sites in Dushanbe and drive the pro-government supporters out of Ozodi square; on the same day the Supreme Soviet was forced to announce a break in its proceedings (Nazriev and Sattorov 2005: 144). With government in chaos, the seizure of the television station may have been most significant as it allowed the opposition to disseminate alternative messages and images, so destroying the last vestiges of state authority (Khodjibaeva 1999: 14). With widespread fighting in the streets, Russian troops, formerly part of the Soviet armed forces, acted to protect Nabiev and broker a compromise between the two sides. On 11 May a Government of National Reconciliation (GNR) was announced. Nabiev would remain as President and retain his key ministerial supporters, while a third of posts would go to the opposition.

The Dushanbe violence began a process of complete *governmental breakdown*[9] between May and September 1992 as the regime rapidly lost its remaining authority. It was in the period from May to November that much of the killing occurred. Very soon the GNR proved unworkable as the regions of Leninabad and Kulob declared they would not take orders from the new government. By July 1992, none of the security forces remained loyal to the coalition government and fighting spread across the south of the country between field commanders and their militias. Such groups pledged their loyalty to a particular region, but ceasefires negotiated between regional leaders were often immediately broken by local commanders. Violence was most intense in those cities and districts subject to inter-regional forced migration and resettlement, especially around the town of Qurghanteppa where different solidarity groups had long been divided by kolkhoz. By September, Nabiev had lost any remaining support that he had on either pro- or anti-government sides with both the Khujandi–Kulobi dominated parliament and the IRP calling for his resignation (Whitlock 2002: 168–169). On 7 September, while trying to flee from Dushanbe, Nabiev was cornered on his way to the airport

Russian and regional support was crucial in establishing Rahmon in power as Dushanbe fell back under Moscow's authority. Russian and Uzbek forces, having provided support for the victories of the Popular Front in November and December 1992, soon moved into a position of support for the status quo. In addition to the border guards of the Federal Border Service of the Russian Federation (RBF), which were until 2004 maintained along Tajikistan's southern border with Afghanistan, Russia led the way in establishing a small CIS peacekeeping force in 1993. The total CIS/Russian presence at one stage numbered 20,000 troops. The agreement to create a CIS peacekeeping force was made on 24 September 1993 with the governments of Tajikistan, Kazakhstan, Kyrgyzstan and Uzbekistan. Whilst one of the parties to the conflict (the Government of Tajikistan) was a CIS member and a signatory to the agreement, the other (the UTO) became the object of 'peacekeeping'. Both Russia and Uzbekistan also assisted the government in establishing new security forces based largely on PFT factions (Jawad and Tadjbaksh 1995: 17). The great fear for these governments was that Afghanistan's instability and Islamic militancy could spill over into the CIS region. President Yeltsin declared in 1993 that Tajikistan's southern border was, 'in effect, Russia's', as he began a policy of consistent support for the Rahmon government both politically and financially (Rubin 1998: 155–156). Moreover, Russian intervention went beyond support and assistance to the appointment of Russian military officers as ministers in the Tajik government, including Aleksandr Shishliannikov who was Minister of Defence from 1992 to 1995 (Atkin 1997: 303). At this time analysts and some members of the Russian government characterised Tajikistan as a 'protectorate' (Whitlock 2002: 191) or 'Garrison state' (Rubin 1994).

The international community's 'third-party' approach was much less significant in these early years. Boutros-Ghali's *Agenda for Peace* (1992) had defined post-conflict peacebuilding, expanded substantially the remit of peacekeeping forces and called for a new era of interventionism. However, it was other places, including tragically Somalia and Bosnia, which proved the primary testing grounds for this new interventionism. In early 1993 the International Community had become involved on the ground in Tajikistan through the presence of the UN Secretary General's special envoy to Tajikistan. Shortly after, in June 1993, an OSCE centre was set up (Goryayev 2001). The beginning of negotiations and the signing of a notional ceasefire had allowed the UN to introduce official observers with a view to 'free and fair elections'. The UN Mission of Observers in Tajikistan (UNMOT) on renewable six-month tours of duty as specified by a ceasefire signed in Iran on 17 September 1994, and authorised by UN Security Council Resolution 968 of 16 December 1994, was set up (UNSC 1994).[13] Before this, from March 1993, a second-track process of facilitated negotiation, the Inter-Tajik Dialogue, began in Moscow between junior figures and associates of both sides, and independent representatives of the intelligentsia under the auspices of the non-governmental Dartmouth Conference (Saunders 1999: 9). The dialogue has been widely viewed as instrumental in creating some kind of organisational coherence among the opposition and providing the beginnings of 'consensus' between elites (Matveeva 2006; Saunders 1999).

The UN-sponsored negotiations in Tajikistan began precariously. At this time there may have been greater unity between the Moscow and Afghanistan wings of the opposition, who were in regular communication and, argue Jawad and Tadjbaksh, 'worked in uniformity' (1995: 18), than there was within Rahmon's government which was divided between Khujandi and Kulobi factions. In the first round of March 1994, a junior minister in the Tajik government met the national-democratic opposition in Moscow. Both the senior echelons of the Tajik government and the Afghanistan wing of the UTO chose not to take part. Despite a lack of progress in negotiations, Rahmon – emboldened by the support he received from Russia – chose to push on with elections. On 6 November 1994, in a simulation of democratic consent, the Kulobi Rahmon defeated the Khujandi Abdullojonov, receiving 60 per cent of the vote in an election which Helsinki Watch (1994) described as 'marred by a climate of fear and flagrant fraud'. Abdullojonov had been Rahmon's Prime Minster from December 1992 until December 1993 in the government that came to power following the retaking of Dushanbe. On being forced from power, Abdullojonov had sought to mobilise opposition to the Kulobis from the Khujand faction of the governing regime, establishing a number of political parties but failing to win a seat at the table for the peace negotiations.

Despite governmental intransigence and divisions in the international community, crucial signs of movement towards an accord were visible in the background. These accelerated once developments in Afghanistan provided a sense of urgency in the region. As the Taliban took Kabul in 1996, both Russia and Iran, who had become significant in the negotiations as a consequence of sponsoring and supporting the Islamic Movement of Rebirth (the new name for the IRP), pushed for resolution of the conflict. Lynch describes how Russian involvement moved from 'unconditional commitment' to the regime (late 1992–1995) to 'differentiated peacekeeping' (from 1996) in favour of the regime and involving, to a limited extent, Central Asian states in a CIS force.[14] Breakthrough talks of December 1996 were held in Afghanistan, under Mas'ud's auspices; a ceasefire was agreed and a draft power-sharing arrangement discussed. In addition, by the winter of 1996–1997 there was considerable 'war weariness' among civilians and combatants; the agreement made in Afghanistan had been foreshadowed by the 'Gharm Protocol', a ceasefire between local commanders on 19 September 1996 (see Abdullo 2001; Whitlock 2002: 230–231). The effects of massive unemployment and hyperinflation (over 2,000 per cent in 1993) meant that underdevelopment and the challenge of 'making ends meet', rather than physical violence, had become the primary threat to survival by this time (Harris 1998: 660–661). While incidents of fighting continued over the winter there was widespread public support for the peace agreement.

The emergent peace

Drawing a line between war and peace in Tajikistan proves an impossible task, save for the official determination that the war ended with the 27 June agreement

– now marked as 'Peace Day' in Tajikistan. The years before and after the peace agreement saw major rebellions against the government by renegade army commander Mahmud Khudoiberdiyev (in Tursonzoda, February 1996, and Khujand, November 1998) and an assassination attempt which almost succeeded in killing Rahmon in April 1997. However, over twelve years, and three overlapping periods between 1993 and 2005, one can see the gradual re-acquisition of legitimacy as the new regime was eventually accepted with varying degrees of acquiescence from local, regional and international actors. Reading peace in terms of legitimate order requires that we pay attention to the emergence of representations as well as the economic relationships of post-conflict change. This is implied in Khodjibaeva's contention in the period immediately after the peace accords that 'a "television reconciliation" between the two sides is more important than anything else' (1999: 15).

Agreement and implementation, 1997–2000

The package of agreements and protocols constituting the *General Agreement on the Establishment of Peace and National Accord in Tajikistan* was signed on 27 June 1997 in Moscow. A protocol on refugees was to facilitate the return of refugees after five years exile in Afghanistan. The military protocol of the agreement provided for a process of Demobilisation, Disarmament and Reintegration (DDR) of ex-UTO fighters into the armed forces. The political protocol established a basis for power-sharing in national and local government on a 70:30 split between the government and UTO, created a joint Central Election Commission (CEC), and agreed to the lifting of all restrictions on opposition parties following the completion of DDR. The implementation process was to be coordinated by a Commission on National Reconciliation (CNR), composed equally of government and UTO members and chaired by a UTO representative.

Implementation of the accords was inconsistent. In keeping with the general agreement, UTO leader Said Abdullo Nuri took charge of the CNR. Strong progress was made on the repatriation of refugees from Afghanistan with the deteriorating condition there and the new optimism in Tajikistan producing both 'carrot and stick' incentives to return. Tens of thousands were repatriated with the assistance of the United Nations (UN Mission of Observers to Tajikistan [UNMOT] and UNHCR) and Russian forces (both border guards and CIS peacekeepers). However, progress was much slower and weaker with respect to the protocol on military issues. The disarmament stage of this process was due to take just two months, with ex-opposition fighters assembling at specified points to deliver their arms to be held in secure depots. In actuality this proved unrealistic. From the early stages of the process the UNMOT officers noticed a 'discrepancy between registered fighters and the weapons returned' (cited in Conrad 1999: 3). By the end of 1998 the CNR announced the registration of 6,238 opposition fighters and 2,119 weapons handed in. Despite these unpromising results, in August 1999 the official disarmament process was declared complete, thus allowing for the legalisation of opposition parties, although only a minority of the weapons thought to be held by opposition forces had been handed in. President Rakhmonov stated that, 'no one knows the number of weapons. You [unspecified, probably referring to the Opposition] have hidden them' (cited in ibid: 3). As the security environment remained uncertain commanders remained armed and independent on both sides. Areas of Dushanbe were divided between them until the early 2000s. Nevertheless the process continued and by March 2000, 4,498 UTO fighters had been integrated into the armed forces, largely within their own separable units (Abdullo 2001).

Implementing the political protocol was an equally troubled process. At a national level the 70:30 split was partially achieved with, for example, Turajonzoda taking the position of first vice-premier and the UTO military commander, Mirzo Ziyoev, appointed to head the Ministry of Emergency Situations (MCHS), a 'power' ministry with its own troops. At the local level, the redistribution of posts was less extensive, heavily complicated by localised loyalties and intraregional rivalries (R.G. Smith 1999: 247). The process was further complicated by periodic localised outbreaks of violence between warlords and by the re-emergence of a 'third force' which had been explicitly excluded from the official negotiations. Former Prime Minister Abdullojonov, operating from outside the country, established the National Reconciliation Movement with allies from the northern area of Khujand, and predicted the failure of the peace accords due to their lack of support from Khujandis. When the commander of the government's First Rapid Reaction Brigade, Mahmud Khudoiberdiev, rebelled against the government and then, in November 1998, made an attack on Khujand, the country's second city, collusion with Abdullojonov was alleged by the government. Over 1,000 troops briefly occupied the centre of Khujand before being driven out by a major government offensive involving the troops of Suhrob Kosimov (MVD) and Mirzo Ziyoev (MCHS) who had been on opposing sides before the peace agreement.

Despite numerous crises, momentum in the implementation process was maintained towards presidential and parliamentary elections in November 1999 and February 2000 respectively. Rahmon's re-election as president with 97 per cent of the vote on a 99 per cent turnout was implausible but was not popularly challenged. Although the IRP had great difficulty in registering its candidate, Davlat Usmon, it seems likely that Rahmon would probably have won anyway by a comfortable margin (Akiner 2001: 59). In parliamentary elections, the President's People's Democratic Party (PDP) won a clear majority of thirty-six out of fifty-one seats, with the IRP – the only opposition party to gain seats – gaining just two. The elections signified the end of the implementation phase, underscored the dominance of the governing elite, and indicated a factionalised opposition which was simultaneously 'included' within the political system and yet marginalised from real power. A new hegemony was gradually being established under Rahmon, yet 'national unity' remained contingent. As Khodjibaeva comments with respect to national television, 'the smallest mistake in editorial policy could cause a new explosion' (1999: 15).

At this stage it is important to assess the impact of the accords and their 1997–2000 implementation on peacebuilding as a whole. Iji contends that, although the peace agreement was not comprehensive, it did 'put an end to the major armed conflict' (2005: 189). However, four qualifications need to be made here. First, major military activities continued after the accords, as further significant battles and systematic political violence took place at least until 2001. Second, the accords were limited agreements and were reached only after heavy international pressure. Hay (2001) notes that the UN mediating team always drafted the initial texts of a protocol, 95 per cent of which was accepted by the parties. According to Abdullaev and Barnes, 'the agreements represented the minimum point of consensus between the negotiators at the time they were drafted and did not attempt to provide a normative blueprint for the future' (2001: no pagination). Third, their content represented an inter-elite 'compromise' which reflected the dominance of the civil war's victors, the Kulobi factions around Rahmon, and the support rendered to them by the dominant regional power, Russia. In other words, the winners further institutionalised their victory by severely restricting the political position of UTO groups, and succeeding in excluding the Khujandi faction, by now referred to as 'the third force'. Finally, the peace agreement contained an informal political and economic subtext which divided the (legal and illegal) resources of the country in favour of the Kulobi factions. 'Divvying up the drug smuggling market', Matveeva remarks, 'was perhaps an unwritten part of the peace agreement, in which both sides had a share' (2006: 20). Nevertheless, while the 1997 General Agreement did not itself resolve the conflict, it became an important symbol of compromise between elites and a crucial foundation for legitimate government. It continues to be affirmed by elites on all sides as the basis for the peace which must continue to be preserved.[15]

Building peace, 2000–2007

While the 1993–2000 peace process provided and implemented a juridical 'peace' between the government and opposition, it was between 2000 and 2007 when a nationwide empirical 'peace' was achieved. However, the way that peace has been consolidated is often diametrically opposed to international norms. This brief sketch provides an introduction to international peacebuilding in Tajikistan over the period 2000–2007 before moving on to introduce three key areas of peacebuilding – democratisation, security and development – which will be explored in the latter half of this book.

The year 2000 brought the creation of the UN Tajikistan Office of Peacebuilding (UNTOP) by Security Council mandate, to replace UNMOT, in order 'to consolidate peace and promote democracy' (UNSC 2000). UNTOP was the fourth 'peacebuilding support office' established by the UN and the first outside of Africa. It was renewed annually until its closure in July 2007 as a result of considerable pressure from the Government which sought to rid Tajikistan of an association with conflict. UNTOP's annual budget stood at around US$2 million and it was composed of around ten international and twenty national staff (UNGA 2002: 4–5; UNGA 2003: 46–48; UNGA 2006: 30–36). With so little capacity relative to the task in hand, UNTOP's official role was to encourage wider international assistance and to conduct a limited number of peacebuilding projects, working with other UN agencies, the OSCE, and international and local NGOs. In the words of the Secretary-General's report of 2006, the activities of UNTOP, in line with its terms of reference, were directed towards 'the consolidation of peace and national reconciliation, strengthening of democratic institutions, promotion of the rule of law and support for national capacity-building in the area of human rights' (UNGA 2006: 31). In order to pursue these objectives UNTOP was mandated by the Security Council to conduct targeted projects, mainly in the form of conferences, workshops and training for officials and civil society leaders. The UN General Assembly reviewed UNTOP's progress annually against its objectives.

From the perspective of UNTOP and international peacebuilders more broadly, it is possible to subdivide the period 2000–2007 into one of cautious optimism and another of increasing pessimism. Until 2003, the last warlord groups were eradicated, high rates of economic growth were experienced, an edifice of pluralism was apparent including new opposition parties, newspapers and a huge number of NGOs and life for the vast majority improved demonstrably. During my first visits to Tajikistan, which took place over this period, I was amazed that the country had so recently experienced a war and was struck by how the reality of life across the country belied external accounts of danger and instability. Around 2003–2004, the political space for the opposition shrunk, parties and media were closed down or denied registration, and new economic problems emerged from a reliance on migrant remittances which was producing a pattern of over-consumption and under-investment. At the same time, the political and military security environment remained stable. Drawing too great a divide between pre- and post-2003 is a clear act of international peacebuilding discourse in laying a temporal marker between the promise of peace and the fear of a return to conflict. As I will explore in Chapter 3, apparent regression in Tajikistan may be understood in terms of shifts in the discursive environment.

An analysis of trends in Overseas Development Assistance (ODA) is equally unable to determine a beginning and end to the peacebuilding period. Aid remains a huge part of gross national income (GNI) and remains a staple for those Tajiks who remain in the country (see Table 2.1). However, it is extremely difficult to distinguish international peacebuilding assistance from other objectives and paradigms of ODA. The discursive nature of peacebuilding means that International Community support to education, healthcare or the macro-economy in the post-conflict period was very often constructed in terms of conflict resolution. International assistance rose following the peace agreement to become 17 per cent of gross national income in 2001.

Since around 2003–2004, however, there has been a visible decline both in the importance of peacebuilding as an aid paradigm for major Western donors in Tajikistan and a decline in Western aid as a proportion of total ODA with a clear shift away from such peacebuilding assistance indicated both in terms of sectors and donors (Table 2.2). A far greater proportion of aid is now given in the form

Table 2.1 Basic social and economic data, Tajikistan, 1997–2003

	1997	1998	1999	2000	2001	2002	2003
Life expectancy at birth, total (years)	67.2	67.5	67.4	67.6	68.3	68.6	63.6
Population, total (millions)	5.9	6.0	6.0	6.1	6.1	6.2	6.4
GDP growth (annual %)	1.7	5.3	3.7	8.3	10.2	9.1	10.2
GNI[1] per capita (Atlas method, 2005 US$)	160	170	170	180	170	180	210
Aid (% of GNI)	9.77	12.71	11.88	13.35	16.79	14.31	9.85
Aid (total, US$ per capita)	14.28	26.21	19.89	20.14	27.27	26.88	22.85

Source: UNDP 2005b: 241.

Note
1 Gross national income is used by the World Bank to measure all production in the domestic economy (i.e. GDP) plus the net flows of income (such as rents, profits and labour income) from abroad. It is a more reliable indicator of wealth in a country such as Tajikistan which relies on labour migration for much of its income.

Table 2.2 International aid to Tajikistan, 2003–2007

Overseas development assistance (US$)	2003	2004	2005	2006
Loans	60.0	77.6	99.3	192.7
Grants	205.0	265.5	245.2	200.9
Total	265.0	343.1	344.4	393.6

Source: Principals Coordination In Tajikistan, Summary Tables, available at: http://www.untj.org/principals/tracking/summary.php, accessed: 23 July 2008.

of loans, reflecting the increased assistance of non-traditional donors, especially China. The Chinese government provided a US$105 million loan in 2006 and a further US$500 million loan for infrastructural investment in 2007. This loan exceeded the total volume of all other ODA for that year and indicates a dramatic shift away from a reliance on International Community (peacebuilding) assistance to, by 2007, a new and highly indebted relationship with China.

One of the key foci of international peacebuilding since 2000 has been democratic reform, although this period has seen democratisation thwarted with the increasing political dominance of Rahmon's Danghara clique. The 70:30 split of posts between government and opposition has gradually been dismantled with few former-opposition figures still in position.[16] However, this retreat from formal power-sharing has not led to the emergence of electoral politics. A June 2003 referendum allowed more than 100 changes to the constitution including Article 65 allowing two seven-year presidential terms and raising the possibility of Rahmon, after his election in 2006, staying in office until 2020. The shrinking of the circle of power has also involved much work behind the scenes, including the use of *kompromat* ('compromising materials', for political pressure) to force out dissenters. Targets included both opposition figures from the war, most prominently Mahmudruzi Iskandarov, the leader of the DPT and ex-commander from the Tajikobad district of Rasht valley, and some of President Rahmon's closest allies, including Ghaffor Mirzoyev, the commander of the presidential guard, who were both jailed in 2005. Quantitative data provide further evidence of this trend to increasing authoritarianism (Table 2.3). The nature of this form of domination by an increasingly exclusive section of elites despite, and at times because of, international assistance will be examined in Chapter 5.

The 2000s have also seen a notable decline in political violence and a broad improvement in the security environment. From 1999 to 2001, fighters of the Islamic Movement of Uzbekistan (IMU) made summer-time incursions from

Table 2.3 Nations in transit democracy score, *Freedom House,* 1997–2006

	1997	1998	1999	2001	2002	2003	2004	2005	2006
Democracy score	6.20	5.95	5.75	5.58	5.63	5.63	5.71	5.71	5.93

Note
7 = least free; 1 = most free.

temporary bases in Tajikistan to neighbouring Kyrgyzstan and Uzbekistan. At least two districts of the country – Darband and Tavildera – were dominated by warlords, and are thought to have provided support for IMU activities. Violence, largely around criminal activities, was frequent in the Rasht valley as a whole including assassinations of government ministers, the kidnapping of foreigners, violence around the trafficking of drugs and rivalries between groups. Across the country during the 2000 elections violence killed a total of nineteen, including two candidates (OSCE 2000). However, these groups cannot be said to have been acting 'independently of the authorities' but rather overlapped with the state as their members often held positions within state structures. Gradually, the Rahmon regime has further co-opted them or has suppressed renegade elements that have become an embarrassment or impediment to their hegemony, for example in the final battles of the conflict against Rahmon Sanginov and Mullo Abdullo in 2001. The annihilation of these two warlords and their groups represents the re-centralisation of military forces to Dushanbe that has characterised the period. This correlates with fewer acts of open violence in the Rasht valley, which is now firmly under government control. However, as will be discussed in Chapter 6, this is more a process of the changing dynamics of securitisation where reintegration preceded demobilisation and disarmament than the completion of DDR and the Security Sector Reform agenda (Torjesen and MacFarlane 2007). Moreover, despite this reduction in political violence across the country, violence is extremely high in the family and home, with perhaps up to 50 per cent of households (Haarr 2005). This is emblematic of Tajikistan's 'peace'.

The economic development picture also equivocates. In the 2000s the Tajik economy achieved impressive formal rates of economic development and rises in GNI per capita (see Table 2.1). However, these figures are hardly representative of the real economy of the country. They do not capture the cotton business and narcotics trafficking through which elites can make huge profits while the poor and children are forced into unpaid work, nor the combination of subsistence agriculture, labour migration and shuttle-trading through which the poor seek to earn a living. Outward seasonal migration by males, largely to Russia, is highly significant in Tajikistan. Figures gathered by the International Organisation for Migration (IOM) estimate that anywhere between 0.6 and 1.2 million left the country for work between 2001 and 2002 (Olimova and Bosc 2003). Significantly, these numbers suggest that perhaps around a half of men of fighting age may be abroad for a significant period over the course of a year. Whitlock notes, 'in the new century far more Tajiks went to Russia than had ever done so during the days of the Soviet Union' (2002: 266). Household and social surveys indicate that whatever rehabilitation of livelihoods has been experienced can largely be attributed to the informal economy, primarily remittances from labour migration, and international assistance (Olimova and Bosc 2003; Hoffman and Buckley 2007; SIDA 2007). Moreover, despite impressive rates of economic growth in recent years, by 2005 the Tajik economy had still only reached 62 per cent of its size in 1991. One study concludes that growth has been, 'largely triggered by *one-time discrete events*' such as the peace and the sudden increase in migration (SIDA 2007: 4). Thus, long-term economic and social trends indicate a development reversal where today's teenagers have significantly reduced educational opportunities and a lower standard of living than their parents did at their age. Whilst overall economic decline has been reversed, it is not clear that decay of the social environment has yet been arrested with higher rates of illiteracy, child labour, HIV/AIDS and drug addiction. As explored in Chapter 7, a reliance on international aid remains a feature but one which can be manipulated locally by those in positions of power.

Conclusions

If the events of the Tajikistan conflict and peace process themselves are contingent and complex, the writing of them is barely a simpler endeavour. Dominant peacebuilding discourses and disciplinary academic ones build on and respond to one another, often according to political and scholarly trends rather than due to practical experience or new research findings. These discourses are intertextually linked. Moreover, as will be explored in subsequent chapters, the writing and practising of history intertwines. Influential English-language reports and journalistic accounts, undoubtedly feed back into the practices of international actors, donor priorities and foreign policies decisions. How the conflict, war and peace process are remembered and forgotten, and how the future is envisioned, is the theme for Chapters 3 and 4.

This review of the history has provided insight into the differences and similarities between war and 'peace' in Tajikistan and thus the character of 'peacebuilding'. Two points stand out. First, regionalism remains the most significant discursive and practical feature of the peace. Yet this regionalism is Janus-faced. As Mullojanov notes, 'the Tajik civil war is a modern phenomenon, the product of the Soviet system and of its regionally differentiated policy of economic development, and the Brejnevian policy of stabilization of the nomenclatures' (2001b: 248). Regionalism can be the vehicle for clashes of ideas and interests which supersede ethnic rivalry. It can serve processes of militarisation, or those of pacification. Today these basic divisions of Tajik political society remain yet, as will be further investigated in Chapter 4, they are somehow constituted into a stable political order. This raises a second issue. In light of the major role of Russia in Tajikistan throughout the period, the impact of the Western-dominated 'international community' remains unclear. On what basis did the UN, OSCE and international humanitarian organisations make space for international peacebuilding in Tajikistan? How did they respond to the privileged position of Russia and to what extent did their policies and programmes respond to their experiences of intervention in practice? The following chapter considers in more depth the nature of international community in Tajikistan and addresses the question of why it was discursively bound to pursue a vision of the liberal peace despite doubts about the practical salience of this vision.

3   International peacebuilding in Tajikistan

> Western ideals of constitutional democracy, human rights, free and fair multi-party elections and political reconciliation are worthy objectives, but they do not necessarily fit within the Tajik's own conceptions of their future.
>
> (Olivier Brennikmeijer, UN official in Tajikistan 1998: 181)

To understand the Tajik peace better we must understand how it is differentially legitimated via popular-subordinate, elite and international discourses. In any setting of the post-conflict there are multiple communities or 'selves' at play. Over the next two chapters I will investigate these communities across three scales of political order: global, elite and subordinate. This short chapter begins with the global. It explores the rise and fall of international peacebuilding discourse in Tajikistan from 2000 to 2007. As such this chapter and the remainder of this book can be read in four ways.

First, this book charts international peacebuilding in Tajikistan – its basic discourse and its public and hidden transcripts. It considers international intervention in terms of the 'international community' in Tajikistan. This self-image, the International Community,[1] shapes peacebuilding discourse and strategy towards the post-conflict other, in this case, Tajikistan. Yet it is not homogeneous or monolithic. Elsewhere I have outlined three basic discourses of international peacebuilding: democratic peacebuilding, civil society peacebuilding and state-building (Heathershaw 2008a). In this chapter I explore the specific practising of these basic discourses in the public pronouncements, acts of programme implementation and diplomatic endeavours of the International Community in Tajikistan. Furthermore I will investigate the 'hidden' transcript of peacebuilding, hinted at in Brennikmeijer's above-cited scepticism. Yet the infrequency of open departures from international discourse also highlights the power of peacebuilding as a hegemonic discourse which makes international intervention meaningful and legitimate.

Second, it is a study of the politics of peacebuilding in Tajikistan. A political analysis of peacebuilding explores not simply the extent to which it achieves its ostensible aims of achieving a more liberal, just or effective political and social system but also its impact on the kind of political (dis)order which emerges in the aftermath of civil war. There is an international dimension to the emergence of legitimate order even if the transition process is quite different from that envisaged by peacebuilders. Many of the resources required to render patronage are provided by 'external' actors which may play a greater 'internal' role than the state itself. By working within this process of the re-institutionalisation of statehood, Western donors, UN agencies and the OSCE also contribute to this transition. They are producing new rules of the game, new modes of consent, and new spaces for politics. In revealing the particular representations of peace-building texts, this section will begin an investigation of the extent to which global political space, identity and ideology extends into Tajikistani territory. Where, it asks, is the world in Tajikistan?

Third, the book is a study of discursive change. The international discourses outlined here are by no means static. In some respects, as will be discussed below, internal emphases and intertextual relations have changed considerably since international peacebuilding was officially inscribed to Tajikistan with the creation of UNTOP in 2000. Today both UNTOP and international peacebuild-ing have expired and the reasons for that are vital to the story of this book. There are three sources of discursive change, none of which can be attributed to objec-tive or extra-discursive causes. First, there is endogenous discursive change which reflects changing ideas of intervention within the community of practice. This form of change will be explored here in terms of the rise of statebuilding over civil society peacebuilding. Second, and also discussed here, discourse may shift when the hidden transcript begins to break through into the public domain. Finally, discursive change can occur in the intertextual relations between com-munities. This chapter closes with a reflection on the response of elites to peace-building and Chapter 4 goes on to outline the elites and subordinates as correspondent communities with international peacebuilding.

Finally, this is an analysis conducted from a position at the edges of the Inter-national Community itself. Many academic analysts have also worked and con-tinue to work in and for national government agencies, international organisations and non-governmental organisations. In this sense, we are or have been part of the International Community in Tajikistan; and any analysis of that community, such as the one undertaken here, is one conducted partly from the inside. Indeed much academic writing seeks to solve the problems identified by policy-makers and found on the agenda of the International Community. Ana-lysts and scholars implicitly or explicitly locate themselves as part of the identity group of the International Community. It is in this sense that the vast majority of writing on Tajikistan is an exercise in 'othering'. It is here that this discourse analysis of the International Community begins.

In the first part of the chapter I explore how Tajikistan is a self-image to the International Community: it is a place of both peril and promise; a place which can transition to peace to the extent that it leaves its essential ethno-national pathology behind and becomes who we internationals imagine ourselves to be. In the second section, I reflect on the contentions in this othering process, between civil society and statebuilding dimensions of discourse and show how these two trends have produced different kinds of engagement in Tajikistan and how their incorporation is reconstituting international engagement 'after peacebuilding'. In the third section I consider the hidden peacebuilding of the International Community in terms of the scepticism of international programme managers towards their own work. I then go on to introduce the tactics of accommodation and discursive practices which justify the adaptation of programmes to local realities.

The international community and the Tajik other

The object of intervention (the 'other') in peacebuilding discourse is determined in comparison with the subject of the International Community (the 'self'). Remaining on the margins of the global solidarity group since independence, Tajikistan has been subject to certain general readings, intrusions and expectations. In such a way the global boundary line between civilised and uncivilised is drawn. Regions and localities acquire their own particular meanings in international discourse with respect to international self-images, as Campbell (1998a, 1998b) and Hansen (2006) have both shown with respect to Bosnia. Peacebuilding perspectives on the Central Asian subject have been shaped through the dichotomy of 'them'/'us' (peril/promise), where the peril that they may regress to traditional solidarities and conflicts can be offset by the promise that they might become more democratic, like who we imagine ourselves to be.

Who they are: the peril in Tajikistan

In international discourse the Central Asian space has often been presented in terms of danger: the perils of re-traditionalisation. Myers (2003) has shown how it has been seen through Sovietological and post-Soviet discourses and has increased in its exotic otherness since the fall of the USSR. There are three primary 'threats' identified by this 'discourse of danger' in Central Asia (Thompson and Heathershaw 2005): Islamic fundamentalism, resurgent nationalism or reawakened tribalism (Heathershaw 2005a: 23–25). Often these perils are combined as in one pseudo-historical popular account comparing Tajikistan's 'valley-based clans headed by petty warlords' with those of Afghanistan, whose own war was, 'a protracted civil conflict that radicalised young Tajiks and promoted Islamic fundamentalism' (Myers 2003: 183–184). Foremost amongst these threats in Western eyes is that of radical Islam – a perception which has been accentuated following increased Western official and popular interest in the region after 9/11. This had special implications for Tajikistan where Islam versus Secularism proved a particularly popular mode of interpretation in the International Community (e.g. Rashid 1994), despite the multiple interpretations offered in the more respected academic literature (see Chapter 2). Thus, preventing the perceived re-emergence of radical Islam becomes a key task of international intervention in Central Asia and Tajikistan in particular (F.S. Hansen 2005: 45–54; Seifert and Kraikemayer 2003). Such analyses serve to internalise the causes of conflict to Tajikistan. For example, the UN Secretary-General's representative in Tajikistan, Vladimir Sotirov, argues that the reasons for the war and any future conflict are not about external factors, as often claimed by Tajikistani political leaders, but by Tajik society's own 'deep problems' (UNTOP/NAPST 2003: 64).

In this vein, it follows that many policy-based assessments are very sceptical about Tajikistan's 'peace'. For some, this reflects regression across the region (Olcott 2005). However, within this discursively constructed dangerous space, Tajikistan represents a particular problem. The Open Society Institute (OSI) reported that despite the peace agreement, Tajikistan was ripe to 'erupt into armed conflict' (1999, no pagination); a judgement that was echoed by Lynch (2001: 69) and Collins (2003: 268–269). This continued perception of peril in Tajikistan expresses a widely held belief that peace will remain elusive while the country remains unreformed (ICG 2001a: ii). Even seasoned analysts have apparently fallen into this trap. For example, Schoeberlein, in a guidebook to conflict prevention work in the region, judged that 'current tensions in Tajikistan are far greater than before the war', and only the 'war-weariness of the population may provide some insurance against any widespread outbreak of violence' (2002: 476–477). Thus, Tajikistan was represented in the first half of the 2000s, as 'the most vulnerable of Central Asian nations' (ICG 2001a: i). Only with the uprising in Uzbekistan and the violent political change in Kyrgyzstan of 2005 came a shift in this relative assessment. International Crisis Group, for example, has not produced a report or briefing on Tajikistan since 2004, switching its focus to Uzbekistan and Kyrgyzstan, particularly after 2005.

The effect of such othering via a discourse of danger is to determine a priori elite and citizen roles, attributing to them particular identities and roles of conflicting parties, active mediators (in civil society) or passive victims. This determinism is strongly reflected in Conciliation Resources' *Accord* special issue on Tajikistan, *The Politics of Compromise*, (Abdullaev and Barnes 2001), one of the most widely cited pieces in international literature and reports, bringing together many key figures from the peace process. The editors praise the 'exceptionally well-coordinated' peace process led by the United Nations (2001: no pagination). Contributors draw attention to the roles of international organisation and 'civil society' as well as equalising the different national parties to the process. On the other hand they note that, '[Tajikistanis] history of war and violence has led many to prefer a government capable of sustaining a "negative peace" based on life without war at the price of not enjoying their full range of personal rights and liberties' (Abdullaev and Barnes 2001: no pagination). Here it is thus implied that the fault for the lack of post-conflict progress lies with not just the Rahmon regime but the Tajikistani people, joined together as the other of peacebuilding. Meanwhile international governmental and non-governmental players are mediators at all 'levels' of the process (Abdullaev and Barnes 2001). The volume unsurprisingly avoids analysis of the role of the informal: the importance of corruption and the role of patronage networks in greasing the politics of compromise, nor the role of narco-trafficking as an alternative source of employment for ex-commanders. There is furthermore little acknowledgement that many Tajikistanis were at different times parties, mediators and victims. Peace-building is thus reduced to a formalist process of compromise and democratic institution-building.

Who we are: the promise in Tajikistan

If the enemy-other of peacebuilding is found in the nature of Tajikistan and the Tajiks then the ideal-other, the endpoint of peacebuilding, is a self-image. For peacebuilders, war is born out of a failure of democratic institutions – a failure, in other words, to adopt some variation of the liberal-democratic government found in the member states of the International Community. This representation evokes a second prism through which Central Asia has been seen in the era of independence, that of nascent, transitional democracy.

The fusing of peace and democracy is indeed mandated in the role of the UN in Tajikistan. The UN Tajikistan Office of Peacebuilding (UNTOP) was estab-lished, according to the Security Council, 'in order to consolidate peace and promote democracy' (2004). In its very existence then UNTOP was premised upon the understanding that Tajikistan's elites and people share these ambitions. Sotirov remarked in 2002 that, 'there is a wish and will in the leadership of the country to introduce democratic principles of governance and development in the society, in an effort to create a vibrant civil society'. Furthermore he noted,

> I am encouraged by the democratic developments so far in this country. I believe if it continues to move in the same direction in the future, it will quickly develop into a pluralistic democracy. However, a lot of difficulties have to be overcome, especially in the field of further separation of powers, mass media, promotion and the protection of human rights, thereby encour-aging civil society, reforming power structures, and continuing with a spirit of tolerance and dialogue in the society.[2]

Such accounts highlight democratic deficits which threaten the peace, whilst being broadly supportive of the government. For example, the US Ambassador to Tajikistan, Richard Hoagland, in March 2004, remarked that he was 'optimis-tic about democracy in Tajikistan' and that 'in the first instance, this is because the government has chosen a democratic path'.[3]

The public transcripts of international actors in Tajikistan consistently invoke the ideal-other of peacebuilding as the goal to which Tajikistan aspires or should aspire. *What Peace Five Years After The Signing of the Tajik Peace Agreement?*, Abdullaev and Freizer's 2003 study for the UK Government's Global Conflict Prevention Pool, follows a similar line of argument. Success is attributed to international intervention, 'as the peace building process resolved many of the power sharing tensions between the former warring parties' (ibid.: 7). A second stage is then determined: statebuilding. The 'state-building process, where the central government has struggled to assert control over the entire country', is seen as a significant but more precarious process given the centralisation of power and resources this has involved, and the 'network of patron–client relations' which it is based on (ibid.: 7). Moreover, they argue:

> While the country has effectively overcome many challenges, it continues to grapple with securing cooperative arrangements with its neighbours, establishing a democratic and decentralised system of governance, and promoting economic development and investment.
>
> (ibid.: 5)

Such text ascribes to the individual the desire for 'rights' and the responsibility of citizenship, while envisioning a state with the right of sovereignty and responsibilities for reform. Similarly, an ICG report which warned of the potential for Tajikistan to slip back into conflict made eight recommendations to the Tajikistani government to further democratisation and power-sharing, none of which have subsequently been fulfilled (2001a: ii).

The resilience of international peacebuilding discourse in Tajikistan is found not in unambiguous evidence of progress but in its self-imagining: the very division of them/us and peril/promise. Tajikistanis from the President down are deemed to oscillate between these two poles; this is the tremendous power of transition discourse to interpret and re-interpret reality. Even where a peacebuilding analyst argues that Tajikistan's process is failing it is still according to the two poles of failure and success by which judgements are made. Transition portrayals of the Tajik subject may be dismissed by some as rhetorical carrots and sticks, yet underlying such statements are peacebuilding's axioms regarding the sustainable post-conflict state. This basic discourse provides the very foundation of international action, space and identity in Tajikistan. While by 2005 few international observers were claiming that outside initiatives could do much to challenge the retrenchment of authoritarianism, this regression had occurred, it was argued, not because of the involvement of the International Community but because of insufficient involvement (Malekzade 2005: 2). In these general terms it is impossible for international peacebuilding to fail.

From humanitarianism to statebuilding

The sketch offered above is not to say that peacebuilding has remained entirely consistent over the period since 2000. Rather, shifts within this structure have been produced both by global trends towards statebuilding and, to a very limited degree, by the experiences working in the Tajikistani context. By the middle of the 2000s this began to affect the advice being offered to international actors. For example, Abdullaev and Freizer's distinction between 'peacebuilding' and 'statebuilding' (2003: 5, see above) advocates the latter as the new challenge for Tajikistan. Public international discourse has shifted towards statebuilding in the wake of 9/11, constituting a Tajikistani environment which is almost universally acknowledged to be 'after peacebuilding' (Heathershaw and Mullojanov 2007).

However, this new discursive environment retains many of the key ethical, spatial and temporal markers of the Central Asian other which have characterised the international debate since the early-1990s. Transition discourses such as peacebuilding never die but reinvent themselves in new civil society and state-building variants.

The rise of civil society peacebuilding in Tajikistan

Civil society peacebuilding in Tajikistan has been primarily driven by aid agencies and international development actors. As such, its genealogy is complex. First, it is imbedded in a post-conflict humanitarianism perspective which highlights the twin perils of poverty and authoritarianism. To humanitarians the conflict is interpreted primarily as a desperate fight for resources, born out of poverty and the dysfunctional post-Soviet economy. The work of BBC correspondent Monica Whitlock (2002), which is perhaps the most widely read English-language account of the civil war, and that of Aziz Niyazi (1998, 1999) focus on the social and humanitarian dimensions of the conflict. There is much to be said for this explanation of the causes of war but what concerns us here are the functions of this humanitarian discourse with its emphasis on the need to build capacity from the 'bottom-up'. For Niyazi, this means that conflict resolution must tackle, 'problems of demography, resettlement policies, of the economy and state system, and of ensuring the harmony of state and society' (1999: 191). In particular Niyazi argues for the involvement of 'social organizations and local organs of self-government' (1999: 192) in environmental protection. Following a reduction in the level of violence in the early 2000s many of these goals were pursued via the community peacebuilding programmes of international non-governmental organisations.

The huge post-conflict expansion of international development industry in Tajikistan in recent years should also be understood alongside a rising interest in civil society in Central Asia and its deployment as a solution for the problems of the region by donor agencies and NGOs. The very idea of 'civil society' is premised upon a political society where the state is emancipated from its constituent individuals, groups and networks. However appropriate this idea in the Central Asian context, its dispersal by international organisations has been almost viral in its intensity and lack of differentiation. Starr approvingly notes the 'breathtaking speed' and 'intensity' of the growth of civil society across Central Asia (1999: 27). Tabyshalieva, deploying the language of donors, views the development of civil society as a process of enhancing 'the capacity and expertise of NGOs in long-term conflict prevention' (2002: 482). While civil society, she argues, 'is still at a rudimentary stage', it is beginning to influence political developments locally and nationally (ibid.: 482–483). In the case of Tajikistan, Harold Saunders argues that under the concept of the multilevel peace process such organisations have facilitated, 'crucial processes of post-conflict peacebuilding by citizens in civil society' (1998: 4). Several NGOs were established by participants in the Inter-Tajik dialogue and a number of university teaching programmes in conflict resolution have been influenced by the concept. International NGOs, certain UN agencies (esp. UNDP) and donor organisations (USAID and DfID) emphasised 'civil society' programmes as they became more involved in the region after 2000, particularly those aimed at conflict prevention or resolution.

Finally civil society peacebuilding must be understood in terms of trends dating back to the 1980s in the global development industry away from direct support for governments. These discursive trends produced a surge of interest in community development programmes amongst donors. This process arguably culminated at the start of this decade with the twinning of macro-economic reform to community development and poverty reduction under the strategy to achieve the UN's Millennium Development Goals (MDG). The MDGs have become a key marker in Tajikistan (ICG 2003; Babajanian 2004) and one that cannot be met without a major role for civil society. Between 1994 and 2001, approximately 400 NGOs were registered with the Tajikistani government (Akiner 2001: 58). After 2001 the sector grew exponentially, yet in recent years the fleeting nature of many of these groups has become apparent. By 2007, the Ministry of Justice had approximately 3,000 NGOs registered but perhaps as many as 80 per cent of these might now be defunct.[4] Many of these organisations were created under international programmes and, despite hopes for 'indigenisation', their life-span broadly matches that of the programmes.

There are broadly speaking three species of such neo-liberal civil society, yet in practice many organisations are of a hybrid type. The first type were explicitly engineered as part of a USAID civil society building programme administered by American NGOs Counterpart Consortium or IREX and can be regarded as donor-organised non-governmental organisations (DONGOs). For example, in Tajikistan the American NGO Counterpart Consortium established Civil Society Support Centres (CSSC) across regional towns and cities under a programme beginning in 1997. These CSSCs were major institutions, most of which continue to exist and hold to similar objectives. For example, although all involvement of the CSSC in Khujand with Counterpart ended in 2003, the organisation has struggled on, winning grants here and there. In 2007 it had contracted substantially but was still known generally as 'Counterpart Consortium – Khujand'. Rather than seeing the break with its parent as an opportunity, as was imagined in international discourse, the director of the organisation presented the change negatively. 'We were set up as a branch (*filial*) of Counterpart', she noted, 'and we had difficulties working with other international organisations'.[5]

A second type of NGO, similar to the DONGO but often smaller and more specialised, are direct sub-contractors of the International Community. They are often urban-based and run by former officials or members of the intelligentsia possessing technical and English-language skills. Such groups are also dependent on a relationship with an international NGO or even a particular programme. One organisation based in Khujand, Ittifok, was a large and buoyant NGO in 2005 as a sub-contractor for Mercy Corps under the Peaceful Communities Initiative (PCI) programme employing ten to fifteen individuals. However, by late

2006, as the programme drew to a close the organisation was wound up. Its executive director found employment in Dushanbe, but the NGO itself expired.[6] Rather than seeing such groups, which are often active one year and expired the next, as local organisations it might be better to see them as vehicles for gifted individuals and extensions of the International Community in Tajikistan. It is in this sense that Hurinisso Gafforzoda, political activist, NGO leader and long-time partner of the International Community, commented in 2007 that, 'compared to Kyrgyzstan and Ukraine, our "civil society" is a project-conducting civil society'. It is composed of hybrid institutions which represent the interests of, and are entirely dependent on, international donors in fund-raising. More cynically, some of these organisations are known locally as 'pocket NGOs' (*karmanyi NPOs*) given that they acquire business from certain agencies on the basis of payments. Corruption, whilst difficult to investigate, is understood to be rife in this type of civil society.[7]

A third type are so-called grassroots or community-based organisations (CBOs), set up in villages by internationals and local NGOs in order to implement humanitarian assistance in a given place. As will be explored in Chapter 7, both MDG and peacebuilding maxims informed an emphasis on CBOs as agents of change. Indeed, CBOs as part of 'civil society' were frequently presented as an antidote to an excessive focus on the state (Tabyshalieva 2002: 482). Several major programmes were conducted after 2000. Some of these programmes endeavoured to create standing organisations with a micro-lending facility; consequently, today such organisations are widespread in Tajikistan. Around a half of the country's rural districts (Jamoats) are covered by either UNDP Jamoat Resource Centres (JRC) or the Aga Khan's Village Organisation (VO) structure with its Social Union of VOs at regional level (SUDVO).

The shift to statebuilding

In recent years 'civil society' has become less fashionable, evinced by a discursive and programmatic shift away from the 'bottom-up' approach of NGOs. This should be understood in terms of interdependent trends including the changing global political context of international development following 9/11 and a move to bring the state back into development through direct budget support. In a more conservative policy environment, the threat of 'terrorism' became increasingly explained in terms of the 'failed state', particularly in the US National Security Strategy of 2002. This was reflected in writing on Tajikistan and, as will be shown in Chapter 6, spurred new interest in and funding for security assistance programmes.

Zürcher's study, although addressing community development and commissioned by the German donor agency GTZ, can perhaps be read in light of the merging of civil society and statebuilding approaches. While the risk of violent conflict is said to be 'decreasing', the author argues that 'poverty, rising inequality, and high dependence on labour migration and donor money', combined with 'uneven access to land' is exacerbating the dominance of an elite which has seized control of the state (2004: ii). Therefore, Zürcher notes, hybrid forms of local governance are emerging which reflect the power of vertical patronage networks but vary greatly from community to community (ibid.: iv). By reasserting the elite as the key providers of order, and exponents of exploitation, the report effectively bridges humanitarian and statebuilding wings of peacebuilding. Abdullaev and Freizer (2003), as we have seen, offer a similar line of argument. Yet there are internal tensions within these works as they describe existing practices and simultaneously prescribe targets. If state–society relations are based on patron–client networks, as the authors suggest, what kind of decentralisation, which they recommend, ought we to expect?

Matveeva's more recent work, *Central Asia: A Strategic Framework for Peacebuilding*, for the British NGO International Alert, seeks to address the tensions in these two reports, both of which she references. Written after spending a period working for the UN in Tajikistan, the report adds to this post-9/11 shift towards statebuilding. Peacebuilding she argues, needs to be revised.

> There is no reason to hide a preference for programmes that ensure full accountability, good governance at every level and democratic participation by all. But it is not the most effective approach to insist at all times on that full agenda, especially when some parties with which donor governments want to work, including governments in Central Asia, find profound cause for concern in the democratization agenda. The suggestion here is to focus on local-level transparency, some long-term aspects of statebuilding and the development of national discussions about the future.
>
> (2006: 12–13)

Moreover, Matveeva notes that Tajikistan has achieved a 'degree of stability' primarily through 'enhanced security – the main plank of the government's legitimacy' (ibid.: 19). It is in the security dimension that common ground between international actors, and the basis for 'engaging with Russia', can be found (ibid.: 10, 12). Such work suggests that it is both global discourse and intertextual relations with elite and local actors which determine shifts in policy advice and analysis. Via both discursive evolution and intertextual relations, moreover, Tajikistan is increasingly inscribed as 'after peacebuilding'.

Both the Abdullaev and Freizer (2003) and Matveeva (2006) reports were written with specific mandates to develop a strategic framework for peacebuilding. It is this discursive dynamic which best explains the disjuncture between analysis and recommendations found in both texts, particularly Abdullaev and Freizer's. The reports exhibit the classic hallmarks of peacebuilding. The authors inscribe the Tajik subject as desiring 'rights' of citizenship, while writing the state with the right of sovereignty and responsibilities for reform. These are the leitmotifs of neo-liberal peacebuilding texts. Yet both reports, especially Matveeva's later study, come down in favour of a shift towards statebuilding and argue that peace-making and peacebuilding have *already overcome* many of the 'challenges' of the war. Matveeva argues that statebuilding is an international strategy more in keeping with the ambitions of local elites. However, the international statebuilding she evokes she supposes as universal and thus entirely in keeping with the transition agenda of the International Community.

Thus, rather than wholesale shift away from the civil society approach we appear to be seeing its contraction, reformulation and incorporation within that of statebuilding. Leading International Community development and decentralisation programmes have reflected this in seeking to incorporate 'top-down' and 'bottom-up' approaches in terms of a good governance approach to local government. One influential study commissioned by the Swedish International Development Agency (SIDA) argued that independent community-based organisations constitute 'parallel structures' and should not be supported (Ramböll Management 2006: 18). In apparent contrast to this, another oft-cited study of local government in Tajikistan concludes: 'at a local level, the boundary between public and private remains murky' (UI 2003: 2). However, in discourse analysis terms it is not just how these approaches differ that is important (indeed their contrasts are not explicitly addressed in the hastily and limitedly self-critical International Community). Perhaps more important is that both reports are used to argue for the subordination of such community-based organisations to local government in order to build state – envisaged as the supreme locus of governance. Such discursive developments have led to programming shifts with DfID, for example, making a £3.34 million investment over 2006–2009 into the Zerafhson valley of Tajikistan where UNDP Jamoat Resource Centres have increasingly been subordinated to state organs (DfID 2007: 1). Moreover, in the wake of this decreased international interest in and funding for civil society and a new and more restrictive state law on civil society, the heavily dependent sector faces a major contraction.[8] Whilst this shrinking of the NGO sector in Tajikistan may not be a direct result of the international discursive shift way from 'civil society', it at least indicates the heavy dependence of the sector and the virtual realities of neo-liberal 'civil society'.

This is not to say that consensus has been established in this merger of security and development (Duffield 2002). Statebuilding accounts are founded in security concerns and start from an assumption that Tajikistan is a 'failed' or 'semi-anarchical state' dominated by warlords, where further war can only be precariously avoided through the presence of foreign troops (Dadmehr 2003: 257). Such analyses of the 'failed state' make plausible, indeed necessary, the application of statebuilding programmes to Tajikistan. Since the declaration of the 'war on terror', such programmes and platforms have been explored and advocated in the work of influential Washington-based analysts (See Blank 2005; Giragosian 2006; Hill 2002; Mihalka 2006). On the other hand, proponents of democratic peacebuilding and civil society approaches begin with a development ethos and continue stubbornly to affirm the value of democratisation in statebuilding. Hill, for example, in 2002 wrote of statebuilding in these terms:

> The primary goal for U.S. policy must also be to enhance Central Asia's development not just its military role. Like Afghanistan, if they are to

transform themselves from potential breeding grounds for transnational terrorists into viable, stable states, the Central Asian countries must liberalise
economically and democratise politically.

(2002: 18)

Similarly, ICG noted that Tajikistan's peace depended to a great extent on its
progress in democratic reform and that a conservative or gradualist 'peacebuilding' had allowed a legitimate settlement to regress into an increasingly illegitimate and resolutely anti-democratic institution-building process (2004: 19).

The international public transcript of Tajikistan's peacebuilding has never
reached a point of absolute consensus – roughly divided as it is between three
basic discourses – yet its 'pragmatic' prescriptions stayed within the bounds of
the neo-liberal political imaginary of the International Community with its peril/
promise and Them/Us dichotomies. The shifts that have occurred should not be
viewed empirically in terms of the objective passing of one phase (peacebuilding) to the next (statebuilding). This shift must be grasped interpretatively. If
'peacebuilding' is less commonly deployed in international texts and testimonies
today, it is not because its challenges have been overcome and its goals have
been achieved. Rather, global discursive trends and local intertextual relations
have both served to shift the discursive environment to the extent that Tajikistan
can be said to be 'after peacebuilding'. That such discursive shifts must be
understood interpretatively, rather than explained objectively, indicates how
public knowledge is intertextually constructed in the International Community.
In this world officials and programme coordinators must try and make their programmes work in a Tajikistan which does not correspond to its representation in
international public discourse.

International peacebuilding in practice

As international peacebuilding texts and testimonies are drawn from the public
transcripts they narrate a simplistic schema of liberal intervention. However, in
countless personal interviews and encounters between 2003 and 2007, I found
many disillusioned or dispassionate members of the International Community
departing from this public aspect. More often than not such opinions were
expressed off the record. Individual programme managers testified that switches
in international strategy were very little about 'realities on the ground' and more
about the coming in and going out of development and peacebuilding fashions
and institutional requirements to declare success in its absence. I came to con-
clude that the regularity of such dissent indicated more than merely the stresses
and strains of implementing challenging programmes in a difficult environment.
Rather these 'hidden' accounts express doubt about the ethical, spatial and temporal parameters of the public transcript. They suggest that particularity and
context is considerably more important than the idea of the universal or univer-
salisable the International Community supposes. There are at least three variants
of the hidden transcript: *scepticism* about the stated success of programmes (as

represented in 'independent' evaluations), *pessimism* regarding the state of the country (as opposed to the optimism of public transcripts), and *consternation* with one another (in contrast to the self-image of a single, relatively coordinated International Community).

Hidden transcripts of international peacebuilding

International officials in Tajikistan often professed *scepticism*, even cynicism, regarding the impact of the programmes they were themselves conducting to further that peace. One NGO officer, for example, conceded that political development in Tajikistan was dominated by the state and claimed there was 'no role for civil society' in democratisation. Furthermore he remarked that the role of the International Community in Tajikistani politics would 'always' be very limited.[9] Another programme manager noted that their work had limited impact in terms of both physical and social infrastructure. He remarked that NGOs in his region of Tajikistan had built 'a million fucked-up water systems'. Moreover, in terms of his project to build civil society and 'peaceful communities' he noted:

> My best case analysis is one step at a time. On my worst day I would say: how can we even talk about building civil society in a country which is a million miles away from such a thing as bringing women into everyday processes? How can we do anything in terms of civil society when we are dealing with people who think women are dogs and rats? Can you define civil society with 50 percent of the population?[10]

Such 'hidden' scepticism and cynicism was common particularly among officials who spoke some local language and/or had been in the country for some time. The gender analysis offered here is not necessarily nuanced but does indicate the exclusions of the Tajik peace as recounted privately by international officers.

In some contrast, *pessimism* is a second variant in the 'hidden transcripts' of the International Community which abandons all hope of the promise of democracy, in resignation to the peril of authoritarianism. 'The next revolution will start from this region', one international official in Kulob noted. 'When people can't access political life they look for something different, and this something is *Hizb-ut Tahrir*.'[11] This view was echoed, on the record, by an ex-diplomat in Dushanbe.

> What do you do as a young Tajik? There's labour migration. Then some get jobs in local administration which are paid low and they have some kind of values and don't pay bribes. [...] The more clever guys, they could probably end up as an office manager, programme manager [for an international organization], but this is the very, very top. The problem is the bottom. The bottom is enormous.

> (Epkenhans 2005: 2)

In such representations it is assumed that Tajiks might react to the strains of extreme poverty in their country in ultimately the same way as 'we' might, and that their ways out are through 'us', however limited those opportunities might be. Such hidden transcripts do not directly contradict public testimonies but simply express more plainly and acutely some of the trends in public discourse.

Clashes between true believers (who largely adhere to a public transcript of peacebuilding), sceptics (who question it), and pessimists (who emphasise peril over promise), lead to *consternation* within the 'International Community'. One recent example can be found in an email exchange between an editor of the open-source intelligence agency Oxford Analytica (OA) and the then US Ambassador to Tajikistan, Richard Hoagland. OA, in an article on 'state weakness', pronounced peacebuilding as a failure and portrayed local and international actors as irresponsive to the problems of authoritarianism. President Rahmon is picked out for particular criticism as his regime is 'too weak and corrupt to cope', while he personally is, 'reported to be unperturbed by the scale and immediacy of the problem' (OA 2006, no pagination). In response to these assertions, Hoagland wrote to OA that,

> Frankly, the 'State Weakness' analysis was without doubt the worst I have seen in my nearly three years here at the US Embassy in Dushanbe and for the two years previous when I was Director for Caucasus and Central Asia in the State Department. The conclusion, '…the country is set to remain a failed state on the brink of civil war' is so far from reality that if one of my staff had turned this in, I would have responded, 'What the hell have you been smoking?'
>
> (Johnson's Russia List 2006, no pagination)

Perhaps, the most revealing aspect of this exchange is the disagreement over basic facts between two expert institutions, OA and the US Embassy. Hoagland rightly questions the OA claim that the UTO still exists as a meaningful alliance as well as their citation of the Islamic Movement of Tajikistan (IMT), which they describe as, 'the local wing of *Hizb ut-Tahrir*', which has incorporated Taleban and members of the IMU (OA 2006). Regarding the IMT, he comments that, 'my folks [at the embassy] who follow such things have only two very sketchy recent reports of something called the Islamic Movement of Tajikistan' (Johnson's Russia List 2006).

To characterise such exchanges as 'debate' would miss the revealing absurdities here; that two highly regarded purveyors of knowledge in the International Community – Oxford Analytica and the US State Department – can't agree on the basic facts about Tajikistan. Despite their pessimism, the OA author and editor, whose reply to Hoagland strongly defended the article, follow the trends of peacebuilding discourse in portraying Tajikistan as a site of peril which can only be overcome by the promise of democratisation. He/she is not objectively reading facts but interpreting them in light of a deeply embedded and ideologically imbued discourse of peace. Hoagland, on the other hand, departs from the peace-/state-building mainstream, in questioning this peril and promise as well as the construction of terrorist threat. This is not to say that he himself – like all of us – isn't influenced by discursive trends. Indeed, Hoagland perceptively makes a point about how discourses are built intertextually when commenting in his response that, 'the problem with a truly flawed analytical report like this one is that it gets into the mix of other sources and can influence other analyses' (ibid). 'Reality', he implies, may at least in part be composed of such 'truly flawed' analysis. Furthermore, this example shows that hidden transcripts can both affirm and deny public representations.

Neo-liberal technologies of peacebuilding

This then is the International Community in Tajikistan: at once extolling its virtues as conflict transformer whilst at the same time betraying the inauthentic character of this vision via exceptions to discourse and adaptations in practice. However, we must interpret the national and international discursive relations in Tajikistan in historical perspective. As international actors became increasingly involved in Tajikistan during the conflict this provided a further set of tropes, concepts and grand ideas to invoke and deploy. The domination and subjection of the Tajik political elite to foreign powers has normalised 'ambivalence in outlook and behaviour' (Rakowska-Harmstone 1970: 4) dating back to the Soviet era. Dudoignan argues that post-conflict intervention has exacerbated a politics of ambivalence in Tajikistan: 'an attitude characterised by a special ability to integrate alien ideological mottos, and to play simultaneously different, sometimes openly contradictory registers of discourse if not of thought' (2004: 122). It is this ambivalence which allows the Tajik political elite to participate simultaneously in international peacebuilding and play elite politics and raises the question of why international peacebuilders may resign themselves to a pale shadow of their ostensible objectives.

To answer this question we must place peacebuilding in its neo-liberal context. I use neo-liberalism, in the sense used by Gill (1995), to locate the ideological moorings of international peacebuilding discourse. Neo-liberalism has developed from its disciplinary origins, via interventionary discourses, to a form of praxis, adjusted and adapted 'pragmatically' in context, but always in terms supportive of market-based order and solutions. Its strategies or 'technologies of governing' (Ong 2006) such as 'structural adjustment', 'good governance' and 'civil society' are born out of these ethics. Critical research discussed in the introduction has considered how international peacebuilding combines a grand normative vision with a technocratic policy-practice which produces a conservative, 'pragmatic peacebuilding' in practice (Chandler 1999; Richmond 2005; Heathershaw 2008a). The presence of both grand vision and technocratic practice generates a 'virtual peace' (Richmond and Franks 2007) where a chasm opens up between the public goals of liberal transformation and technocratic representations and practices of programmes and projects. In this sense international peacebuilding is not strictly speaking a solidly liberal discourse but a hybrid liberal one which combines conservative, liberal and humanitarian elements in technocratic policy practice.

Recent research in Tajikistan has shown that the technocratic implementation of privatisation and provision of structural adjustment packages in the late 1990s and early 2000s before significant public sector reform enabled the emergence of centralised control by an oligarchic civilian regime (Nakaya 2008). Yet, far from being aberrations, these incoherent combinations of, in Foucauldian terms, bio-political and disciplinary techniques, remain integral to the workings of the International Community. UNTOP itself presents clear examples of the move from the transformational public discourse to policy practice. Table 3.1 presents an extract from the Secretary-General report on progress against UNTOP's objective for 2005–2006 and planning for 2006–2007 (UNGA 2006: 30–36). It shows how the objective of consolidating peace is transformed into achievement indicators, performance measures and outputs such as trainings and seminars. This example is typical of UNTOP strategic planning (see also UNGA 2003: 46–48) and is, in fact, common to modern international development's new public management ethos (see Chapter 7). These accounting concerns have the effect of reducing conflict transformation to specific, measurable but in them-

Table 3.1 Example of UNTOP expected accomplishment, 2005–2007

Objective: To consolidate peace in Tajikistan
Expected accomplishments
(a) Increased ability of the Government and political parties to maintain stability in the country and prevent conflict

Indicators of achievement
(a) Progressively strengthened dialogue and
involvement of political parties and civil society in decision-making processes

Performance measure: Number of policies introduced to broaden citizens' participation in government, in particular that of women
　　2005: 2
　　Estimate 2006: 3
　　Target 2007: 4

Outputs
• Provision by the Representative of the Secretary-General of good offices and advice
• Four national dialogue sessions on political pluralism and the role of parliament in peacebuilding
• National dialogue recommendations published online and made available to stakeholders
• On-the-job training, two study visits and assistance in capacity-building for Parliament
• Twenty seminars for parliamentarians, political party representatives and NGO activists on conflict prevention and resolution
• Ten in-depth training-of-trainers workshops on conflict prevention for local officials and representatives of civil society
• Eight training sessions on improved government reporting to the public for 200 representatives of local media and press secretaries of government agencies in different parts of the country

---

Source: adapted from UNGA 2006: 33.

selves superficial changes. Tajikistan is not short of policies and laws which look good on paper, but in practice are disregarded by officialdom or superseded by an inchoate regulatory framework which functions to enable rent-seeking and clientelism. The 'virtual peace' generated by this technocratic approach will be discussed in more detail in Chapters 5 to 7.

This reflection on international peacebuilding practice supports a rethink of the position of the International Community in post-conflict Tajikistan. It is not only the negative repercussions (the failure to meet the overall objective of the liberal peace) which we must consider but the positive functions of this post-conflict order (in terms of self-legitimation and resource allocation to support the status quo). We must grasp how this new order is sustained via political as well as economic relationships which allow the incorporation of different regional groups into state networks. If the International Community were hypothetically to attempt to force through comprehensive neo-liberal reforms for greater accountability and the reduction of the bloated public sector this might jeopardise the peace. Dudoignan notes that the, 'non-coordinated and often redundant' role of overseas aid 'has accentuated the attitude of ambivalence of the Tajikistani authorities, which had a long habit of dealing with contradictory and unconsequent [*sic*] demands from Moscow during the late Soviet period' (ibid.: 137). This leads to perestroika-style 'reforms', involving 'a cosmetic commitment to norms enunciated by the international agencies coupled with a total lack of political will for change' (ibid.: 137). As such neo-liberal technologies of peacebuilding grease the wheels of international intervention and enable the continuance of parallel discourses. However, this 'positive' role acts directly against hopes for liberal transformation. The role of the International Community in Tajikistan, according to such an account, is that of a supplier and mediator of material and symbolic resources which support the current oligarchic order. This supporting role is not that of a third party, nor that of a powerful and relatively homogeneous agent, but that of a dispersed range of actors, each under the influence of discourses beyond their individual control.

Conclusions: the intertextual politics of peacebuilding

Whilst the basic structure of the peacebuilding debate is visible in the Tajik context, its parts and borderlines shift and fluctuate in context. On the one hand, the terms 'conflict prevention', 'peacebuilding', 'democratic transition', 'state-building' and 'conflict transformation' are often used interchangeably, and merged with goals for economic development, health and education, and 'civil society'. On the other hand, sometimes a slippage from one term or goal to another indicates a shift between discourses and thus in the nature of international assistance as a whole. Whichever concept is deployed, and whatever slippage in discourse occurs, the international writing of the 'other' of Tajikistan remains relatively consistent as it is derived from a discursive environment structured in terms of a reasonably stable self-image. The formal end of international peacebuilding in Tajikistan must be seen in light of its self-referential nature. It is this defacement of the Other which ensures that that which comes after (in this case, a statebuilding discourse) shares a great deal in common with its predecessor.

UNTOP ceased at the end of July 2007 after seven years of UN peacebuilding.[12] Vladimir Sotirov, the head of UNTOP, joined international colleagues and state officials to draw a line under international peacebuilding. As UNTOP expired, so international peacebuilding, according to temporal markers of transition and progress, was reaching its finale in Tajikistan. Sotirov, speaking to me in an interview one month before his departure, and in keeping with the public transcript, argued that, 'nation-building and the consolidation of power to the hands of the President was [pause] in general a positive development, building a sense of one nation, with one past, present and future'. Since 2006, he suggested, Tajikistan had entered the 'last stage of peacebuilding', involving the 'strengthening of the rule of law and media freedoms', and 'establishment of institutions'. In Sotirov's account, the feeling of a peacebuilding reversal since 2003, widely acknowledged by international officials in private, was erased in favour of an account of linear progress towards consolidated peace and a stronger state. As evidence for his optimism he recited numerous examples of projects undertaken, seminars conducted and workshops provided. However, even in this reductive account dissonance between elite 'nation-building' and international peacebuilding could not be completely elided. A symbolic problem remained. There had been 'an understanding', Sotirov remarked, that the mission would continue for one more year, until July 2008, but what he termed 'subjective factors' had prevented this. The Government, he commented, 'felt that the title "peacebuilding" was embarrassing [pause]. that it was damaging the reputation of the country'.[13] For a regime wishing to put the civil war to one side, 'international peacebuilding', however technocratic in policy-practice, had become an intolerable representation.

This chapter has begun a discourse analysis and participant observation of the International Community in Tajikistan. It has argued that international strategies and programming in Tajikistan must be situated amidst the global discursive trends of international peacebuilding. Thus oft-mentioned 'realities on the ground' are highly subjective factors which are interpreted in terms of a global shift towards statebuilding. As such the public transcript of peacebuilding-cum-statebuilding generates policy-practice and constitutes the parameters of what was legitimate for international intervention in Tajikistan. It serves to justify the disbursal of tens of millions of dollars of international assistance and continues the image of Tajikistan as a positive partner for the International Community. Increasingly success is defined in terms of a statebuilding discourse framed in terms of security rather than a peacebuilding discourse framed in terms of humanitarian assistance and democratisation. In practice this 'success' is achieved *despite* intense but often inexplicit scepticism, pessimism and consternation within the International Community and *because of* a reduction of the transformational goals of international peacebuilding to technocratic objectives and outputs. These two features of practice lead quite naturally to the adaptations and accommodations made by programme managers and their staff as they seek to make their programmes succeed in the local context. However, it should be clear from the above that this 'success' is deceptive. A fuller picture of the politics of peacebuilding and the concomitant emergence of legitimate order comes from a study of the intertextual relations, in their public and hidden aspects, between these shifting international discourses and those emanating from Tajikistan and Central Asia. Before going on to consider Tajikistan's elites and subordinates as correspondents with the International Community, we must consider them in their own terms.

4   Elite and subordinate discourses of peace

The Tajik people have entered the new millennium firmly convinced that peace, unity and creative work, a formula for advancement – which was instigated by President Rahmon and which became the quintessence of the previous ten years of independence – will give a powerful impetus to our further movement towards democratic, secular and legitimate statehood and towards integration into the world community.

(Fatoev 2001: 104)

These days the people in power are former communists. The only difference is that now they are members of the President's party, but their ideology has hardly changed at all.

(Isroil Ismoilov, pensioner, February 2005)[1]

Don't hidden transcripts themselves constrain underdogs' definitions and awareness of overdogs' vulnerability?

(Tilly 1991: 599)

The post-Soviet continuity imagined by the pensioner Ismoilov nicely illustrates the productive nature of discourse in creating legitimate political order. Such views, widely held in Tajikistan but often understated, indicate the ambiguity of hidden transcripts. On the one hand they can generate the social relations of resistance. On the other, as indicated by Tilly, they produce apathy and resignation. It is the contention of this chapter that the new state–societal relations that have emerged in post-conflict Tajikistan should not be regarded exclusively in terms of *either* governors versus resistors *or* leaders versus followers, but rather they should be considered as an intersubjective relationship between elites and subordinates. Governmentality is spatio-hierarchical but also discursively constructed and thus remains fragile and contingent. It faces popular disquiet and cynicism yet also public accommodation and avoidance. Moreover, the two categories of elites and subordinates are themselves not mutually exclusive. Many Tajiks find themselves playing a dual role in this respect: *both* as an authoritative guarantor of the stability of their family unit *and* as a subject embodying traditional values of deference to patriarchal authority.

Before embarking on this analysis we must discuss a preliminary question of definition and the distinctions of elite from subordinate. In the post-Soviet context, 'elite' must be understood in broader terms than that of the power elite, as it has been classically rendered in political science. Moreover, whilst Soviet-era academicians and cultural intelligentsia have lost influence, political authority continues to be produced socially and culturally as well as politico-economically. Therefore, I understand elites to be all those who exercise political authority – where the personal and familial are political. Such a broad definition is appropriate in a study of the politics of peace. It is consistent with a discourse-centred approach and it has been adopted elsewhere for the study of power relations in Tajikistan where twin legacies of Sovietism and communalism have combined, in basic terms, to 'reinforce the power of the community over the individual' (Harris 2004: 174). This is not a functionalist or formalist definition; it is one which makes the exact composition and qualities of the elite fungible to discursive change, social space and political contingency. It is the subject role of *rais* or *aksakal* which is socially constructed imagined communities of contemporary Tajikistan.

I justify this definitional move empirically via discourse analysis and participant observation of the performative exercise of 'authority'. An individual can play the role of subordinate at one moment (in the workplace or at a government office) and elite the next (on the street or at the teahouse). Moreover, most married men and persons of maturity (old men and women) at times perform political authority over their spouse, siblings or other relatives – although their authority is circumscribed within a family network.[2] By this definition the elite may include state officials from the President himself to heads of local authorities, villages and neighbourhoods. In keeping with the legacies of the Soviet era it can also encompasses members of the academic and cultural elite and members of state agencies of administration and regulation. Even well-connected small business people and traders who have not formerly received state assets directly, but are dependent on patrimonial relations with tax inspectors and permit granters, may take a role within elite networks. *In doing so*, they take their place in a network which constitutes an elite community of discourse and practice.

This chapter is a study of these doings, in public and hidden discourse and practice. It shows both the productivity of these discourses and their practical limits. The chapter is divided into three sections. The first section shows how elites deploy a public transcript of peace enforcement (a discourse of *mirostroitelstvo* [peacebuilding]). The second section investigates popular responses to the regime in terms of subordinate public transcripts of conflict accommodation (a discourse of *tinji* [peacefulness/wellness]). The final section of the chapter explores the hidden transcripts where elites deny the ideals of 'authority' in their corrupt practices and subordinates negate their consent to the regime through practices of avoidance and limited expressions of dissent. In light of this analysis, it goes on to draw some preliminary observations about the nature of both the state-idea and state-system of Tajikistan. The chapter concludes that in order to understand the state of peace in Tajikistan we must grasp the intertextualities of public and hidden transcripts – between (the publicly professed) state-idea and (the largely hidden functioning of the) state-system.

Elite *mirostroitelstvo*

The above quote from Fatoev, the author of the official history of Tajikistan's first ten years, emerges from the broader concerns of social order which are found in contemporary Tajik political discourse. This is as true of an official discourse of *mirostroitelstvo* (peacebuilding) as it is of the oft-deployed notions of *ayb* (shame) and *nomus* (honour). Thus, with the translation of UN concepts of peacebuilding and peacekeeping, more than the original English is lost in translation. For example, whilst formal Russian-language *mirotvorchestvo* (peacekeeping) doctrine borrows much from UN language, its practical interpretation both in Moscow and across the region bears little resemblance to liberal ideals of the International Community. This is less a technical matter of translation than an issue of a 'travelling concept' which takes on a new meaning in a different political context. Thus, across the post-Soviet space, peacekeeping has come to represent a distinctly authoritarian approach to conflict resolution (MacKinlay and Cross 2003). *Mirostroitelstvo* can equally be understood as emanating from a post-colonial context and the product of 'a system which is', according to Atkin, 'qualitatively neo-Soviet' (1997: 278). As discourse, it invokes not just questions of conflict resolution but must be seen as part of a wider constitution of political order. Thus in studying a given register of discourse we study it alongside other registers which are similarly constitutive of and constituted by this ideologically saturated order.

This section highlights three dimensions of *mirostroitelstvo* discourse:

- *Temporal*: the remembering of *perestroika* as the cause of war, and the idealising of national progress as a managed process of statebuilding
- *Ethical*: the idealising of communal 'stability' and political 'authority' over individual rights and freedom of choice
- *Spatial*: the locating of authority with the basic idea of the territorial state, locally, nationally and internationally

These three dimensions feature in a *mirostroitelstvo* discourse which legitimates the political ends of regime stabilisation. In this sense, neo-Soviet elite discourse in a post-colonial setting is much like Liu's conception of a post-socialist political imagination, which 'envisioned eventual economic and political liberalisation within solidly Soviet assumptions about the role of the state' (2002: 192).

Before this chapter goes on to explore these dimensions of discourse some words must be said about the formation of elite discourse in Tajikistan and the sources used in this study. Elite discourse in Tajikistan is principally produced and reproduced performatively via speech at ceremonies and official events as well as in official practice behind closed doors. The performative function of discourse is considered in greater depth in later chapters. Here sources for discourse analysis are found in the books and newspaper articles of leading elites (such as President Rahmon's multi-volume, quasi-academic and ghost-written account *The Tajiks in the Mirror of History* [*Tojikon dar oinai Tarikh*]), transcribed speeches given by such people at national and international fora (e.g. Mahmadsaid Ubaidulloyev's 'The strengthening of civil society in Tajikistan') as well as works of official history (e.g. Fatoev's *Tajikistan: Ten Years of Independence* [*Tajikistan: Desyit lyet Nizavisimosti*]) and political theory (Ibrohim Usmonov's *Treatise on the State* [*Traktat o Gosudartsve*]). These texts are neither exhaustive nor properly sampled but are the most prominent and public examples of Tajik political discourse. They are important texts which deploy the key features of elite discourse.

A further problem lies in analysing the relationship between texts and authors. It is difficult to chart intertextual production of discourse as there is little practice of citing other sources, with the exception of references to various sayings of the President. However, some effort is made to achieve a genealogical perspective as I draw reference to pre-Soviet and Soviet authors and ideas which are taken on and developed in modern political discourse (e.g. Usmonov's extensive use of Ahmad Donish). I have furthermore attempted to provide greater context to this discourse analysis via secondary sources on the development and deployment of ideas in Soviet and post-Soviet Central Asia.

From Soviet to neo-Soviet

The notion of progress is clearly important to Tajikistan's post-conflict and post-Soviet elites. However, their sense of the temporal is imbued with a different set of meanings and signifiers than found in neo-liberal peacebuilding. Indeed, to denote Tajik political discourse as post-Soviet or neo-Soviet is itself a discursive move which would be vehemently opposed by many in the regime. Moreover, that the Tajik elite can be considered neo-Soviet is not to say that they are wittingly nostalgic for the Soviet system. Many in authority in Tajikistan explicitly turn their back on this era and some deploy nationalist tropes against the imperial past. However, they do this whilst enacting roles, practices and policies which developed during a twentieth century where a localised communalism and modernistic communism combined to create a new social and political order across the Central Asian region. I understand Sovietism in the Tajik context as a hybrid system which emerged from the partial transformation of Tajikistani political society during the Soviet era. This transformation created, according to Rakowska-Harmstone's analysis of the 1960s, a 'political system of which the legitimacy is not in question' and 'a new elite, whose interests can be satisfied only through the system' (1970: 272). It was a discursively constituted system of power rather than an ideology.

The doctrine of Sovietism began as an archetypal form of what James C. Scott calls authoritarian high modernism that lay behind the collectivisation of the early Soviet period. Scott observes,

At its centre was a supreme self-confidence about continued linear progress, the development of scientific and technical knowledge, the expansion of production, the rational design of social order, the growing satisfaction of human needs, and, not least, an increasing control over nature (including human nature) commensurate with a scientific understanding of natural laws.

(1998: 89)

Yet the disillusionment with such grand narratives was apparent well before the traumatic fall of the Soviet Union. During Stalin's reign Sovietism was 'gutted of living content and reduced to mere instruments of power' (Sakwa 1998: 170). 'Over the years', Sakwa remarks, 'Soviet ideology became transformed into the ethos of the system, and by the same token lost some of the characteristics of philosophy' (ibid.: 174). Soviet ideology continued to provide the ostensible basis of legitimacy for the Soviet Union but was never properly remade – and the final attempt to do so played a large part in the system's collapse. Elitism became more pronounced in late Sovietism as during Khruschchev and Brezhnev eras more emphasis was placed on the development of Soviet Central Asian cadres through technical training and higher education. As a consequence many of the 'new' elites of contemporary Tajikistan hold technical and/or higher degrees acquired in the late Soviet era.

Today's neo-Sovietism is practised in derivative discourses which emerge from a post-colonial context. They have flimsier ideological moorings and bear an impoverished resemblance to their Soviet parent. The writers of neo-Soviet discourse are much less involved with the accumulation of knowledge, scientific and human progress. Sakwa draws similar conclusions regarding the political make-up of Putin whose politics are 'imbued with a post-Soviet face whilst often taking on a neo-Soviet aspect' (2004: 47). Putin's success in stabilising Russia is admired by many leaders across the region. In a region with few examples of post-Soviet progress, the Putin presidency provides markers by which interest can be defined and apparently provides a justification for 'sovereign democracy'.

One feature of neo-Soviet *mirostroitelstvo* discourse in Tajikistan is that of the deliberate obfuscation of recent history. President Rahmon's public statements rarely address the war. However, in his few pronouncements on the topic, he has associated the war with *perestroika*, which created 'a vacuum, which was formed as a result of the break-up (*raspad*) of the old state [the Soviet Union]'. This breakdown of power was followed by 'attempts to fill in [the old state] with all possible kinds of extremism at the beginning of the 1990s' (Rahmon 1999). Elites deploy particularly negative images of the formal end of the USSR and the 'anarchy' it is thought to have brought about. Such readings serve powerful political functions as they inscribe war as an exception to authoritarian rule, rather than a product of it. Similarly, they allow Rahmon to portray his rise to power in late 1992 as that of a saviour rather than of a placeman for the country's powerful and brutal warlords. Elite accounts of the war, to the extent that they detail political violence, do not link this violence to the process by which the current regime became ascendant, but rather associate it with non-state factions.

In the public transcript, war is discussed only in terms of 'peace' – specifically the progress being achieved under the present government. This narrative is even found in texts whose publication is funded and supported by the International Community. For example, the second volume of *The Republic of Tajikistan: History of Independence*, which narrates 1992, a year when perhaps tens of thousands of Tajiks died due to the conflict, portrays the collection as,

> an attempt to reconstruct the history of the making of Tajikistan as an independent sovereign state, to analyse and generalise the unique experience of peacekeeping work [*mirostvorcheskoi deyatelnosti*] of the leadership and all fruitful [*zdorovykh*] forces of the country in the search for a way out of the political crisis, upon the resolution of which the existence of the Tajik state itself depended.
>
> (Nazriev and Sattorov 2005: 3)

A further discursive move is to link 'peacebuilding' and 'statebuilding' to the person of the President. This situates the Tajik people under the authority of the President who is leading them to an eventual state of prosperity. Readings of the civil war are regularly accompanied by accounts of recovery and progress under the person of the president. *Tajikistan: Ten Years of Independence*, remarks:

> These years which saw civil war followed by long-awaited peace, the implementation of economical and social reforms unprecedented for such a complicated period, these years which symbolised the tragedy and triumph of our Tajik people will be forever linked with the thoughts, hopes and work of one man whose name has become widely known all over the world – Emomali Rahmon.
>
> (Fatoev 2001: 95)

This official text draws a clear distinction between government and opposition factions in typical fashion. An independent Tajikistan was hijacked, in Rahmon's own words, by 'hostile forces inside and outside the country' whereby 'the history of our nation and state sank into oblivion and the achievements of unity and independence were forgotten' (2001: 12). Such texts represent Tajikistan as a modern nation-state, suggest that the sources of past problems are externally supported oppositionists, and at the same time overlook the fact that the most significant and hostile external intervention came from Russian and Uzbek land and air forces in support of the Rahmon regime. Thus, elite accounts differ from international portrayals by remembering government as above the conflict rather than as an active player in the civil war. They deploy not only the temporal markers of elite discourse but ethical and spatial signifiers.

Ethics of 'stability' and 'authority'

The ideals of 'stability' and 'authority' found in elite ethics of *mirostroitelstvo* are central to discourses across the region (Heathershaw 2007a: 252–254). They are intrinsically linked. This is an authoritarian state-as-guardian view where the regime not only demands political stability and economic growth but quiescence in social relations and the maintenance of public morality. These ethics ascribe roles to the elite as well as inscribing a wide range of rights and functions to political authority.

First, the ideal of 'stability' (*stabilnost*) is used to explain the priority of economic development over political liberalisation. It denotes a state of increasing economic prosperity and political inactivity. Political opposition is considered necessarily 'destabilising', and reform is seen as secondary or subsequent to economic growth (Gaffurov 2005: 3). This perspective on political progress is shared across the elite, from the intelligentsia to the state class. Abdullo, a Tajik political analyst, comments that political stability, equated to 'the further strengthening of peace', is tied to the provision of growth and 'development of the national economy'.[3] This seems uncontroversial but it is the dismissal of political reform and democratisation in these accounts which is telling. 'Democratisation' here is a gradual process which can be brought to fruition after significant economic development has been achieved (Usmonov 2003b). According to Mahmadsaid Ubaidulloyev, an ex-commander and long-time Mayor of Dushanbe, democratisation initiatives should not supersede 'the important fact, that the basic aim of every citizen of our country and society as a whole consists of the acquisition of the fruits of a peaceful life, the strengthening of activities in the economic sphere' (2003: 66). Moreover, 'the perfecting of a political system for society, in our view, must be planned [...] and must not bear spasmodic character, but be smooth, consistent (*posledovatel'nym*) and expedient' (ibid.: 63). Tajikistan's *National Development Strategy* (NDS) for 2005 to 2015 should been seen in this light. For President Rahmon, 'economic independence' is 'the foundation of true independence'.[4]

The second ethic is that of authority. The term 'authority' (*avtoritet*) is often used to signify a person who has command over his peers.[5] In political discourse, it is inscribed as primarily residing with official and unofficial leaders, first the President, and those appointed or supported by the President, to the exclusion of non-governmental actors (Fatoev 2001: 95). This authority is both personal and official. Within his own political party, the PDP, Rahmon's personal authority is explicitly analogous with that of the party. In answer to the question why does the PDP have such a strong position in the politics of Tajikistan, Asozoda, the party's third-ranking official, proclaimed,

> Firstly, this is something that everyone accepts. The position of the party became so strong when [President] Emomali Sharipovich Rahmon – a person who has colossal authority – became our Chairman. Why? First, he promised the Nation that he would end the war. Second, he at once said that

all political migrants and forced evacuees should return to the homeland. Third, he said, that he'd resolve the problem of hunger. That's how the authority of this person came about! Our party did not increase his authority. He gave this authority to the party.

(Asozoda 2005: 3)

This personification of stability and authority with Rahmon is a pervasive feature of the symbolic order of peace in Tajikistan. Iconography put in place by officials reconfirms their acceptance of presidential power. The huge increase in the number of portraits and sayings of Rahmon hanging from public and non-public buildings often alongside other Tajik 'national heroes' is a feature of the period since 2000. For example, the three-storey-high portrait shown hanging on an apartment block in Khujand (Figure 4.1) signifies consent by regional elites to the 'colossal authority' of the President. It reads 'The health of the nation is a priceless wealth'; the structure blocks the light to numerous occupied residential apartments. Faced with such public deference, Rahmon has at times stepped in himself to deny a cult of personality which he may have found embarrassing. On several occasions he has publicly called on state bodies not to engage in a 'cult of personality' or the 'eulogisation' of his personality, particularly around his fiftieth birthday in 2002.[6] Tellingly, only he of course is able to call for portraits to be taken down; for others to challenge him publicly would break with the public transcript and potentially spark conflict within elite networks.

Figure 4.1 Billboard of President Rahmon, Khujand.

However, rather than being bound exclusively to the person of Rahmon, 'authority' is impersonated by elites across Tajikistan's local and regional political spaces. Whilst government is portrayed as possessing a common interest with the people (Fatoev 2001: 96), subject roles differ where 'we' are invoked with the qualities to lead 'them', lacking these said qualities. The invocation of the noun *vlast* ('government', 'power', 'the authorities') is often accompanied by its personification with an official or other figure of headship. The title *rais* ('head', 'boss') is deployed to denote the heads of regional or district government, local authority, village or neighbourhood (*raisi Khukumat, raisi Jamoat, raisi kishlak* and *raisi mahalla)*. The title dates back at least to the time of the Emirate of Bukhara when *rais* and *aksakal* (headmen) were appointed in villages to maintain public order. It is used generically to indicate authority in contemporary Tajikistan and sometimes compared with emir, sultan or other historical titles of political leadership (Usmonov 2005b: 69). However, the head as inscribed in the public transcript is not one with unfettered power but those who 'know their powers and know how to call on them' yet 'don't have the right to take for themselves all power' (UNTOP/NAPST 2002b: 32). Lurking behind this self-image of the elite is another image of a subject people in need of being controlled and limited by an authoritative elite. The Soviet-era notion of a people of 'low self-consciousness and high respect'[7] is widely cited.

Political scholarship, both polemical and academic, reproduces these ethics to varying degrees and often with implicit or explicit references to ideas and authors made popular in the Soviet era. It is widely accepted by Tajik political scientists that Rahmon was able to harmonise national interests by stepping in as an authoritative arbiter and overcoming the disorderly struggle amongst the parties (Olimov 2003: 120–121). However, the Khujandi Ibrohim Usmonov is a rare example of a figure within the regime whose writings engage directly and extensively in substantive political analysis. A former peace negotiator, senior presidential advisor and deputy Minister of Culture – in that order of demotion – most of his work was written whilst a member of the regime. A recent work of political theory by Usmonov (2005b), *Treatise on the State*, written whilst he was still deputy minister, is a prescription for a strong state based on the personage of a 'just ruler' with ethics of authority and stability. It develops the patriarchal worldview of the late-nineteenth-century Bukharan scholar Ahmad Donish (1827–1897), who was rehabilitated and represented as a humanist thinker in Soviet Tajikistan in the 1950s and 1960s.[8] Indeed, the idea that national unity requires political unity is a long-standing feature of Tajik political discourse (Wennberg 2001: 8).

From the outset of *Treatise* Usmonov explicitly links the state to power and wealth; 'power protects wealth', he notes, 'and wealth, in turn, breeds the power' (2005b: 67). On one level this is a work of political realism that emphasises the turbulent environment of the state. Usmonov quotes Donish in arguing for stability under a just ruler: 'one should not forget that "stability in politics is the principle of prolongation of reign and handling of state affairs"' (ibid.: 78). On another level it is a normative account. He goes on to affirm Donish's ten principles of a just ruler (e.g. '5. If the decision of the ruler is fair, then he should not be afraid of spawning grievance'), and picks out two of Donish's five conditions of living as of particular importance to the state: 'strong and just ruler' and 'truthful and just officials' (ibid.: 90, 92). Yet from a political liberal perspective *Treatise* is notable for its omissions. Foremost amongst these are the absences of any discussion of constitutional limits, separation of powers, the role of the opposition or civil society. Such omissions are all the more interesting for the fact that Usmonov was considered one of the more open-minded figures in the Rahmon regime. It was clear from my two interviews with him that he was a sophisticated thinker who was able to elaborate on the differences between contemporary Tajikistan and a liberal-democratic society. In 2006 he was finally removed from government.

The downward spiral of Usmonov's career is emblematic of the decline of political discourse in contemporary Tajikistan from the relatively hetrogeneous and dynamic pre-war period of *perestroika*. The authoritative state which is advocated in elite discourse appears as something of an oriental caricature. Yet the tepidity of the discursive environment should not lead us to dismiss it. However superficial they appear, these testimonies of an ideal of 'authority' correlate with a basic level of legitimacy. They can also be compared with Liu's findings regarding 'good authority' among ethnic Uzbeks in southern Kyrgyzstan. Such a person is imagined as 'a strong and ruthless but benevolent and wise paternal figure whose influence would hold sway over neighbourhood, city, and state' (Liu 2002: 1).

Spaces of 'the state'

In *mirostroitelstvo*, political spaces are also inscribed in neo-Soviet terms. 'The state', ethically, spatially and temporally conceived, is considered the locus of the elite. Moreover, as it is personified or 'impersonated' (Reeves 2006) by its representatives, it becomes a social and personal actor. In the case of Tajikistan, the person of authority is habitually referred to as the rais (head), and exists at all levels of 'the state' from the unofficial authority of the mahalla to the presidency. However, while 'the state' provides a degree of identity for a collection of patriarchs who constitute the regime or political elite, 'nation' is a peculiarly ambiguous trope in elite discourse. It remains so because of the multiple layers of identity and political community in the Tajik context, not least regional communities which served as vehicles for the war. Statist (often denoted as 'nationalist') discourse often reproduces both inter-regional tensions and, more importantly in the post-conflict period, the supremacy of the ideal of national statehood in elite public transcripts.

Nationality (*nationalnost*) has remained an, at best, secondary signifier through much of Tajik history. In accordance with Stalin's nationalities policy the Soviet government of the Tajik SSR undertook a grand project to create the historical legitimacy for the Republic's borders. The historian Bobodjan Gafurov was one of the leading figures in crafting a creation myth for the Tajiks as an eastern Iranian people whose culture predated that of the Persians. He served as first Secretary of the Central Committee of the Communist Party of Tajikistan and the effective leader of the republic from 1945 to 1956. Writers Sadriddin Aini and Mirzo Tursunzade (re)discovered a Tajik literature and cultural history which from the 1930s were incorporated into educational and political discourse. Of course, in the context of a policy of 'national in form and socialist in content' this national story was told in humanistic and class-conscious terms. 'Collective identity linked to nationality did not matter', Geiss categorically remarks, 'as Soviet power obviated its politicisation and limited the range of possible public representations and interpretations of this identity' (2003: 246). However, the establishment of the Tajik SSR and its territorial and administrative basis within the Soviet Union at least engendered a 'basic commitment to the [form of] system' and a national-territorial unit which outlasted the Union itself (Rakowska-Harmstone 1970: 5, 230).

Following independence and war, the ruling elite have sought to garner legitimacy and remake formal ideology through reference to the 'national idea'. Public debate over the nation-state of Tajikistan takes place via the following signifiers:

- An explicit link to the Somonid Empire – in order to justify and legitimise itself the Tajik regime tries to present itself as the inheritor of the Somonid legacy.
- Unity of the Nation (*Vahdati Milli*) – typically described as the key factor for the survival and existence of the Tajik National Statehood.
- National Statehood (*Davlatdorii Milli*) – typically described as the critical factor for the survival and development of Tajik nation and culture.[9]

This national elite discourse reflects a widely held belief that without their own national statehood Tajik people are doomed to assimilation in a predominantly Turkic region. Following the 1997 peace agreement the regime renewed and furthered the Soviet-era campaign of representing the Somonid dynasty of the ninth and tenth centuries as the historical basis for the modern-day nation-state.[10] It is described as the last Tajik State and its fall as a national tragedy which led the nation to 1,000 years of genocide, disintegration and gradual assimilation. Monuments to national icons such as Ismoil Somoni were constructed, including a very large arch and memorial complex in the centre of Dushanbe to mark the 1100th anniversary of the Somonid state in 1999. To this extent, the Tajik elite constitute a 'nationalising regime' (Smith *et al.* 1998: 139) yet one that has inherited its form and many of it tropes from the Soviet era.

These ostensibly *national* discourses and symbols are the object of contestation between *regional* elites who in different ways celebrate the benevolence and authority of the *state* (see Chatterjeee 2002: 21–25). Consequently, official 'nationalist' discourse has taken two contrasting directions. The first of these consists of catering to ethno-nationalist histories of Tajik intellectuals which seek clearly to identify the pre-Somonid origins of the Tajik nation and language. History-writing was one pre-war object of conflict for elites and some scholars argue that such discourse was again politically powerful after the peace accords, in the late-1990s, for a government that in denigrating the domestic and foreign 'other' appealed first to natives in its regional homeland (Nourzhanov 2001). These narratives are most common among intellectuals from the south – particularly the Vaksh and Kulob regions, from where Rahmon hails. However, this official discourse barely conceals inter-regional rivalries over the ethnic origins of 'real' Tajiks – descendants of 'Bactrians' from the South, specifically understood as the area of present-day Kulob, or descendants of 'Sogdian people', as argued by Northern ethnic groups. Inter-regional debates continue today in a moderate form and reflect the struggle of regional cadres to justify their right to political power, as exemplified idiosyncratically by 2006's 'Year of Aryan Civilisation' (Shozimov 2005). The President himself has set the terms of this debate. Rahmon's volume one (2001) of *The Tajiks in the Mirror of History* follows the Soviet historian Gafurov in extolling the humanistic virtues of the prophet Zarathushtra. It identifies Bactria as the 'cradle of Zoroastrianism' and thus challenges the professed Muslim identity of Tajikistan. However, unlike during the civil war, these questions are pursued exclusively between elites and intellectuals, and have little impact upon a less educated post-civil war generation.

A second register of nationalist discourse supersedes these ethno-nationalist variants. National Statehood (*Davlatdorii Milli*) is the foundational idea and part of a political project to inscribe a national community under the state, reflecting the ethics of 'stability' and 'authority'. Tajikistan's statebuilding, consistent with 'nation-building' across Central Asia, is based on the notion that prosperity and stability can only be guaranteed through state leadership and control of transition (Smith *et al.* 1998). In Tajik elite discourse, several stages or moments of state-building are invoked in terms which inscribe the authority of the contemporary regime. Nourzhanov (2001) picks out six axioms in Rahmonov's account found in the President's 1996 newspaper article version of 'The Tajiks in the Mirror of History'. To paraphrase, these include: the Tajiks have a civilising mission to Central Asia; 'Tajik' and 'Aryan' are synonymous; Tajik wars were defensive against outside invaders; Tajiks acquired sovereign statehood before the Mongol invasion; Soviet rule reawakened Tajik statehood, despite the injustice of border delimitation; independence in 1991 was a good which was attacked by enemies of the state (ibid., no pagination). In the post-Soviet era new state-building moments have been identified and inscribed. Some of these are predictable (the 1997 peace agreement) but others less so. The 1994 constitution, written whilst the government was at war with the opposition and amended several times since, for example, is still frequently referred to as the key text of state law and thus the legal basis for peace (Ubaidulloyev 2003: 63). Following 2000, Rahmon has often referred to a 'new stage of statehood'. For example, in his 2000 address to parliament, he noted:

> Tajikistan is at a new stage of statehood. The irreversible process of peace and national accord has reached its final stage. Measures for the democratisation of the country's political life are continuing.[11]

Such discourse, from its rediscovery of the Somonids to this 'new stage of state-hood', has formed the foundation of the official history of Tajikistan which is built on the temporal, ethical and spatial precepts found in *mirostroitelstvo*.

We must then reconsider regionalism and inter-regional dynamics of war and peace in the light of this statism. State and region are intrinsically intersecting identities for political and economic elites in Tajikistan. Tellingly, the nation-state was a key space for national, inter-regional breakdown which took an exclusively endogenous form until forced migration produced refugee communities in Moscow, Afghanistan and elsewhere. Long-term Tajik diaspora communities in neighbouring and far-flung countries never played a major role in the conflict. Roy highlights state-national spaces as the crucial locus through which regionalism's (*mahalgero'i*) dynamics are produced (2000: 98). Long-term political success for elites during the Soviet Union was only possible through a solidarity group *at the national level* of the interpersonal network, which extends across tribal and regional divisions, as well as a constituency *within the republican boundary*. Political status and economic interests were maintained and enhanced by these networks 'created around leading public figures or important families', often sealed with intermarriage (ibid.: 99). Such elite networks can equally be orientated towards politico-administrative control or military action, as was the case during the civil war. Thus it is not the superseding of regionalism that has caused the Tajik peace but its reconstitution in civilian form and into official spaces. This is underpinned by a vision of Tajikistani statehood which continued throughout the period since national territorial delimitation in the 1920s (Bergne 2006). It was the nation-state which provided the spatial boundary within which Tajikistan's regionalist conflict emerged and which today provides the locus for the resolution of that conflict.

Subordinate *tinji*

The relationship between inter-regional rivalry and state-national unity in the elite debate over the nation reflects the ambiguous nature of the terms of 'state' and 'society' – terms that in Tajikistan are best understood as discursively constituted. The regime itself can certainly not be considered emancipated from society, many of whose divides it has incorporated. But at the same time the regime claims sovereign supremacy over society via the state. Hierarchies clearly exist yet their boundaries are inscribed discursively and practised substantively and thus remain institutionally indistinct. When the boundaries between elite and subordinate vary in space as well as time, as they do most acutely in locales, individuals may play the role of elite one moment and subordinate the next. This section explores the discourse of *tinji* and the practical know-how of subordinates in Tajik localities and trans-localities. This is what Scott calls *mētis* – the symbolic and heuristic resources of individuals and families to avoid, accommodate and defy the interventions of elites and internationals. However, this is no 'culturalist' argument for the immutability of traditions, cultures and mentalities. Rather, despite the differences of religious persuasion, 'clan' or region, a fairly consistent popular discourse of getting-along has emerged in the form of a public transcript which I denote as *tinji*.

In Tajiki there are numerous words for peace. However, the commonly used notion of *tinji* (wellness/peacefulness) perhaps best conveys the feelings of many who avoid conflict socially and especially politically. Unsurprisingly there is no word for 'peacebuilding' in the vernacular and so Tajiki-speaking NGO workers and associates, for example, might use *mirostroitelstvo* or a similar phrase in Russian in its stead. The discourse or ethos which I am seeking to describe and interpret here is not strictly bound by the limits of the Tajik language (not least because I also found this worldview amongst other local communities in Tajik-stan whose first language is Russian, Kyrgyz or Uzbek). *Tinji* has ethical, spatial and temporal dimensions in its public transcript:

- *Ethical*: the idealising of 'unity' and 'patriarchy' where social 'cohesion' ought to be retained.
- *Spatial*: the preservation of the local 'community' (mahalla) as a social, apolitical site.
- *Temporal*: the search for post-conflict 'modernisation'.

There are of course historical and genealogical roots to these markers, albeit ones which are hard to trace. Whilst my analysis characterises elite discourses as neo-Soviet, Kandiyoti points out that it is 'at the level of the quotidian that one finds the clearest expression of habits and expectations acquired during the Soviet period, as well as important generational differences in their expression' (2002: 253).

Analysis of subordinate or popular discourse proves particularly challenging. As *tinji* is deployed exclusively in oral communication, semi-structured inter-views, open-answer surveys and focus groups are utilised to establish a basic public transcript. The following analysis is based on research conducted in five communities across two sub-regions (Asht and Panjakent raiyons) of Sughd oblast where international organisations had just begun to work in 2005 (Heath-ershaw 2005c).[12] These results are broadly consistent with my experiences and findings from the Rasht valley and Khatlon. However, intertextual relations are less formalised and more difficult to assess. Here discourse analysis requires an approach which reveals not just forms of public representations but how wider practices emerge which sustain or challenge them. Accessing such ethnographic data was a persistent challenge of research and one that was only ever partially overcome. This section reveals the findings of discourse analysis but first explores the historical origins of society, locality and spaces of subordination.

'Society': the evolution of local spaces

Mann (1988) has noted that to speak of society, just as to speak of state, is to cheat. Tajik 'society' can be broken down into regions, sub-regions and various identity groups based on gender, ethnicity, confession, education, profession or social status. Yet, in the post-conflict period a relatively consistent *public* transcript has emerged across the country and thus forms the basis for dynamics of conflict avoidance and accommodation in the *public* square. This common ground paradoxically demands the apartness of communities from one another via a parochial and patriarchal vision of the village. The very emergence of this discourse and its attendant practices of avoidance and accommodation is in itself a major indicator of peace. This conciliating trend did not emerge from nowhere: it has its roots in historical processes that have created bases for cooperation as they have simultaneously spawned vehicles for contention.

Under various empires, power in what is today Tajikistan was always effectively dispersed as 'local rulers established themselves in strategic positions, carving out small, independent principalities' (Akiner 2001: 10). Despite this, an inconsistent process of the integration of local spaces was taking place before and during the Soviet period. Tajiks do not speak directly about 'clans' or 'tribes' but use alternative terms to express local and familial ties. The *avlod* (extended family group) was the fundamental social unit of pre-Soviet Tajik society but it did not take the dominant position in public or political space at that time. Rather it was the mahalla (community), often including numerous *avlods*, which provided a public space for festivities and the resolution of questions of local governance (Geiss 2003: 9). In this respect, pre-Soviet Tajik society differed from the tribal societies of Central Asia where kinship was more important and perhaps remains more important today. Both Uzbeks and Tajiks of present-day western Tajikistan – whose ethnic distinctions are not very clear now and were even less so in pre-Soviet times – often resided in larger *kishlak* (agricultural settlements) made up of several mahallas.

One can consider this puzzle historically in terms of the modern conjoining of local spaces over several centuries as present-day Tajikistan moved from being a collection of local fiefs under a khan through the Soviet period to being an independent nation-state under a president. In practice to the extent that integration of local spaces occurred it was extremely stratified. So-called 'detribalisation' took place under the influence of the khan who administratively divided subjects on the basis of *kishlak* or mahalla, and took over the duties of conflict regulation, to erode the political power of the *avlod* or larger clan (Geiss 2003: 92). This residential unit was the basis for their further political integration into the 'state' structures of consecutively the Khanate of Kokand (for northern Tajiks) or Emirate of Bukhara (for southern and eastern Tajiks), the Russian Tsarist empire, and the Soviet Union. However, *avlod* remained the base social unit as the larger units of mahalla and *kishlak* became absorbed into imperial power structures. According to Geiss, this process, where the Khans successively ceded more ground to Russian Tsars, undermined the bases of legitimacy in nineteenth-century Central Asia. 'Thus', he remarks, 'patrimonial state structures in tsarist Central Asia were based on domination rather than authority, due to the lack of shared legal and political community structures' (ibid.: 239). Multiple, overlapping claims to political authority continued to exist at this time.

However, an incomplete Russian colonial integration process was superseded in the Soviet era by re-communalisation and inter-regional migrations. It is worth returning to Olivier Roy's (1998, 2000) reading of this period, discussed in Chapter 2, in order to understand better the formation of Tajikistan's local spaces. Roy argues that the Tajik conflict must be seen as a distinctly post-Soviet conflict – a 'war of the kolkhoz' – reflecting a re-constitution of Soviet-era regionalism.[13] For example, during the 1992 battle in the Vakhsh valley between the Gharmi-dominated Turkmenistan kolkhoz and Kulobi-dominated Moskwa kolkhoz, the border between the collective farms was the frontline in the fighting. When the Gharmis were defeated in November 1992 it was minority Kulobis from Turkmenistan kolkhoz, that had fled to ally with Moskva, who then returned with a number of Kulobi allies to lead the kolkhoz, with the Gharmis who remained as their labourers. When Gharmi refugees returned, aided by UNHCR, they similarly took up lowly positions under their new Kulobi masters. 'Thus what one had here', he notes, 'was the reconstitution of a social differentiation arising out of the combined effects of war, predation and neo-tribalism' (2000: 95). This raises important questions about the terms under which the defeated came to accept their subordination under a new hegemonial elite. Moreover to speak of a single condition of subordination which is broadly similar across the country we must justify this judgement empirically in terms of the discourses of peace emanating from local spaces across the regions.

Harmony and patriarchy

The first element of the discourse of *tinji* is the denial or downplaying of conflict in the community. 'Conflict' (*konflikt*), 'tension' (*naprazheniye*) or 'disquiet' (*bezspokoystvo, raznoglasiye*) when acknowledged are attributed to brief disputes caused by a lack of resources. Less common is the acknowledgement of tension with local government (*khukumat*) or with other villages (where the dispute is again over resources). Table 4.1 shows that although the international NGO Mercy Corps had identified the villages as places where there was inter-

Table 4.1 Acknowledgement of tension – what kind of tension (*naprazheniye*) are there in the community?

Community	Tension:					
	Over water	*Over other resources*	*Between villages*	*With Hulumat[1]*	*None/ it's calm*	*Grand total*
Koshonar	5	1	2		4	12
Margedar	3		1	2	6	12
Navabad				2	10	12
Navbuned	2				10	12
Tajik Okjar		1		1	10	12
Grand total	10	2	3	5	40	60

Note
1 Regarding taxes/call to army/elections.

ethnic conflict, or at least the potential for such conflict, two-thirds of respondents refused to acknowledge the existence of any kinds of tension. Only in the villages of Koshona and Margedar, where violence had taken place in a dispute over access to water and land, was there widespread acknowledgement of conflict.

When asked to identify threats, again there was significant agreement between community leaders and members – with both identifying the lack of work opportunities and the consequent effects of unemployment and labour migration as the most significant threat to 'peace' (*tinji*; *spokoystvo*).[14] Table 4.2 presents a categorisation of the answers of all sixty respondents in five villages to the open question: 'What is the greatest threat to peace in the village?' Economic (lack of resources) and social deficits (illiteracy, addictions) were cited as potential threats. Inter-ethnic tension and political or military threats to security were not cited at all.

Such a public transcript of conflict denial has elsewhere in the Central Asian context been denoted as a 'harmony ideology' (Bichsel 2005). Under a harmony ideology, community members refuse to acknowledge any disagreements or even any personal opinions for fear of breaking from the group. However, such statements are not merely those of negation but have 'positive' functions of avoidance and accommodation to elite demands. This harmony ideology was, ironically, particularly strongly represented by the elected community groups which had recently been established by the international NGO Mercy Corps. Perhaps the most acute demonstration of this worldview in my research was provided during a bilingual Russian/Tajik SWOT analysis conducted with a group in Novabad where the mixed-sex members were asked to identify the strengths and weaknesses of the village, and the opportunities and threats that they face (Table 4.3). Their responses inscribed 'unity' (*edinstvo*) and 'cohesion' (*splochonnost*) to the village, whilst weaknesses and threats were found in insufficient unity. Whilst a harmony ideology is a thin simplification, it is important to recognise that even such tropes can be, to a certain extent, productive. They do not end perceptions of inequality, or stifle all tensions and arguments, but they can to some extent engender self-censorship in public spaces.

The theme of harmony is also conveyed in patriarchal understandings of community management and leadership. Gendered and ageist dimensions are appar-

Table 4.2 Perceived threats to village – what is the greatest threat to peace in the village?

Community	Unemployment and labour migration	Lack of water and other resources	Illiteracy/ alcoholism/ drug addiction	There are no threats	Grand total
Koshonar	7	2		3	12
Margedar	11	1			12
Navabad	6		6		12
Navbuned	2	6		4	12
Tojikokjar	1		1	10	12
Grand total	29	9	7	17	60

Table 4.3 SWOT analysis, Novabad, Panjikent district

Strengths	Weaknesses
• Respectful culture (*Izati Ehtirom.* [Taj.]/*Uvazhaemaya kultura*) • Unity (*Yagonay.* [Taj.]/*Edinstvo*) • Mutual understanding (*Yakdigarfahmi* [Taj.]/*Vzaimoponimaniye*) • Friendship (*Dusti* [Taj.]/.*Druzhba*)	• Provocative or insubordinate behaviour (*Ighvo* [Taj.]/*Provokatsiya*) – including people who do not follow the leadership • 'People who know head of the police and report lies to them about our community, because they are jealous of projects' • 'People who dig up our pipes before'
Opportunities	Threats
• To teach the youth and direct them on the right path • Solving problems with mutual understanding and without quarrels	• Not being able to agree • Belittling one another • Some people don't obey the head of the community

ent in the public silence of women in the presence of older males. The two most common descriptions of community problem-solving are 'cohesion' and 'activeness' (*aktivnost*). Often they are used together to imply that an active community is one that coheres, and a coherent community is one that is active. When asked, 'do people listen to your voice?' the Koshenar community leader (*raisi mahalla*) noted, 'Yes, of course. The village represents one family, from one root [*koren*].'[15] The community leader in Margedar, who served forty-five years as a collective farm brigade leader (*brigadir*) from the first day the community was opened until 1997, described his leadership role: 'because I worked with them from the first day. All men and women grew up under my eyes. The people trust me and would not be able to deceive me.'[16] Community leaders in all five villages were keen to communicate examples of collective work projects (*hashar*) as they knew that the international NGO expected them to contribute to projects in this way. Indeed the local project officers of the NGO consistently told them that they needed to be mobilised and work together under the Rais as part of the programme.[17] But 'mobilisation' here is understood as calling on people to provide free labour for a community goal which has been decided by the Rais and the CIG, composed of other 'respected' (*uvazhaemye*) community members or even local government. This was indicated in the results of street and group interviews. A majority of men, particularly older men, interviewed cite that they feel listened to, while just two out of fifteen younger women felt that their voice was heard in the community. The Koshenar CIG leader was quite open that 'the voice of women has no kind of meaning'. The women in his group, being amidst male authority figures (including myself), vociferously agreed.[18]

To probe this public transcript further it is interesting to look at testimonies with regard to communal and personal livelihoods. Local elites give the impression that while the situation remains difficult, the material conditions of the community have improved over recent years. Testimonies from villagers (their subordinates), however, were somewhat mixed. Attempts to measure individual perspectives were often thwarted by an insistence to interpret 'you' in the plural – part of a broader public transcript of community togetherness. The majority (forty-four out of sixty) declared that their quality of life had improved over the previous year, from 2004 to 2005. However, whilst only one of twenty-nine men responded that their quality of life had not got better, half of all women (fifteen out of thirty) admitted it was the same or worse (Heathershaw 2005c: 9). Almost all of these fifteen were young women, most of whom were housewives living with their in-laws.

On the one hand these testimonies indicate some of the difficulties of conducting social research which lacks a substantive ethnographic aspect. Yet as public discourse these scripts are significant. Rather than being 'traditional', this highly gendered and generational form of social organisation has a distinctly post-Soviet aspect. While in other parts of Central Asia attempts have been made to formalise the mahalla committee or equivalent body by making it an organ of local government (Uzbekistan) or advisory council (Kyrgyzstan), in Tajikistan the mahalla has remained informal notwithstanding the attempts of international organisations to formalise it through the registration of community-based organisations. In Tajik villages 'mahalla' is often used interchangeably to denote both the community as a whole and its leadership[19] as made manifest in daily 'teahouse' (*choihona*) meetings. The young and, especially, women are rarely present at these times – a feature which has been exacerbated in the post-conflict, post-Soviet era. Since 1991, Tajikistan has lost many official instruments for gender equality and has lost much of its ethnic and cultural diversity with an exodus of Russians, Germans and other émigré families of European descent. Dushanbe, in particular, has felt this change. Previously one of the most Russified cities in Central Asia, its demographics have shifted markedly with whole streets and areas associated with one sub-regional group or another, with a particular influx of Kulobi people since the ascent of Rahmon to power fifteen years ago. Such demographic change is met by contrasting trends of the increasing impact of the Internet and the greater availability of Western popular culture (Harris 2006). Nevertheless, this has come relatively late to Tajikistan, which only in recent years has seen the arrival of Internet cafes and foreign voluntary workers in significant numbers and rarely outside the capital and Khujand.

Post-conflict anti-politics and modernisation

Whilst post-Soviet transition away from a planned economy towards integration into the periphery of the capitalist global market economy has been less evident in Tajikistan than other Central Asian republics, this is not to say that progress towards the material and technological conditions found in wealthy countries is not a goal for Tajikistan's elites and subordinates alike. Indeed, and importantly for this analysis, peace is understood publicly in terms of modernisation. For example, CBO members in Komsomol were particularly enthused by the prospect for modernisation through their involvement with Mercy Corps. 'We don't want anymore war', one commented, 'We want a modern country.'[20] The group's plans for their activities in the coming years amounted to a programme of cottage industrialisation including 'a sewing factory [for twenty-five girls]', a 'mini-factory [for processing fruit and vegetables]' and a 'workshop' to bring employment, as well as a 'pumping station' to deal with water shortages.[21] Other CAGs similarly associated conflict resolution with the development of core economic and social infrastructure including bridges, electrical transformers, school improvements and health clinics.

This ideal of modernisation and progress is markedly post-conflict in that it contributes to a forgetting of the past which nicely complements elite history-writing. In subordinate discourse this is concomitant, not with the performance of authority, but with an avoidance of the political sphere. This anti-political outlook is temporally founded on memories of the divisive pre-war election, particularly the 1991 presidential elections. Community leaders in Margedar provided a particularly strong example of this. 'In our village', one man noted, 'peace (*spokoystvo*) is one of our strengths'. Another man added, 'there are no tensions, no kind of political parties'.[22] At this point he was quietly chided by fellow group members for mentioning politics. Another leader (the *raisi mahalla*) in a later interview agreed that there was no political tension. He acknowledged that 'there are political parties'[23] but contended that 'there are no contentious (*sporni*) questions between them'. This anti-politics seems to be rooted in a rendering of time as post-conflict where conflict is a period of the past associated with political activity. The above example offers a glimpse of the retreat from active political participation which has taken place in Tajik society since the numerous popular political movements of *perestroika*, prior to the civil war. The association of democratic politics and political Islam with war is extremely strong. Accordingly, the political becomes a place for elites, represented by the state and the domain of the Other. Ironically, this makes anti-politics profoundly political and constitutive of Tajikistan's peace.

The hidden state of peace

The two discourses of elite *mirostroitelstvo* and subordinate *tinji* affirm apparently complementary ideals of 'stability' and 'harmony', 'authority' and 'unity'. They are a product of relations of power where elites demand affirmation or at least acquiescence. This is not to say that both discourses are mere instrumental effects of power, deployed cynically as post-facto justifications for domination. Rather, they constitute, in Humphrey's terms, 'some combination of previous ways, beliefs, and habits of mind, many of which could be characterised as Soviet or Post-Soviet repertoires by means of which people can make sense of their activities' (2002: xxi). In the schema of Scott these 'repertoires' have public and hidden aspects with the latter taking the form of testimonies of avoidance, dissent and resignation. A study of hidden transcripts makes visible the 'habits of mind' and relationships of power which are obscured in public discourses of peace.

State-system against 'the state'

Tajikistan's elite navigate between the public and hidden spaces of the state. The role of officials at all levels in collecting unofficial payments, providing favours and selling official posts is an aspect of elite discursive practice which is vital to any understanding of peace and politics. The state as a networked institution and an ideal provides cover (*krisha*) for patronage and clientelism (what is often denoted in international discourse as 'corruption'). In this sense these elite networks constitute the state itself. However, whilst the hidden practices and discourses of rent-seeking and favouritism may constitute everyday life in the *state-system* they challenge and seemingly undermine the *state-idea* ('the state', as expressed in the public transcript).[24] Here, in advance of the main body of empirical work of Chapters 5 to 7 which explore in detail such practices and testimonies, the general effect on the state of this post-Soviet, post-conflict corruption will be introduced.

The particularist and localist form of the actual practices of the state-system coincides with the institutional and material degradation of the state that has taken place since independence. The party apparatus has gone. Local government heads are not necessarily required to be members of the dominant party. Even where parties are ostensibly significant and dominant – such as President Rahmon's Peoples' Democratic Party of Tajikistan – the real bases of power are networks based around individuals and families. However, the extent of this shift from the party to individuals is not as great as often implied. During the Soviet Union, informal networks within and between 'clan'-based solidarity groups formed the basis for party nomenklatura (Roy 2000). Many of these cadres have re-emerged in the current system where they deploy neo-Soviet tropes ambivalently as ideals embodied in the past (during the Soviet Union) or in other spaces (e.g. Russia under Putin). Moreover, their elusiveness in practice serves continually to undermine the productive power of the *mirostroitelstvo* public transcript.

Numerous examples of how state practice challenges the ideal of 'the state' are found in Tajikistan's post-Soviet privatisations, which took place under the auspices of the international community. In the later stages of the war significant macro-economic assistance, including IMF credits and a World Bank-assisted privatisation programme, had begun to stabilise the economy (Akiner 2001: 60). However, it was state elites that benefited from a process where state industries were transferred from the public hands of the ministry to the 'private' hands of the minister, his family and supporters. For example, the Tajik Khizmat company, run by ex-minister Sayfuddin Turayev, came into existence simply by the privatisation of the ministry 'with the profits being pocketed by the minister in question' (Roy 2000: 184). In other cases which Roy describes, an industry is kept in 'public' hands but its profits are siphoned to a controlling elite faction. He notes:

> The state is thus effectively leased to networks of power. In Tajikistan, a
> deputy-minister is in a position to resell for convertible currency cotton that

he has bought from the *kolkhoz* in roubles, and banks his profits in a foreign account. As in the case of privatisation, state control can be equally illusory. Here the maintenance of the statist structure does not necessarily mean control by the state, but the use of that structure in order to better satisfy private interests.

(ibid.: 184)

What Roy is describing here is exactly the kind of public/hidden divide in the life of the post-conflict Tajikistani state where an all-pervasive state-idea is denied in hidden practices of the multiple parts of the state-system. This puzzle of the 'state-against-itself' (Migdal 1994) and the 'strong/weak state' in Central Asia (McMann 2004) will be explored further in subsequent chapters.

However, before we move on, we must consider one quite straightforward explanation for this anomaly: that is, strong regime versus weak state. This answer at first sight seems plausible in a system where power-holders are increasingly representative of a regime based around President Rahmon, in which both former civil war allies and opponents are gradually being excluded. Thus, it is argued by critics of the regime and critical advocates for greater international statebuilding that we see the strengthening of the regime but not the strengthening of the state. The litmus test offered as proof for this assertion is the transfer of power from Rahmon to another President. How, it is asked, could such a transition take place? If the President fell ill or was killed by an assassin's bullet, what mechanism exists to bring a new government to power without descending into another civil war? Such questions invite speculation but, like all counterfactuals, offer little prospect of resolution. The problem here is demarcating the state from the regime. In elite public transcripts 'the state' and 'state officials' are inscribed as being synonymous. As neither opposition nor popular discourses clearly distinguish between 'state' and 'regime' this implies that an unambiguous divide is not socially and politically meaningful, and thus not analytically valuable. I will continue to use the term 'regime' to identify the multiple and divisible state-actors of the state-system, at times identifying particular local factions of state-actors. These hidden transcripts and factions will be explored in more detail in Chapters 5–7.

Popular avoidance, dissent and resignation tactics

During my research I found that the silent stories of the poor were less hidden and more accessible than the stories of elite relations of patronage and corruption. Indeed it was their very exclusion from political and economic power that made some people, although often fearful of the consequences, willing to speak out. Yet their hidden transcripts revealed three aspects of subordinate social life immediately relevant to the emergence of legitimate political order, only one of which approximates to 'resistance'.

First, the Tajik poor practise conflict avoidance in the form of everyday subsistence living and seasonal labour migration. In the communities I lived in and visited from 2003 to 2007, those who were not somehow linked to elite networks which gave them privileged access to land and/or rent were preoccupied with the difficult process of scratching out a living and coping with poverty. The young – both male and female – testify increasingly to the burden of making a living locally, going on labour migration to Russia (for men), and coping as head of the household without their husbands (for women). During street interviews, I asked the question: 'What changes would make your life easier?' Fifty-three out of sixty interviewees named 'work places' as one of, or the only, change that would make a difference. A representative selection of answers is below:

JH: What changes would make your life easier?

24-year-old, female, housewife: 'First, there's no work places. Second, there's no libraries for us to be able to study. I can read but there's no books. I want to study but there's no possibilities. We need to raise the level of education.'

18-year-old, female, housewife: 'There's no work places for us, for women. If they opened a sewing shop for us, we'd be able to make our lives easier.'

28-year-old, male, unemployed: 'Work places. I want to work.'

20-year-old, female, housewife: 'If there were work places in our community that would make our life easier. I would undertake any work as a migrant and with this earn myself something to live off.'

26-year-old, male, unemployed: 'A way out (*vyezd*) to Russia'[25]

Such testimonies, which are extremely common across Tajikistan, whilst hardly qualifying as dissent, depart from the harmony ideology that is typically portrayed to internationals and outsiders. They lead to an acceptance of the necessity of migration and the creation of translocal communities between Tajikistan and, typically, Russia. Tajik film-maker Jamshed Ushmonov's 2006 film, *Angel on the Right*, similarly represents this form of conflict avoidance for an ex-fighter returning to repay post-Soviet debts. Migration as a form of conflict avoidance will be examined further in Chapter 6.

Second, the poor can be heard to dissent quietly against the new order. Dissenting voices are more likely to occur amongst the young and the women of the village, the two groups which are particularly excluded from the patriarchal system. While publicly women claim that they accept their lot as second-class citizens, a small minority are ready to speak out. As a male researcher, I found cynicism behind closed doors towards the regime in particular and older males in general. There seem to be two directions of dissent: anger about poverty, and hopelessness with the local community. They may exist among groups of female cotton workers, peasant farmers, male labour migrants, or within the extended family, mahalla or ex-kolkhoz. For example, in one village in the Rasht valley some young male peasant farmers noted how the actual arrangements for 'water management' were less equitable and harmonious than the village leadership claimed. One noted that the members of the *dekon* farm which was attached to the sovkhoz received priority access to water and when they used it there were shortages for poorer members of the community who had their own plots. More-over, one remarked, 'if you want to irrigate your land you have to monitor it', in order to stop others redirecting the water.[26]

Third and finally, this dissent extends to limited collaborative resistance. For example, female cotton workers in a village near Sharituz reported that they hadn't been paid in six months and that the community priority was not that officially decreed by the community leadership during the international NGO-sponsored planning workshops but, simply, to 'get paid'. 'The head [rais] promised', one claimed, 'but it hasn't yet come'. The women noted bitterly that they had simply received left-over cotton stalks to sell in the bazaar.[27] When I tentatively inquired with the rais about this situation he acknowledged that the women had been to see him but laid the blame for their non-payment with the businessmen who finance local cotton production, to whom local farmers are indebted. A lack of trust in the local elite contrasts strongly with the 'unity' and 'harmony' maxims of *tinji*. In a few cases it may also be contributing to apparently increased support for radical Islamic movements, such as Hizb ut-Tahrir.

This raises the question of religious faith, which must be considered in terms of its significance as a source of the temporal and ethical markers of subordinate dis-course and practices. Unlike some representations of it as a transformational vision of change or a driver of radicalisation, amongst many of the faithful in Tajikistan Islam appears to provide sustenance for resignation as well as sources for resist-ance. In this sense, the local mullos I interviewed offered responses similar to those of other village leaders. As such, 'Islamic' political discourse and practice emerges from the wider and politically moderate social environment as has been noted by scholars of Islam in Tajikistan (Hiro 1994: 203, 217; Atkin 1995: 254). In Harris' terms, 'everyday Islam is largely mediated through the honour-and-shame system, which has become intimately bound up in [Tajikistan's] local cus-tomary laws' (2004: 34–35). It may be that there is a hidden transcript of political Islam, inaccessible to this research, which would indicate nascent resistance to the Rahmon regime.[28] However, most empirical research conducted in Tajikistan sug-gests that the wider Muslim population remains largely indifferent to politics in the post-war period (Mullojanov 2001b).

Inter-subjectivities of family and state

How is one to make political sense of elite–subordinate relations in the contexts of both contending public and hidden transcripts and a contrasting state-idea and state-system? One route not to follow is the familiar Western sovietological move of equating public with (neo-)Soviet and personal–hidden with traditional. Rakowska-Harmstone, for example, entertains speculation on the existence of, 'a "shadow elite" of people who enjoy prestige and power in the community by virtue of traditional criteria, and whose activities have been carefully concealed from the authorities' (1970: 282, 284). A second route best avoided is that of the neo-institutionalist pathway of assuming the dominance of the hidden state-system over the public state-idea to the extent that 'the lack of a coherent idea of state' necessitates that we 'dissolve the state into concrete coercive and institutional functions in order to see how bodies that in theory should counter the problem adhere to a very different logic in practice' (Engvall 2006: 835, 851). The general problem here is one of reification. Answering questions of the politics of peace and the emergence of order necessitates attentiveness to the politics of space and a consideration of the shifting boundaries of public and hidden which limit possibilities for resistance as much as they provide some room for alternatives to hegemonic order.

Such a line of inquiry has been pursued in Collette Harris' (2004) *Control and Subversion: Gender Relations in Tajikistan.* Harris explores patriarchy in the Tajik family alongside its functioning in the Tajik state in terms of the gendered code of honour and shame (*nomus* and *ayb*). She studies how gender 'masks' – which she regards as a substitute for the physical veil which was outlawed from the 1920s (2004: 58) – allow order *both in* the family *and of* the state. Yet Harris finds Tajiks living in 'multiple layers of contradictions' as they are subject to control and subjects of subversion according to their sexual and generational identity (2004: 170). Masks operate as 'shields' which 'permit the existence of individuality beneath the surface conformity, albeit within the relatively narrow limits possible in the restricted environment of Tajikistan' (ibid.: 173). In a context where representations are used, apparently instrumentally, by their subjects it appears legitimate to ask questions about *real* beliefs and the degree of 'internalisation'. This, however, Harris argues, is a problematic move. Mask-wearers are 'not just pretending' but they are playing a role much like an actor in the theatre (2004: 23). Women and men in Tajikistan feel bound to their 'public' gender performances and the continued playing of this role constitutes their own subjectivity – their identity in social and political order. What is important is not control as such but the public demonstration of control.

It is in this sense that the parallels between family and state in Tajik society must be understood. Where gender roles are so binding, public space extends through the spaces of the mahalla (where male heads of households are responsible for the chastity and right conduct of their womenfolk) into the home (where fathers must reaffirm these gender boundaries for the children) and even the bedroom (where husbands might assert demands for sex). It is only here, in the bedroom, where Harris finds potential for limited forms of interpersonal relations not bound by gender masks (ibid.: 171). Perhaps here she is being overly deterministic in denying the existence of social practices of resistance or at least alternative forms of association (public or hidden) across the mahalla. Yet the parallels between the gendered social order of Tajikistan that she describes and the ideals of political 'stability' and 'authority' discussed above are considerable. Family and state in Tajikistan are two different aspects of the same sociopolitical order. Tajiks often draw such parallels and President Rahmon frequently plays up to this image, presiding over a presidential youth movement in the Soviet tradition and frequently issuing public pronouncements on appropriate forms of dress and conduct for young people. As such, political order in Tajikistan begins with family, gender relations and sex.

Adherence to gender masks in public has functions for individuals as well as for public order. It allows them limited space for individuality and personal expression in hidden spaces. In turn, the confinement of subversive practice to hidden space concomitantly reaffirms the hegemony of the public transcript – that is they affirm that which they supposedly negate. When hidden transcripts remain hidden they are better understood as resignation rather than resistance. In this sense, public and hidden transcripts, if stable, are not so much contrasting as concomitant. As Scott notes (1990: 202–203), it is only when what's been hidden bursts through to the public sphere (whether that is the family, the mahalla or a city street) that 'political electricity' surges and resistance develops. Family is a forum for such 'resistance' or, more likely by Harris' analysis, a bulwark against it. For most Tajiks, the family not only provides the foundational unit of political order but it provides the point at which 'resistance' or 'subversion' to that order is either given birth or left still-born.

Conclusions

In the years since the 1997 peace agreement a multidimensional order of complex legitimacy has emerged in Tajikistan. Chapters 3 and 4 have outlined the discursive constitution of peacebuilding in terms of three basic discourses – international peacebuilding, elite *mirostroitelstvo* and subordinate *tinji*. With the three discourses in mind we can chart post-conflict international intervention in terms of their intertextual relations, the reproductions and adaptations of the three discourses, and the opposition to them found in the hidden transcript. This gives us some basis to assess the politics of peacebuilding and emergence of legitimate order as a process with dynamics of continuity and change.

In the following thematic chapters the points of intersection of contending discourses and spaces will be identified as I seek to chart how discourses have accommodated each others' contrasting representations. For example, an expatriate working for an international NGO on a community self-governance project may find his international peacebuilding mediated by the *mirostroitelstvo* of local government leaders, and the disengagement from public life of community members operating in terms of *tinji*. Similarly, a local government leader conducting a self-legitimating 'election' may find he has to adjust his behaviour in moments and places to satisfy the OSCE observers, and simultaneously mobilise a disengaged population to do their 'duty'. In such a way intertextual political practice is spatially differentiated and temporally contingent. Furthermore, the accommodations and fudges made between internationals, elites and subordinates very often enable self-seeking opportunism by well-positioned individuals across all three scales delineated above. In short, grand narratives are compromised in favour of messy solutions that don't correspond directly to any single discourse. Yet this does not necessarily mean that these visions diminish or become unproductive. For reasons explored below peace-builders and peace-enforcers often press on towards the goal regardless of its inauthenticity in their minds and others. This is perhaps best conveyed in

Žižek's rendering of Sloterdijk's 'cynical subjects' who 'know that, in their activity, they are following an illusion, but still, they are doing it' (1989: 29).[29]

In the following chapters, I suggest that it is from this discursive environment that properties of *authority* (Chapter 5), *sovereignty* (Chapter 6) and *livelihoods* (Chapter 7) emerge. But in investigating the sources of these three properties – and the discursive environment which sustains them – we must look in some places which are unfamiliar to international peacebuilders. Sexual and familial relations are by no means independent of questions of political order or of building peace. Similarly, practices of migration and shuttle-trading, withdrawal to the home and reliance on subsistence agriculture are no less part of the material foundation for submission to this authority than are public performances of consent to elite hegemony. Corruption and patronage relations, migration and subsistence may be far more important to the emergence of legitimate order in Tajikistan than *democratisation* (Chapter 5), *security sector reform* (Chapter 6) and *community development* (Chapter 7). It is to these practices and interventions that this book now turns.

5 Democracy and authority

[The elections] were a show (*spektakl*) where our government and the poor played the leading roles.

(Dilbar Samadova, Social Democratic Party of Tajikistan 2005: 5)

Free and fair elections conducted under a multiparty system are seen as the essential marker of international peacebuilding's success. 'Indeed', Jeong notes, in a major survey of the field, 'conducting *elections needed to establish a legitimate government* has been the overriding objective under which all other international activities are generally subsumed' (2005: 103, emphasis added). The International Community has invested considerable time and resources to improving electoral law, increasing civic engagement and the monitoring of national elections in Tajikistan. Such investments reflect policy priorities set by donor-funded research that in turn adopts the generic priorities of peacebuilding discourse. For example, the 2003 'peacebuilding framework' for Tajikistan identified people's opportunities to '*non-violently express their dissatisfaction* with government, ruling elite policies and programmes *through the democratic process*' as one of five priorities. Its recommendations included support for opposition parties and 'a democratic multiparty system', the 'creation of open spaces for dialogue', assistance for 'holding free and fair elections' and, in particular, 'technical assistance and training to improve election procedures' (Abdullaev and Freizer, 2003: 54–55). However, whilst the Tajikistani government has consciously incorporated the language of democracy into its legal framework and public pronouncements, it is largely unconstrained by democratic institutions or norms. Multiparty elections in Tajikistan serve purposes other than those of democratisation.

This chapter explores how democracy has been denied and authority has emerged in post-conflict politics. It reveals the role of international assistance in the *performance of authority*. I argue that these performances constitute the very nature of 'political parties' and 'elections' in a way which produces a conveniently fungible form of authority, personified by some and impersonated by others. The chapter is divided into four sections. The first section introduces the role of the International Community and the parties themselves through a consideration of the 2000 elections and the subsequent attempts to reform the law on parliamentary elections. The second section considers the function of the 2005 parliamentary elections in this hybrid system; how, as a 'spectacle of consent', they are performed as the authorisation of elections and the election of authority. The third section looks at the attempts to generate multipartyism and provide an outlet for opposition via dialogue between the state, political parties and civil society. It shows how 'opposition' is enabled in the in-between spaces of the International Community, which concomitantly re-inscribe the hegemony of the regime in the public square. Finally, the fourth section outlines ongoing post-conflict processes of the re-centring and de-centring of authority, and raises the question of what role international assistance plays in generating these processes.

Political transition after 2000

International intervention to support and develop political parties and elections in Tajikistan takes place in a political context of party structures formed around elite networks. Some of these parties predate the civil war whilst others emerged in its aftermath. Equally, earlier elections in Tajikistan have provided key moments of conflict and become key markers of international peacebuilding. At the beginning of the 2000s the relationship between government and opposition parties remained tense whilst elections provided points of contention and violence.

The elections of 1999 and 2000

Post-conflict multiparty politics faced difficulties from the beginning. In August 1999, following the UTO's declaration that its armed units had disbanded, confirmed by the CNR, the ban on political parties was lifted. However, pressure increased on political parties with six of the eleven registered since 1998 being suspended, banned or deregistered in the run-up to the presidential elections of November 1999 and the parliamentary ballot of February 2000.[1] It was not until 26 September 1999 that an amendment was passed to the constitution which extended the presidential term to seven years and created a two-chamber parliament (*Majlisi Oli*).[2] A last minute deal between President Rahmon and UTO leader Nuri introduced the parliamentary election law on the eve of the presidential elections less than three months before Tajikistan's first post-war parliamentary elections.[3] Rahmon was duly re-elected with 97 per cent of the vote in farcical presidential elections where he was, for most of the campaign, the only candidate standing.[4] Subsequent to his victory the election law was adjusted to, amongst other things, legally guarantee opposition parties 20 per cent representation on district election committees (DEC) and polling station committees (PSC). Despite some significant violence, the parliamentary elections also passed off without a serious challenge to the results despite the overwhelming majority of seats going to the President's party and his supporters. The new parliament included the presidential People's Democratic Party (thirty-six deputies), the pro-governmental Communist Party (thirteen deputies), and non-affiliated 'independent' candidates who were largely staunch allies of the government (ten deputies). The IRPT won two seats, both via the party list (OSCE 2000: 24).

This gesture towards 'multiparty politics' led many international observers to praise the elections as a great advance in pluralism. 'It is absolutely certain', Lavrakas, for the OSCE, notes, 'that the possibility of electing deputies by party lists played an important role in the development of pluralism in Tajikistan and meant an increase in the role of the multi-party system in society' (OSCE 2004: 20). For the International Community, the headline conclusion related to the explicit goals of peacebuilding. 'The most significant accomplishment in this peacebuilding process', the official OSCE report noted, 'was the inclusion of the former warring parties and others in the electoral process' (2000: 1). Although international observers also noted deficiencies in terms of both the legislative framework, campaign and election-day irregularities (ibid.: 1–2), it is understandable that the International Community would emphasise positives over negatives in Tajikistan's first post-conflict parliamentary elections. However, the inclusion of opposition elites within a 'multiparty system' does not necessarily constitute democratisation. Elections can be a symbol of unity and homogeneity through cooperation and subordination and thus produce the reverse of pluralism. They can also allow for the inclusion of new elites, the rotation of old ones and provide for the exclusion of parties deemed to be a threat. These alternative functions can serve to exclude popular participation and inhibit diversity, yet this does not necessarily mean they are illegitimate.

The parties after the elections[5]

To reduce Tajikistan's politics to its formally existing parties and elections does not begin to capture the underlying political dynamics, of which parties are merely a superficial representation. Such parties are formed from regionally-based elite networks which deploy 'authority' and 'stability' in public testimonies and practices. Thus any exploration of political parties needs to consider the constitutive role of *mirostroitelstvo* discourse, the regional basis of their members and their discursive practices.

The winners

The Peoples' Democratic Party (PDPT) is the youngest of Tajikistan's parties which gained seats in 2000. The history of its development is one of the formation of a regional elite centred around victorious Kulobi warlords and apparatchiks. Formed in 1993 as the People's Party of Tajikistan, and registered in 1994, it was initially a party of the Kurghon Teppa regional elite and headed by Abdumadzid Dostiev. As Rahmon worked to consolidate his power, Kurghon Teppa elites found their authority diminished and Rahmon's network moved to use the party as a vehicle for their power. After President Rahmon became a member in March 1998, he was elected party leader at the 4th Party Congress of 18 April 1998, with Dostiev named his deputy. The party was renamed the PDPT and political elites at all bureaucratic levels (province, district and local) were advised, cajoled or instructed to join. This process, shadowing the growth in Rahmon's personal power, constituted the widening of his patronage network to include old and new allies from regions across the country. Joining the party, in most cases, was concomitant with taking a position in local or regional government. For example, Kadirah Jurayev, a party leader in Gharm district, became a member in 2000 after he was given the position of head of a *dekon* farm. 'The head of the *Khukumat* explained that this is the party in power now and only this party can change things'.[6] Whilst as an institution the PDPT suffers from many of the weaknesses of other political parties in terms of organisational limitations and financial shortages, by sum of its members' wealth then it is by far the best financed party in Tajikistan.

If the PDPT came to be the new representative of the party-state, the Communist Party (CPT) was the previous version in decline. The party still intertwines strongly with government. In parliament, the thirteen-strong communist faction of 2000 to 2005 was openly pro-governmental. Some CPT officials themselves present this as a constructive relationship where they support the government on most issues but can quietly dissent on others (Anon 2005: 3). However, this role within the government has taken place alongside a haemorrhaging of party membership to the PDPT. In Kulob, for example, cadres retained their membership of the CPT whilst joining the PDPT in order to gain favour with local authorities and maintain their positions in the local administration.[7] CPT officially supported the local PDPT candidate in 2005 in return for places in the local assembly (Dinkayev 2005: 3). Such close relations between the PDPT and CPT reflect the network relationships that constitute multiparty politics in Tajikistan. Two new self-declared 'pro-governmental' parties, the Agrarian Party of Tajikistan (APT) and the Party for Economic Reform of Tajikistan (PERT), were created in late 2005 and enjoy a similar relationship with government.[8] The CPT, APT and PERT all fielded candidates in the 2006 presidential elections.[9]

The losers

As discussed in Chapter 2, the Islamic Renaissance Party of Tajikistan (IRPT) grew out of the revival of political Islam across the Muslim world in the late twentieth century. The party maintained a moderate public platform and describes its members as 'Muslim-citizens' of Tajikistan (Himmatzoda 2003a). Although the IRPT won two seats in the 2000 elections, this was significantly below what it had hoped for. It is traditionally strongest in the Rasht valley (esp. Tavildara raiyon), as well as in various pockets of Khatlon (e.g. Vakhsh) and Soghd (e.g. Isfara) oblasts. However, it has been outflanked on both sides, losing support both from those who have been co-opted by government and from those who are turning their back on the party in favour of more radical Islamic groups. In 2006 its long-time leader and former head of the UTO Said Abdullo Nuri died. He was replaced by Muhiddin Kabiri, a modern man with significant business interests who is favourably regarded as a 'moderate' in the International Community.

The Democratic Party of Tajikistan (DPT) was also founded during *perestroika*. It has since undergone a gradual decline, being riddled by internal splits and tensions. Early in its history it lost its ethnic Russian faction (from the city of Chkalovsk) and the conservative group of Akil Akilov (Olimova and Bowyer 2002: 20–21) to become an ethno-regional party of elites of the Rasht valley, united with the IRPT. In 1995, after overtures from the government to return to Tajikistan and isolate the IRPT, it split once again between the Almaty and Tehran platforms. The Almaty platform, with the election of Makhmadruzi Iskandarov from Tajikabad in the Rasht Valley, achieved a rapprochement with Rahmon and continued to fill a number of state positions under the terms of the peace agreement. Despite these ties with government, they failed to gain any seats in the 2000 elections (receiving only 3.5 per cent of the votes). As a consequence of this schismatic history, the DPT has now lost the regional power bases it once had. In 2004, it lost its charismatic leader, Iskandarov, who was arrested, tried and convicted on terrorist charges. Following the conviction, the party split again when Masud Sobirov was elected leader by his supporters in April 2006. Today there are three separate DPT factions representing Sobirov, the imprisoned Iskandarov and Saidjaffar Ismonov. The Ministry of Justice recognises the Sobirov faction as the official DPT.

The Socialist Party (SPT) was founded towards the end of the peace negotiations. Between its genesis in 1996 and his assassination in 1999, it served as a vehicle for Safarali Kenjayev, a leading figure of the nomenklatura who played a major role in the onset of war. The party grew in popularity in Kenjayev's home region of the Zerafshon valley and garnered some support from Khujandis in some areas of Soghd oblast and Dushanbe. However, following Kenjayev's death, and his son Sherali Kenjayev's ascent to the leadership, the party descended into what one prominent leader labelled as 'some kind of crisis' (Horisova 2005: 2) and began to suffer from what Asadullaev calls 'a lack of prominent people' (ibid.: 21). While the new leadership supported Rahmon in the presidential elections of 1999, the membership preferred to support the candidate of *Adolathoh* (Party of Justice), Saiffidin Turaev.[10] The party split again in 2004 as Mirhussein Narziev was removed from the leadership by members ostensibly unhappy about the party's entering into coalition with other parties for the 2005 elections.[11] Abduhalim Gaffurov, the new leader, is officially recognised and ran as a candidate against Rahmon in the 2006 presidential elections receiving 2.8 per cent of the vote.

Despite these features of factionalism it is inadequate to dismiss political parties as distractions from self-interested, regionally based economic networks. Underlying these shifts in power networks are relationships founded in patrimonial co-optation and authoritarian control. However, the extreme fluidity of political formations in Tajikistan challenges the idea that either parties or the informal networks which underlie them are sufficient frames through which to view the new ruling elite. In reality both government and opposition networks are constantly in flux with the co-optation of 'opposition' figures and expulsion of 'governmental' representatives. For example, Akil Akilov, Prime Minister since 1999 and now a senior member of the PDPT, was once a leader of the DPT before rejoining the CPT. Similarly, Qazi Turajonzoda, although he has never been a party member, sided with the IRPT during perestroika before returning to the ruling elite as Deputy Prime Minister. Elites on both sides shift strategically between parties and factions. While this chapter will investigate cases of personnel and institutional change, its focus will be on the discourses and practices which distinguish insiders from outsiders in Tajikistani politics. It is these discourses and practices which constitute authority, 'opposition' and resistance.

Reforming elections, 2002–2005

Tajikistan's elections were considered by the International Community to be a 'first step' on the road to multiparty democracy. Therefore, certain democratic deficits were identified which might be addressed before the next elections in 2005.

In early 2002 the government began work on rewriting Tajikistan's electoral law. The OSCE led attempts at reform following the deficiencies identified by their Office for Democratic Institutions and Human Rights' (ODIHR) report on the 2000 elections.[12] In late 2002, it began a process of informal consultation and in April 2003 convened a formal conference for opposition parties and the government under the project, 'In preparation for the 2005 elections'.[13] The OSCE Centre in Dushanbe created a working group to consider the amendments, formed of a deputy and a vice-chairman from three parties (CPT, IRPT and DPT). The most marginalised opposition parties – the SPT and a new party, the Social Democratic Party of Tajikistan (SDPT) – were excluded from this group and confined to formulating amendments, involvement in relevant seminars organised by OSCE, the International Foundation for Electoral Systems (IFES) and the National Democratic Institute (NDI) (Lavrakas 2004: 35). ODIHR reviewed the draft and advised the group to strengthen it to address issues such as the increase of the number of seats in the lower house, independence of the electoral commissions, financing of campaigns and the inclusion of non-partisan domestic observers.

At this point, as the draft was to be discussed formally by parliament, the initiative began to hit difficulties. Fearful, the working group refused to sign the draft. Moreover, as the group worked outside parliament, it was ridiculed as illegitimate by some deputies and PDPT representatives were instructed to oppose it. As one OSCE official described, 'Well, you know, there was a lot of trouble: they said "How can you challenge the authority of parliament?", "This is a matter of national sovereignty".' By late February 2004 two drafts appeared in parliament: a CPT/IRPT draft with some similarities to the OSCE-supported text and a PDPT draft which appeared ten days later. ODIHR analysed the drafts and found them both to be deficient. Marti Ahtisaari, personal envoy to Central Asia of the OSCE president-in-office, passed the comments directly to the Speaker of the lower house. According to an OSCE official, both Ahtisaari and the then Bulgarian president-in-office 'pressed the government and conveyed the message of importance'. Following these interventions President Rahmon stepped into the breach in the manner of an arbiter and announced that parliament should invite opposition parties to discuss the amendments. On 10–12 June 2004 they held public consultations for three days which were attended by OSCE, UNTOP, a number of NGOs and representatives of the Presidential Administration. However, the protocol drafted by parliament largely reflected the PDPT draft. The law was passed by the lower (16 June 2004) and upper (8 July 2004) chambers of parliament. While opposition parties appealed to the President to veto the law in two letters signed by five parties (all legal parties except the PDPT), Rahmon labelled it a 'compromise solution' and signed it into law.

For the International Community this law contained some small improvements and some significant new problems (OSCE 2005g: 4). Prohibiting governmental interference, for example, was meaningless as so many government officials 'double-hatted' as election officials (ibid.: 4). Asadullaev in a CIMERA-edited elections guide noted that Article 32 of the new law had 'the most anti-democratic character' in that it required a pledge or deposit per candidate of the equivalent of 200 minimum monthly wages (equivalent to US$1,400 in 2005), which made it difficult for anyone outside the most wealthy to stand for parliament (Asadullaev 2004: 36). One government official later conceded that this change made the law less democratic than its predecessor (Usmonov 2005a: 5–6). However, despite these problems UNTOP and the OSCE pushed on with support and observation of the 2005 elections.

This outcome raises the two major themes which this chapter explores: the simulation of 'democratisation', 'opposition' and 'multiparty politics'; and the performance of authority. First, democratisation is declared present in its absence by representatives of the International Community. Despite some limited public and more extensive private criticism of the new law (see also ICG 2004), senior international officials often softened their criticism with recourse to the promise of international peacebuilding. Hoagland, the US Ambassador, in a 3 March 2004 speech remarked:

> Although not all political parties have been registered, there is a multiparty system, including the only legal Islamic party in the whole Central Asia. What is more inspiring is that the government is adhering to the democratic practice of decreasing the central government control over local affairs. I am confident that democracy will prosper in Tajikistan.[14]

The 'only legal Islamic party in Central Asia' is a familiar refrain of internationals in defence of Tajik democracy, one that seems to excuse a multitude of democratic deficits and rescues the possibility of international peacebuilding (Dinkayev 2005: 4).

Second, the performance of authority is witnessed by the regime's occlusion of international criticism. The right of the state to consent to elections, formally and informally, and interpret laws consistent with the interest of ruling authorities is intrinsic to the 'stable' and 'authoritative' politics imagined in elite discourses. This state-as-guardian approach does not only provide the right of state intervention but the state responsibility of ensuring safe elections occurring without incident.[15] For example, the proposal for independent, non-partisan observers was one suggested improvement that was ruled out in the electoral law reform process of 2002 to 2004. The idea of NGOs providing independent advice or monitoring is simply implausible and unacceptable to state officials. The International Research and Exchanges Board (IREX), IFES and NDI have all had experiences with this elite discourse. One IFES seminar on election law reform in spring 2004, including representatives from the Presidential Administration (PA) as well as the Central Committee on Elections and Referenda (CCER), discussed the question of non-partisan observers. One PA representative questioned, 'even if we passed a law for this what kind of people will you put on there? What do they know?'[16]

These two dynamics come together in the politics of peacebuilding in Tajikistan. The hostility of government towards 'political' actions by NGOs, according to one programme coordinator, demands that they follow the maxim: 'get government permission in advance, always invite the *Khukumat* [local administration]'.[17] When the *Khukumat* is unwilling to give permission, even for very small events, it is often necessary to involve the PA. Following the 'Orange Revolution' in the Ukraine (December 2004) this centralisation of control increased. In one meeting in early 2005 regarding an IFES local publication, 'The Journal of Democracy', a PA official gave a forty-minute lecture: 'Tajikistan is not America', 'we're not ready for this', 'demonstrations in the street are not appropriate for Tajikistan'.[18] Working in such an environment, the goals of international organisations are diluted in practice. One example from the testimony of the same programme officer noted:

> We organised a workshop with 70 participants and asked the local government to participate in order to work with them – you know the idea was to increase the role of citizens in taking about issues in their area, to have roundtables on priority issues to feed into local government who normally don't listen at all. In actuality the *Khukumat* had the say in who is invited and who speaks, but I think you can say that it was a step in the right direction – to get anyone to participate is a positive thing.[19]

A 'step in the right direction' is all that remains of international peacebuilding in this case. However, it is an important remainder; it simulates a process of democratisation despite the absence of any substantive evidence to support that notion.

The 2005 parliamentary elections: the spectacle of consent

On 27 February 2005, Tajikistan held its second post-war parliamentary elections. Unlike the 2000 elections, where eleven people – including one prominent candidate – were killed in pre-election violence, both the campaign and election-day itself passed off peacefully. International Community representatives saw the elections as a crucial moment of peacebuilding. A UN Needs Assessment Mission in April 2004 thus recommended 'the provision of electoral assistance within the peacebuilding strategy of UNTOP' (UNDPA 2004: 2). The hope was to keep state manipulation of the elections to a minimum, to increase the role of opposition parties, the media and the general public, and to see the beginnings of a strong opposition bloc emerging in parliament.[20] However, similar to 2000, the PDPT won an overwhelming victory, actually increasing its share of the vote from 64.9 to 74.9 per cent.[21] There was a great deal of continuity between 2000 and 2005, reflecting two general trends in Tajik politics: a decrease in violence and instability, and a further consolidation of presidential power. The role of elections in the Tajik 'peace' can be understood not as an obstacle to authoritarian retrenchment but as a spectacle of consent which was constitutive of this very process.

Authorising elections

The elections of 2005 were *authorised* by the elite, in terms of inclusion on the ballot, voter education, the nature of media coverage and space for campaigning.

Authorising candidates

Candidature for the elections was authorised by reference to two broad techniques, familiar to post-Soviet politics: control and co-optation. The role of 'authority' is clearly apparent in these practices; its performance is more important than party membership as a marker of inclusion in the elite. Control can include the barring of candidates as well as direct pressure on candidates to withdraw (Ghafforzoda 2005; OSCE 2005g: 22). More pervasive was the deterrent provided by the expensive electoral deposit which could be returned if the candidate withdrew before the election. For example, all three self-nominated candidates in one constituency where I observed, Vakhdat (DEC 10), withdrew on 17 February, just ten days before the election (2005f: 1). These moves suggest that such candidatures may not be bona fide but are submitted in order to give the impression of competitive elections (2005g: 10).

While most opposition party candidates were directly excluded, many self-nominated, CPT and SPT candidates were co-opted by the ruling elite (2005b: 2–3). Self-nominated candidate Dustov in Faizabad (DEC 11) was de-registered by the CCER on the 19 February and put his support behind the official PDPT candidate. He had previously stated on 5 February that he was 'affiliated' to the party of government. During the campaign he regularly appeared together with the official PDPT candidate, and his posters were prominently displayed alongside those of the PDPT (2005d: 3). In Rasht (DEC 12), the candidate for the PDPT, Saidullo Khairulloyev, was not a member of the party, but his nomination was supported by them. As chair of the lower chamber of parliament, he, like many senior elites, played the role of a leader whose authority exceeds that of the party. Together these intra-elite, anti-democratic practices exhibit a variety of different forms of co-optation which constitute horizontal legitimacy or consent to authority within the elite. Performing loyalty to the party in an ultimately unfulfilled candidacy asserts membership of the 'authoritative' elite, and offers the prospect of position or privilege in the future. It would be misleading to dismiss these as purely economic relationships of patronage as they exhibit elite norms and affirm the privileged space of 'the state'.

Authorising information

State control of information was a pronounced feature of the election, and became a challenge for numerous international projects. More than half a million dollars was funnelled through the American NGOs IFES, NDI and IREX, in an election-related grants programme particularly targeted at women and first-time voters. One such IREX-supported NGO was *Elim* in the Kulob region which administered a small grant to educate women voters through a project entitled 'Vote and Win!' (Rahmonova 2005: 5). It is revealing to hear the testimony of the head of *Elim*, Latifahon Rahmonova.

> The events that we organised were political events. Moreover, our organisation was non-governmental. That's why we faced many problems. In the first instance this seems to be a very simple thing, but as one gets involved many difficulties come along. For this reason during these four months that I was occupied in this field – firstly because it was my field and secondly because it was a political field – it was a little hard to work with the Jamoats [local administration]. The residents of Shahrvand village know that while we were waiting to receive letters from the Ministry of Foreign Affairs and IREX, this created opposition between us and the Khukumat [local government]. However, after receiving the letter we came to a consensus and together with the Khukumat and the chair of the [official] women's committee of this community could gather all the women and explain to them their voting rights. Until this moment not only the housewives but also women with qualifications did not know the essence of elections. [...] I am glad that I came across lots of literature that was made available for us from the American organisations, that we are living in a democratic society, that our community is following this path, and we have to support it.
>
> (Ibid: 5)

What's interesting here is how tension between local government and an NGO working on 'political events' in a small number of rural villages were overcome by a letter of permission from central government and a subsequent 'consensus' where the *Khukumat* acquires a leading role in implementing this ostensibly non-governmental project. There is a clear acceptance of patriarchy: that women need to be taught to participate (ibid.: 6). Moreover, the voter education material of IREX is presented in essentially conservative and disempowering terms – 'that our community is following this path, and we have to support it' – rather than as empowering personal choice and highlighting democratic deficits of Tajikistan.

These same features were apparent in media coverage of the elections. In many rural areas, such as Rasht, there are no newspapers and (if the power is on) only a few Russian TV channels and state-owned *Televizioni Tojikiston* (the only national TV station). Significantly, there was a complete lack of debate or critical programmes in the media and many reports of 'self-censorship' across the country. In the month before the elections *Televizioni Tojikiston* devoted just twenty-five minutes in total to the elections.[22] The coverage that was provided was either technical, with significant time given to the CCER to explain the election process, or focused on senior governmental elites. For example, a documentary crew followed Khairulloyev during his campaign (OSCE 2005d: 4). OSCE monitoring found that 63 per cent of total state TV news coverage before the election was devoted to the President (although he was not standing for election) while only 6 per cent covered the elections and candidates (2005e: 10).

Authorising campaigning

The campaign *(agitatsiya)* entailed the public performance of quiescence. Control and co-optation practices marshalled the line between the politically included and excluded. At times this bordered on the absurd. For example, fellow OSCE observers in the Rasht Valley documented the 'cow case' which involved one IRPT candidate who was questioned three times by the head of Faisobod district over 19 and 20 February 2005 concerning a cow he was alleged to have stolen in 1994 during the civil war. The rais noted that new evidence had been found and the case re-opened. The candidate was threatened with being beaten and an attempt was made to force him to sign a confession. Intimidation tactics also included the removal of campaign leaflets and posters,[23] the withholding of permission for meetings (OSCE 2005d: 2–3) and direct threats to candidates and parties. In such cases local political rivalries often drive clashes between 'the state' and 'the opposition' which originate from the time of the civil war. However, to reduce these actions purely to the pursuit of interests may be misleading. They also construct party politics itself as a 'threat'.

The public performances of elites also performed the opposite of threat: 'authority'. The use of 'administrative resources', government vehicles and official spaces by the PDPT and some favoured self-nominated candidates was a dominant feature of the campaign.[24] For example, a meeting on 10 February in Gharm's Cultural Centre was organised jointly by the DEC and the Khukumat. It was packed with 750 people who had been told to attend by their bosses or the local authorities. After a short speech by the IRPT candidate, the Chairman of the lower house, Khairuloyev, gave a speech of seventy-five minutes with reference to Tajik history and literature and the importance of patriotism. After this speech, five members of the audience 'spontaneously' entered the stage to praise the work of the PDPT and encouraged people to vote for Khairuloyev. After a speech of about fifteen minutes by the CPT candidate (cut short by Khairuloyev), the head of the Khukumat entered the stage to praise the PDPT and once again urged people to vote for the Chairman (OSCE 2005b: 2–3). The meeting contained no debate or questioning of candidates. Similar events were common across the country (OSCE 2005d).

As a consequence of this performance of unity, consensus and legitimate rule, opposition candidates abandoned the more public and prominent spaces of towns and cities to authorised 'governmental' candidates and retreated into their 'hidden' spaces. They held meetings in people's homes, choihonas and mahalla premises. 'Some candidates expressed a preference for this kind of low-key activity', the OSCE report notes, 'which they believe guaranteed them a greater level of security and freedom of speech than official meetings' (2005g: 11). Whilst democratic elections require that state actors stay neutral during an election campaign, this axiom is not accepted by political elites in Tajikistan. In an environment where all public space is political, a different and more long-standing distinction is salient: that between the public/official and the hidden/unofficial. The latter is the acceptable space of 'opposition': a space which extends to the private homes of sympathisers and a few local choihonas and mahalla premises out of the eyes of the governing elite.

Electing authority

The elections themselves were extremely subdued. This performance indicated subordinate resignation and elite consent to the ruling order. As an OSCE short-term observer (STO), I witnessed elections where elites from the President down to the members of Polling Station Committees (PSC) enacted a normative preference for the status quo: an election seemingly scripted as a *spectacle of consent*, yet constituted by thousands of autonomous acts by elites, voters and international observers.

Voting for authority

In an environment where public political space is subsumed under 'the state' – where the ruling elite authorises candidates, information and campaigning – the day of polling itself is reduced to a mere simulation of popular decision. However, this simulation remains an important part of elite legitimacy, in its signification of consent amongst the ruling elite and the resignation of subordinates. In a TV broadcast before polling day, the President remarked that he had given 'appropriate instructions' to the electoral commissioners who must now 'set an excellent example of patriotism'.[25] There were many huge hurdles to overcome in conducting an election in a high-mountainous country in the middle of winter. I put this to the head of DEC in Rasht who nevertheless assured me there would be absolutely no problems with the elections despite the extreme weather conditions (including snow drifts of one to two metres obstructing parts of the main road and making branch roads impassable), and the fact that many PSCs were cut off.[26] Sure enough at 8 am on the morning of 28 February – twelve hours after polling stations officially closed – almost all results were in. However, as the DEC had closed down by this time, we visited the Khukumat where the deputy head (who should not legally have been involved in the elections) gave us a district turnout figure of 92 per cent. In this act, as on election day itself, 'authority' trumped legality.

The performances themselves contained many elements which were familiar from the 2000 elections. In terms of the voting itself these included:

- *Orchestrated voting*, where voters had been instructed to turn up early to do their duty.
- *Group voting*, where groups – often women – enter the ballot box together and make a collective decision.
- *Proxy voting*, where one person votes for others.
- *Family voting*, a specific form of proxy voting where the patriarch votes for the whole family.

I observed all of the above directly in the Rasht valley area and all were recorded by observers across the country (OSCE 2005g). The practice of group voting, in particular, indicates the fine line between resignation and consent. It had a strong gender dimension. Men would often tell women that they should choose this man or that man because he is from the Khukumat. Such practices gave a 'communal' feel to the polling station which reproduced *tinji* principles of unity and patriarchy. We witnesses men distributing ballots to the female members of their family and people identifying together who they should vote for before entering the booth in groups. We frequently heard male voices naming the candidate of the PDPT as the correct choice. While power and influence are at work here it would be an oversimplification to attribute such practice solely to elite manipulation. Resignation was an active process.

Counting authority

Nevertheless elite manipulation did play an important role. In terms of the administration of polling the major trends were:

- *Direct participation by local authorities* in polling station commissions.
- *Exclusion of opposition observers* from the counting and tabulation process.
- *Simulated counts* where the concern is for making the paperwork look correct rather than actually counting the votes. Here overall figures are made equivalent to the number of signatures – this often led to the direct manipulation of results.
- *Polling stations closing early*, completing the count and then bringing the result to the DEC ahead of schedule.

One example of early closing which we witnessed in polling station number 75 in the Faizabad constituency is particularly illustrative. When we arrived at 2.45 pm, the polling station had already closed (at 2 pm, six hours before the scheduled closure of 8 pm). Counting was ongoing with the PDPT 'observer' directing the PSC members who were separating the votes into piles. At this point the number of people on the voting list, the ballots received, ballots used, valid ballots and ballots spoiled had been entered into the protocol. Astonishingly, the numbers of voters, received ballots, used ballots and valid ballots were exactly the same: 276. This supposed that there were no excess, unused or spoiled ballots on a 100 per cent turnout. In our presence, PSC members began counting the ballots for each party and candidate and found it impossible to make the votes add up to the number of 276. The PDPT observer who was still orchestrating the process jovially blamed this on the 'Chinese calculator' he was using. After several recounts the figures were adjusted to reflect the actual number of votes the candidates had received, which had the effect of reducing the number of votes for the PDPT candidate, increasing slightly the number of votes for the IRPT and reducing the 100 per cent turnout. However, a 'fair' calculation of the vote still meant that over 80 per cent of the votes were for the PDPT. After the count had finished, the IRPT observer stood up and, without a trace of irony, thanked the PSC for doing a professional job.

This may or may not be an extreme case of a simulated count. According to the OSCE, 'ballots were not properly controlled or accounted for' (2005e: 2) in most polling stations. However, it illustrates a variety of ways in which 'authority' and subordination were performed. Many local PSCs simulated counts to show their adherence to the discourse of the ruling local and national elites for a well-organised election which supported the status quo. Prime examples were found in the many closed polling stations on the afternoon of the election day; their inactivity symbolised the deafening silence of resignation to authority which the elections performed. Such violations did not determine overall results in themselves. They were affective rather than effective. The PDPT was genuinely popular in the sense that local people had resigned to 'authority' and cast their votes accordingly. Moreover, given the temporally idealised 'anti-politics' of *tinji*, there was perceived to be no credible alternative.

Contrasting international and subordinate interpretations

The argument I have made in this section is that authorised non-democratic elections have a 'positive' as well as negative function in that, for example, they provide a mechanism for elite personnel changes. However, more important still is how they are interpreted popularly, nationally and internationally. They enable the elite to accrue vertical legitimacy with subordinates, horizontal legitimacy amongst itself and even legitimacy from the International Community. Local and global testimonies about the elections indicate these functions.

International discourses: finding a measure of pluralism

Privately, international observers were disdainful of the elections of 2005, expressing a widespread view that they were a product of elite manipulation. For one

OSCE observer in Gharm, it was a 'Brezhnev election', whereas for another it was 'just how things work here'.[27] A senior member of the OSCE/ODIHR EOM, commented, shortly after having had his requests to publish the EOM's preliminary findings in a paid-for advertisement in a Dushanbe newspaper declined, 'I've never seen an election which was to such an extent managed by elites.'[28]

By contrast, in public transcripts international discourses represented an attempt to rescue a 'promise' of democracy from this morass. The final report of the organisation was somewhat less critical than these private discourses, using routine language to state that the elections 'failed to meet many OSCE commitments and other international standards on democratic elections', and listing a number of 'large-scale irregularities' and 'serious shortcomings' (OSCE 2005a: 1). The elections were qualified as, 'the first major test of Tajikistan's progress in consolidating democratic processes in the post-war years' (OSCE 2005c: 3). Via the deployment of this temporal ideal, the promise of democracy was rescued from the peril of authoritarianism in the 'measure of pluralism' (ibid.: 1) provided by six registered political parties (OSCE 2005a: 1–2). In such texts, international discourse serves to reduce the political context to the technical, legislative and physical environment. It was a 'lack of implementation' of electoral law which was the problem (OSCE 2005c: 1). As a consequence, any criticism remained constrained by peacebuilding's hope of long-term progress towards reform.

Subordinate discourses: resigning to authority

The elite demand for popular participation in parliamentary elections would at first sight seem to provide something of a challenge to *tinji* discourse. However, the extraordinarily staged nature of the elections enabled conflict avoidance practices as opposed to genuine electoral competition. The predictability of results has been a recurring feature of elections in Tajikistan's history (Ghani 2001). During the Soviet era elections were an annual event of state management. Indeed the only period in the country's history where elections have been somewhat competitive was the civil war years of the 1990s. In particular, the country's rancorous first presidential elections in 1991 are remembered in such a way as to associate 'elections' with 'civil war'. The widespread acceptance of electoral results is a return to the historical norm that perhaps began with December 1999's presidential elections. It is in this historical and historiographical context that popular perceptions must be understood. They reflect widespread apathy and dismissal of the process as something which had little bearing on their lives. Unlike in the neighbouring country of Kyrgyzstan where fraudulent elections prompted a popular coup or 'revolution', elite manipulation of elections was almost universally accepted by subordinates.

Once again representations of the vote were marked by modernist-communalist notions of duty and obligation. Rahmonova, who administered the 'Vote and Win!' project, for example, considers the goal of the project to be the 'participation' of women, i.e. simply being present and going through the process, often for the first time, and thus reducing the amount of family voting. 'Groups of girls and women came to vote themselves', she remarked, 'which was one of our goals. They participated directly, in person. This was exactly our purpose' (2005: 6). But both men and women were seemingly voting for the status quo. One middle-aged man in Dushanbe noted to me why and how he was voting.

JH: Will you vote?
Man: Yes, of course, it's the duty of the citizen. I'll tell you: I'll vote for democracy, for the democratic party.
JH: For the Democratic Party of Tajikistan (DPT)?
Man: Yes, for the President, the head of democracy (*glava demokratii*).

There is some confusion here. Whilst the president is the Chair of the NDPT, the DPT is an opposition party that was part of the UTO during the war. This conversation is not necessarily typical but the lack of knowledge and interest which it reveals was widespread. In other cases, a preference for political continuity was presented in terms of disdain for the President, more often total disinterest in 'democracy'. I was told in several conversations that those in power are better candidates because they have good connections and thus are more likely to be able to do things for people.[29] For some, family or group connections offer the hope that a local elite can provide some assistance to ease their difficulties. For others, having experienced a relatively effective single party during the Soviet Union, there is perhaps a preference for such a unified system (Olimova and Bowyer 2002: 10).

These subordinate representations of process and uniformity – a performance of powerlessness – differ from the public transcript of elites, yet they resign to *mirostroitelstvo* in that they affirm, in terms of *tinji*, that peace requires 'unity'. One explanation for this resignation is that Tajiks are 'happy slaves' (Herzog 1989) who are resigned to structures of domination because they offer no meaningful alternative. Opposition elites present such people in terms of an 'uneducated' population which is 'easy to manipulate' who are thus open to 'threats' and 'false information' about candidates.[30] However, this does not seem to be an entirely accurate description of either the spectacle of the elections or the range of public attitudes in post-Soviet Tajikistan. For the majority, there is an observable ambivalence where it becomes normal, justifiable and even a moral requirement not to know or care about politics. One young woman in Kulob remarked,

> I don't know anything about the elections […]. There is no gas, no television and no radio. In circumstances like these, how are you supposed to know what the election is about and who the candidates are?[31]

Indeed, disinterest and disdain for politics all become more understandable when one grasps that most Tajiks have little frame of reference for 'democracy' outside their experiences during and since the fall of the Soviet Union.

Via analysis of international and local discourses and practices we can see how the elections simultaneously constitute a 'spectacle of consent' to authority both horizontally and vertically. At the same time they are of little importance to Tajikistan's citizens who play a role as much as they make a 'choice'. Moreover, these roles can distract from the actual functions of elections. This was acutely illustrated in an election fair organised by IFES in Dushanbe. The event took place in a fanfare of traditional Tajik trumpets, following welcome speeches by senior representatives from CCER and IFES. Inside, representatives of international organisations mulled around while young Tajikistanis took bundles of flyers and information leaflets from the various party desks. Surprised by this enthusiasm, I asked a group of young people outside why they had taken so many leaflets. They reported that the leaflets could be used to make *stakanchiki* – paper cones used to sell popcorn. This story echoes the findings here that elections in post-conflict Tajikistan provide a stage for the performance of consent within elite networks, and a spectacle for the consumption of the International Community, but have little discernible effect on the lives of the vast majority.

Dialogue and 'opposition': discourse in an in-between space

Facing difficulties in their attempts to democratise electoral politics, the International Community pursued other, ostensibly complementary avenues. Western-sponsored inter-communal and Secular–Islamic dialogue projects have a long history in Tajikistan dating back to the early stages of the civil war. Today such projects have been continued in order to create new rules and beliefs between government and opposition. However, it will be argued that in contemporary Tajikistan this 'opposition' constitutes an evanescent in-between space found between international intervention and the amorphous political space of the official elite. Without a wide political environment supportive of diversity and dialogue such projects merely flounder or, worse, simulate pluralism in its absence and conceal the Rahmon regime's increasing authoritarianism.

In international peacebuilding's terms dialogue is a fundamental element of peace and a necessary dimension of any peace process from the start. The Dartmouth Conference project under Hal Saunders introduced the idea of the 'multi-level peace process' to Tajikistan in 1993, initially meeting in Moscow for a track two mediation process and eventually trying to link civil society to intra-elite dialogue. In 2000 and 2001, inspired by the Dartmouth process, UNTOP and the OSCE began dialogue projects. UNTOP's Political Discussion Club (PDC), in partnership with the National Association of Tajik Political Scientists, held around ten roundtable meetings each year in towns and cities across the country involving heads of local government, political party representatives, civil society and the media. Each year had a theme which was cognate to UNTOP's peacebuilding aims.[32] The OSCE meanwhile began a high-level dialogue supported by the German and Swiss governments and the Centre for OSCE Research (CORE) in Hamburg discussing the role of Islam in Tajik politics, leading to a document of confidence-building measures and two publications (Seifert and Kraikemayer 2003; Bitter *et al.* 2004). In addition to this major project, regional OSCE centres conducted occasional dialogue forums between political parties, known as 'Political Plov'.[33] Such projects have been lauded by one practitioner as 'substitutes [for] the lack of open political discussion in the parliament'. At the same time the same individual acknowledged that dialogue relies 'on the good will of the government to continue the dialogue that they started through the peace process' (Malekzade 2005: 1). This tension raises questions about the limits of international intervention when faced with local discourses and spaces. If international projects truly allow 'open discussion' then, at a bare minimum, we should see some of the testimonies of hidden transcripts begin to penetrate the public spaces of dialogue in the form of opposition discourses to the regime.

Opposition discourses

At first sight Tajikistan's opposition discourses can appear to be a critique of the ruling elite. However, a closer look at the publications produced by internationally supported dialogue projects illustrates that the picture is more complex. Opposition discourses oscillate between unpublished dissent from *mirostroitelstvo* and published conformity with the statements of the ruling elite.

The 'hidden transcripts' of opposition figures often provide stronger criticism and, in some cases, appear to reflect sincerely held commitments to pluralism (Narziev 2005: 8). Some political party leaders will routinely criticise the statements and policies of the government behind closed doors. For example, one noted, 'now there's no stability (*stabilnost*). It's just that people are afraid of the ruling regime – and indeed they stop at nothing!'[34] In another example, opposition activist Mohinisso Horisova noted how the dependency of the Tajik press on the government made the idea of independent election broadcasts – which, she noted, were praised by the OSCE in their report – a 'myth' (Horisova 2005: 8). While such views may be common outside of the limelight, public statements of this kind are unsurprisingly few and far between.

In consequence, opposition figures, including some of those who might openly protest if public space allowed, take on more conformist elite perspectives. This is reflected in the conclusions of dialogue exercises, which represent a 'compromise' between ruling and opposition elites, and can be so bland as to be almost devoid of meaning. For example, the headline conclusion of the German–Swiss dialogue exercise between 2001 and 2004, involving some very senior elites from government and opposition, noted:

> The harmonisation of the correlation of state and religion is the important prerequisite for the protection of national consolidation, of the political and moral wholeness of the young Tajik state, and also of the stability of the process of its further formation.
>
> (Bitter *et al.* 2004: 41)

It went on to emphasise the separation of religious organisations from the state (as guaranteed by article 8 of Tajikistan's constitution) and opaquely describes

Islam as 'the organic ingredient of Tajik society and national culture [that] has a real influence on social-political processes' (ibid.: 42). It highlighted the importance of overcoming 'disunity between Islam and secularism' through 'unifying factors' (ibid.: 42). This, the authors argue, involves taking a common front against external threats principally emanating from Afghanistan (ibid.: 42–43). It is extraordinary how closely these findings echo official pronouncements.

Exponents of dialogue exercises argue that it is the process rather than the results which are important here (Saunders 1999). However, when this process is one of subordination to 'authority' it is difficult to see what difference dialogue is making. The conclusions of dialogues function as floating signifiers that can be accorded different meanings by different audiences. To international officials, the conclusion outlined above might be interpreted as a call to fundamental democratic reform. To elites, an evolutionary process of elite-led economic development in an ordered society can overcome poverty and the conditions for radicalisation (see also Olimova 2003a and Usmonov 2003a). Many dialogue participants from the opposition as well as civil society representatives express similar viewpoints (Himmatzoda 2003b; Gaffurov 2005: 4; Kamollidinov 2005: 4; Zoirov 2003: 224–225). Rahmatullo Valiev, the deputy chair of the DPT-Iskandarov faction, for example, argues that 'there should be rotation in government (*rotatsiya vo vlasti*)' for the elections to count as 'free' and 'democratic' (2005: 3). By such an account it is the failure of the state to provide places in government for the opposition which is the weakness of democracy. The paucity of alternative viewpoints to the public transcript of the elite indicates the failure of dialogue exercise to generate even a nascent pluralism.

IRPT discourses of peace

IRPT testimonies mirror this oscillation between a modicum of hidden dissent and public displays of conformism. While many party members have become disenchanted with the peace process, the leadership, many of whom have gained financially from the peace agreement and their relationships with international donors, has stayed committed to the 'peace'. IRPT leaders' accounts seek to overcome elite representations of political parties and political Islam with the war and justify their own profits from the peace. The leader of the party until 2006, Nuri, emphasised the compromises that were made for 'people's general interests' and 'unity and mutual understanding'.[35] Underpinning this perspective were elite beliefs of the Tajik subject as backward and politically unaware ('they used to live like slaves in Soviet times and, in fact, did not have any political views')[36] and that Tajik space has its own political conditions ('Tajikistan is not Europe and does not yet have developed democratic traditions').[37] Nuri was frequently complimentary about President Rahmon, never entered into harsh criticism of governmental elites, and had even suggested that an IRPT–PDPT coalition would be possible.[38]

Given such public conformism, the IRPT has apparently lost members to radical groups (Olimova and Bowyer 2002: 29). In an increasingly authoritarian environment, its ability to represent political Islam for a wider audience is extremely limited. However, with both 'conservative' and 'liberal' orientations in the party, IRPT discourses should not be characterised monolithically. These wings are to some extent represented by the vice-chairs of the party under Nuri, Muhammadsharif Himatzoda and Muhiddin Kabiri. Himmatzoda (2003a) presses for an increased role of Islam in politics, questions the separation of church and state as a Western idea inappropriate for Islamic societies, and objects to the interpretation of article 8 (on the secular state) of the constitution in these terms. Kabiri, however, tends towards a more liberal interpretation of the role of Islam in Tajikistan, which is popular with the International Community. His writings and public comments have particularly accentuated the differences between the IRPT and radical groups such as Hizb ut-Tahrir (Kabiri 2003a), and emphasised cooperation with international organisations (Kabiri 2003b). Indeed, as an English speaker who often travels to Europe, Kabiri has been involved in many international programmes and is a frequent interviewee of visiting international journalists.

Despite these differences, both 'liberal' and 'conservative' wings of the IRPT have remained moderate in the face of increased pressure by the government and shrinking space for political action. The party has largely kept to the rules of 'authority' and consequently has weakened vis-à-vis the regime. Some have argued that this constitutes a 'de-Islamicisation' of the IRPT which has created increased support for radical organisation Hizb ut-Tahrir (Karagiannis 2006). In this sense the possibility for new conflict may be one outgrowth of Tajikistan's process of peacebuilding. However, investigating these nascent hidden spaces of radicalism would require substantial ethnographic research beyond the scope of this inquiry. What is clear is that internationally supported dialogue exercises do have certain functions for all parties, yet not those envisioned by design.

In-between spaces and the international community

Both the opposition in general and the IRPT in particular oscillate between a 'hidden' critique of Tajikistan's post-war authoritarianism and public conformity with the state. This highlights the temporal and spatial dynamics of intervention where the international creates moments for 'dialogue' and 'opposition'.

Between UNTOP and a hard place

The programmes of the International Community are predicated under the assumption of a public sphere that somehow exists a priori to government restrictions. If only this space can be opened up, it is implied, then democratic politics can emerge (OSCE 2005g: 10–11). In such a way, it is assumed that if specific institutional and observable impediments are removed, a pluralistic political culture can take root. The International Community seeks to support this process through dialogue programmes and events where 'political parties sit round one table and listen to one another and more or less tolerate the opinions of each other' (Shoyev 2005: 5–6). Many political party representatives praise the space they are given to speak out in such low profile events out of the public eye and the opportunities and insights afforded by overseas visits and seminars. 'You know', Horisova remarked regarding an NDI-organised trip to observe elections in Poland, 'for a Tajik, when travelling overseas the most important and best thing is the freedom. For me it was very interesting to see how people vote. No one forces them, they simply go and vote for the party that they want' (2005: 7).

Such international fora, whether those of the Polish elections or seminars in OSCE or UNTOP buildings, represent an *in-between space* where a debate can take place. They exist contingently and non-territorially, rather than representing the irreducible opening of space for alternative voices. In Tajikistan, in-between spaces create space for 'opposition' (a simulated alternative to opposition) rather than meaningful political opposition which is idealised in peacebuilding discourse. These in-between spaces produce their own institutions and practices that exist apart from government and leave its authority unchallenged. They thus *simulate* democracy among Tajiks rather than actually democratising elite and popular spaces of Tajikistan. This apartness of the 'opposition' is maintained through participants' roles as recipients of international aid and as functionaries of international programmes. Many of the senior representatives of political parties who I interviewed also ran their own NGOs to provide a sideline income. In addition, before the elections they received grants to support their activities around the elections and provide personal incomes for party representatives – almost $US1 million was dispersed in total in 2004–2005 (UNTOP 2004). Supported by international programmes, political parties can seem even more detached from local realities; their primary constituents are international rather than local. Yet it is by playing to the international audience that they are able to continue to exist and function.

This simulated and internationalised 'opposition' is most apparent where international spaces touch elite spaces. I received numerous complaints over 2004 and 2005 from opposition figures about the OSCE and UN's failure to speak out regarding, among other things, the spurious constitutional referendum of 2003, and the violations in the 2005 elections. A CPT official in Gharm district, for example, noted that international training seminars produced 'general comments' (*obshchie frazi*) but 'very little of substance'.[39] When such internationally supported events gain any kind of profile they become politicised and are controlled by the regime. For example, in Khujand in 2004 the PDC was dominated by governmental elites who used it as an opportunity to perform their loyalty to the state. The meeting was held in government buildings while initially opposition representatives were shut outside as the head of UNTOP and senior officials of the OSCE sat inside. A series of governmental speakers praised the regime in front of an audience of hundreds of state servants (*goschin-novniki*) who applauded every speech. When the opposition parties were allowed in they had to stand at the sides. After they were eventually given a few minutes to speak they were met with silence.[40]

The SDPT as an internationalised political party

The SDPT, as the youngest opposition party and a party of the intelligentsia, rather than a regionally based party, is a particularly strong example of a party which exists in an in-between space. The SDPT began after a meeting between various opposition party representatives who were excluded from the 2000 elections, including Ramatillo Zoirov, leader of *Adolat va Taraqqiyot* ('Justice and Progress') and Shokirjon Hakimov, a member of the Congress of Popular Unity of Tajikistan.[41] By this time Zoirov had also become a senior advisor to the President and this facilitated the eventual registration of the party in 2002.[42] However, he was quick to assert his independence from Rahmon. He resigned from his position in response to the 2003 referendum which allowed the President to be elected for two further terms in office and publicly argued that, as the referendum was illegal, Rahmon's presidency legally ended in 2004.[43]

After this falling out with Rahmon, the SDPT found itself in the in-between space of the internationalised 'opposition'. Hakimov, the deputy chair, characterises the party as 'intelligent, secular, democratic opposition' (Hakimov 2005: 2). It has gained supporters in this mould, having a few thousand registered members, professionals and NGO administrators, from Dushanbe, Sughd and Badakhshon. Hakimov notes that because members face 'pressure' from the authorities and may lose their job, the party tries to recruit those who 'in economic terms are relatively independent' (ibid.: 4). Its membership has stayed relatively small and it stays afloat partly because many of its leaders run NGOs which subcontract for international organisations. Zoirov, for example, has often worked as a consultant for the International Community including for the UNTOP dialogue project, the PDC (UNTOP 2001a: 16). Hakimov observes, 'as for us all avenues [to government] are closed, we are able to participate in the projects of International Community' (2005: 6). Here, international programmes serve as an alternative to, not a conduit for, real politics.

On the other hand, this involvement with international actors has entailed the further exclusion of the SDPT from the corridors of power. Dilbar Samadova, SDPT deputy chair in Khujand, cited how the party in Khujand has been increasingly marginalised:

> When we talk and criticise this doesn't mean that we hate our homeland and we wish for something to happen to the state. But nevertheless they [the government] doesn't want to understand this and doesn't want to cooperate, I think then we need to work more with international organisations to find some kind of way. For example, you know the Political [Discussion] Club, the first time I participated I was glad and was thinking that this was of some use. But after I participated, you know, that everything stayed the same. There was no response on the part of the Khukumat. It's as if 'the dog barks but the caravan goes on' (*kak budto sobaka layet, a karavan idiot*).[44] Our opinions don't interest them. They don't consider us. For example, they never invite our party anywhere.
>
> (Samadova 2005: 6)

I quote at length from Samadova in order to illustrate how those who do not perform according to 'authority' and 'stability' face exclusion and sanction. SDPT members have been pressured to resign from the parties by their bosses (being asked 'Why do we need more than one party?'), whilst two candidates in the 2005 elections for the Jabor Rasulov district were jailed after insulting a judge who turned down their candidacy (ibid.: 13).[45]

The SDPT is one case among many which illustrate how discourse functions to create political space, and vice versa. Zubaidulloev, a Tajik political analyst, interprets SDPT's difficulties in terms of 'the crossing of a line' set by the authorities. 'People know that the judge was not correct [in the Jabor rasulov case]', he noted, 'but you do not challenge the judge – he's a state servant (*goschinovnik*)'. Furthermore, the SDPT 'may have been able to win one or two seats' had they not made a couple of errors: entering a coalition with other political parties and offering places on their party list to the Tarraqiyot party of Sulton Quvatov who had 'fallen out of favour' with Rahmon.[46] We might characterise such 'crossing a line' as the discursively constructed boundary between simulated 'opposition' of the in-between spaces of the International Community and the public spaces of contemporary Tajik politics. Whilst the SDPT may look at first sight like a political party, in practice it functions more like a travelling dancing troupe – performing for internationals but unknown at home.

Authority

The example above brings into sharp relief the first property of Tajikistan's emergent, legitimate and post-conflict order: *authority*. The trials of the SDPT illustrate that it is according to elite discourse of 'authority' that lines or rules are made and ritualised consent to authority takes place. This state-idea obscures a corrupted state-system: a 'state against itself' (Migdal 1994) where under the cover of 'the state', statesmen are able to steal state resources (Solnick 1998). However, we should not assume that the nature of this authority and this state derives directly from the elite discourse and practice, public and hidden, described in Chapter 3. What this chapter illustrates is that far from being determined by a single hegemonic discourse, this post-conflict authority and state derives from the international/intertextual relations of peacebuilding. As emergent properties of legitimate order they are processes rather than stable attributes. International and local actors accept and adapt to 'authority' and thus legitimate the new regime, the authoritarian state-idea and, indirectly, the corrupt state system. In short, in the midst of international intervention, authority is simultaneously and dialectically *re-centred* (under the idea of 'the state') and *de-centred* (across a state-system which incorporates a range of personal and local agendas).

Re-centring 'the state'

The reconstruction of the Tajikistani state has relied not only on international assistance to finance institution-building and social expenditure but on the widespread acceptance of regime authority globally as well as locally. Elite discourse has proven remarkably fungible and yet robust in incorporating the vocabulary of international peacebuilding and *tinji* in its public transcripts whilst retaining a neo-Soviet discursive form. 'Pluralism' (*pluralizm*) and 'democracy' (*demokratsiya*) have become frequently cited norms in Tajikistan. In his speech before the PDC, for example, Ubaidulloyev emphasised 'the political pluralism of political parties enabling the formation and expression of the will of the people' with the existence of six parties which 'are not "departments" of the state, nor its "branches" of government, but independent links of the political system' (2003: 63, 65). However, there are qualifications to this reflection of peacebuilding ethics. Even within the public fora of dialogue projects, we can look a little deeper and acquire a 'thicker' sense of the variety of meanings of 'pluralism' in context. Ubaidulloyev, accepts the need for 'criticism' (*kritika*) but this must be 'based on facts'. 'However', he goes on,

> criticism for the sake of criticism, criticism from an irrecoverable, dated point of view, criticism in order to wound people, is not fruitful since it leads [...] not to the resolution of problems, but to a mirage or to the idea 'to grab and to divide' which is not acceptable.
>
> (ibid.: 64–65)

Elites also reflect subordinate discourses of 'anti-politics' and posit the state as the guardian against threats. For governmental elites, the 2005 parliamentary elections and the 2006 presidential elections raised the fear that foreign governments might back opposition movements and led to further restrictions being placed on the work of international organisations. This fear, accentuated by memories of the civil war, makes the threat of 'democratic revolution' a powerful limit to the meaning of 'pluralism' in Tajikistan (Lavrakas 2004: 25). Ubaidulloyev, for example, remarks:

> I at once want to note that it must not weaken the ability of all branches of government (*vlast*) to command and regulate the situation as it takes shape, and it must not set one group or party against another, and in such a way as to divert it from the fundamental work of supplying rapid economic growth and the reduction of poverty.
>
> (2003: 62)

This 'fundamental work' reduces 'democracy' to the provision of basic physical wellbeing, and prioritises 'stability' over openness. Such scripts represent the PDPT as the exceptional party which is 'post-conflict', 'non-ideological' and beyond 'political struggle' (Safarov 2003: 129–130). They represent both the values and interests of the consolidated political elite, and reflect subordinate concerns.

This construction of threat is evidenced in discourses and practical responses to the phenomenon of 'coloured revolution'. Following successful uprisings in

Georgia and Ukraine in 2003 and 2004, respectively, elites feared that the 2005 elections could provide a kickstart for popular rebellion against the government. The discourse of 'coloured revolution' gained momentum among authoritarian elites across Central Asia in 2004 and 2005, and was given a further boost after the ousting of President Akayev in Kyrgyzstan in March 2005 and the Andijon uprising in May 2005, despite the fact that these individual uprisings were quite dissimilar. Tajik elite responses reflected neo-Soviet political thinking that sees public protest as necessarily violent and disorderly and justifies rules against even peaceful expressions of public dissent. These rules were deployed widely in Tajikistan during the 2005 elections and immediate aftermath, with elites forbidding even minor demonstrations (Hakimov 2005: 5), and placing restrictions on the work of international organisations with civil society. 'Everything that's happening with them', Asozoda comments, raising the events in Kyrgyzstan and Uzbekistan, 'we have seen with our own eyes.' He goes on:

> God forbid that they have what we had [referring to the civil war]. We're watching everything very carefully. Indeed we've already seen. But they – Uzbekistan, Kyrgyzstan, Ukraine, Azerbaijan – they haven't seen all this. The first democratic transformations in the USSR began in Tajikistan, already in 1989. But when we announced independence, the USSR was still strong. We now watch all these events carefully, not interfering. And we give our opinion: no problems can be resolved with violence (*putyami krovi*).
>
> (2005: 9)

Elites found an audience both amongst themselves and subordinates as well as across the former Soviet Union for these hyperbolic visions of instability. Even opposition and civil society representations implicitly and at times explicitly adopted these assumptions of the dangers propagated by political competition (Pochoyev 2005: 4). It is in this sense that the state-idea has been inscribed and 'authority' re-centred.

De-centring the state-system

Under the cover of this re-centring of authority, hidden practices continue as state actors re-appropriate 'administrative resources' to local networks. This is visible in the manipulated reform of electoral law to serve established elites, the violation of this law during campaigning and polling for the 2005 elections, and the attacks on opposition political parties such as the SDPT as well as countless other examples in contemporary Tajikistani politics. These practices serve to decentre the state as they make it a creature of its various parts.

The de-centring of the state may be dialectically produced by re-centring. As Scott notes (1990), the public transcripts of the dominant demand that the elite perform the particular role that has been inscribed for them. Thus, as impersonators of 'authority', statesmen can act above the law and decide on exceptions to state law. An emphasis on personal 'authority' necessitates that practices that are *de jure* codified are de facto dependent on the person who implements them. In such a situation, universal and consistent implementation of the law, regardless of the identity of the individual implementer, would be deeply delegitimating for the ruling elite. The 'authority' of 'the state' rests on the elite's ability to monopolise local public spaces *not* make them work effectively for the general good. Indeed, such monopoly would unavoidably be weakened if statesmen dropped their particular agendas and functioned exclusively according to a universalist political discourse such as international peacebuilding. The ethic of 'authority' demands that information and law are used and abused to maintain control, rather than being in themselves regulative of social control. Senior officials are said to hold 'black files' containing such evidence of formal rule violation which can be used on those below them if they violate the rules and modes of consent.[47] The irony is that adherence to 'authority' demands rule-breaking. Where official information becomes a hidden weapon of 'authority' it is unsurprising that its public transcript is reduced to the provision of bland statistics, or is completely withheld. Such a state-idea paralyses the general functioning of the state-system. It is this dialectic, between state-idea and state-system, which explains the particular way in which the state fails to live up to its image and, to international observers, appears as a 'strong/weak state'.

The states-people produced by this re-/de-centred state are by and large a cynical and dissembled bunch. Although there are a few genuine believers in *mirostroitelstvo* within post-Soviet power structures, most are merely dismissive of the contradictions between public representations and hidden practices. Shoyev, a political analyst, notes that the expansion of the PDPT mirrors the communist party in this way:

> That's why it's very similar to the communist system, which was also like that. The communist party led but its members were largely people which themselves didn't believe in communist ideals. They were members of this party so that they could occupy certain posts to move on in their work (*prodvigalis po sluzhbe*), but in their hearts they knew that it wasn't correct, that the policy of the party is probably not correct. That's why I even know such people who, although members of the PDPT voted for other parties at the elections. I asked them why they did that and they answered, that of course the idea of their party isn't correct. Simply they are members for the sake of employment (*dlya sluzhbe*), in order to occupy a good post, but in the election, they say, 'I will be voting honestly and with my heart'.
>
> (2005: 3–4)

Shoyev's account is quoted here at length because it is a sympathetic portrayal of a party elite who despite caught in the mode of 'cynical subjects' are not so much hypocritical as opportunistic. The public/private dichotomy here represents the kind of elite ambivalence analysed by Scott (1990) where the dishonesty of the public discourse produces a desire for hidden honesty, a need to negate the lie.

This picture of Tajikistani states-people calls into question the limits of the Rahmon regime, never mind the state. However, therein may lie the rub. As Foucault has noted, the state may be 'no more than a composite reality and a mythicised abstraction' (1991: 103). This is the character of the strong/weak state of Tajikistan, where the idea of 'the state' has been mobilised variously in popular, elite and international discourses as the means by which war can end and order be re-established. It is this idea, this myth, which is vital and produces moments, such as at election time, of apparently choreographed collective action. Yet this statism is effective only at certain scales (e.g. international conferences) and moments (e.g. elections). Beyond these scales and moments the state once again is reduced to little more than the sum of its localist and personalist agendas. Authority is practised in similar ways across the region. As I have argued elsewhere (2007b: 266), it relies on, 'stories which are told to reproduce the identity, boundaries and values of a (political) community'. The myth of the Tajik state continues to be told and simultaneously continues to be betrayed by the practices of the various parts and representatives of the state-system. The consequence of this is a multiplicitous state which is corrupted systematically by statesmen according to local and personal agendas, avoided where possible by citizens, and at certain moments and scales resigned to by both.

Effects and affects of international peacebuilding

To return to our first question, of the politics of peacebuilding, the above analysis casts new light on precisely what role the International Community has in the emergence of this state of affairs. For good or for ill, international peacebuilding supports a parallel political society – a simulacra of multiparty politics. An argument can be made that this is a vital role that establishes a basis for a pluralist political system at some uncertain point in the future however far removed this parallel society may be from the actual allocation of political power and functioning of government today. Yet international discourse and programmes also contribute directly and indirectly to the reproduction of the state-idea and state-system that are intrinsically at odds with democratic transition. International actors have a perfomative role in a discursive and political environment which produces the re-centring and de-centring of authority described above. At least three consequences of international peacebuilding can be identified.

First, as shown in simulating the first steps of 'democracy' and 'opposition', international programmes *legitimise the regime and delegitimise radical political opposition to the wider International Community*. The continued existence of the IRPT in particular, however weakened, is central here. It allows Tajikistan to be represented as a multiparty system with 'the only legal Islamic party in Central Asia' and maintain the appearance of being 'on the road to democracy'. This representation is vital to continued donor support for Tajikistan across a variety of areas which helps legitimise the government in the eyes of both the wider International Community and the Tajik people. The

International Community and even many 'opposition' parties are sensitive and adaptive to this, but it is the government itself which is perhaps most aware of the danger of appearing too authoritarian. 'It is in our interests', Rahmon announced on TV a week before the 2005 elections, 'to ensure that elections are free and transparent, and that they conform to international standards ... so that this important political event promotes Tajikistan's image in the international arena'.[48] However, against Schatz (2006a: 263–284), I argue that the Tajikistani government's occasional and cosmetic concessions to the international actors have not led it substantially to emulate the role of an agent of democratisation inscribed for it by the International Community. Rather, the emulation has primarily occurred on the part of subcontracting partners and the International Community itself who must always 'invite the *Khukumat*'.

Second, international intervention *enhances the authority of the regime currently impersonating 'the state'*. This consequence particularly relates to the horizontal authority of the regime within itself and amongst marginal elites. International acquiescence is not determined exclusively by the discursive environment but is also produced by specific policy decisions which are taken in that environment. For example, the decision to monitor the 2005 elections illustrates how international actors adapt their discourse in context, and how this then serves to perform governmental authority. Before the 2005 elections, the OSCE Needs Assessment Mission noted that 'some independent journalists advised [the Mission] not to send election observers as the OSCE/ODIHR observation efforts may increase the perception of integrity to a potentially flawed process', while political parties noted 'that staying away might send a negative signal regarding the political process in Tajikistan' (OSCE 2004: 6). The OSCE ultimately concurred with the parties rather than these journalists.

Finally, international peacebuilding *institutionalises the marginalisation of the opposition*. Internationally supported elections and opposition parties are habitually greeted with disdain or apathy by most Tajiks who see them as irrelevant to their daily lives. International peacebuilding is, in this sense, complicit in the popular lack of hope in politics. The degree of domination by the elite, and consolidation of that elite into government, differs region by region. However, as acknowledged by Malekzade (2005: 7), wherever it went the PDC reproduced these power dynamics rather than challenged them. To this extent this analysis accords with Matveeva's conclusion that dialogue programmes in Tajikistan lost whatever agency they had after 2000 and served to 'reflect' the political process (2007: 29–30). Moreover, the 'consensus' they did achieve prior to 2000 may also have been a product of the broader, evolving political context of the reconstitution of legitimate order. Thus, democratisation through Huntington's processes of 'replacement' or 'transplacement' (Schatz 2006a: 279) cannot be said to be either at a first step or near completion in post-conflict Tajikistan. The regime's 'soft' authoritarianism (ibid.: 279) is increasingly hardening.

Given this debatable record, doubts about the peacebuilding paradigm have increased in the International Community in the 2000s. One former diplomat noted that dialogue projects themselves were 'crap'. Moreover, he argued,

Dialogue is cheap. You can send some persons to Germany and show them around. The Tajik mafia guys can do some shopping. Everybody's happy. The government's not too heavily involved. It's not too expensive.

(Epkenhans 2005: 4)

On the other hand, an UNTOP official contends that there is 'a need to maintain a political dialogue and not to give away the achievements of the peace process' (Malekzade 2005: 3). Assistance to political parties and elections, particularly through dialogue projects, continues but to a far lesser extent than in the early part of this decade.

Why then continue with a failing strategy? At a basic level the answer lies, first, in the discursive environment which sustains it and is bereft of a better alternative. Second, the identities and vested interests created by the international peacebuilding business. The simulation of 'opposition' is not without its own functions for the marginalised groups involved.[49] Moreover, it is doubtful whether without international support, opposition parties such as the DPT and SDPT could continue to exist. Similarly, without these 'partners' it is questionable whether organisations such as NDI could continue their work in Tajikistan. In this sense the International Community and its subcontractors develop interdependent interests which give them a stake in maintaining the myth of democratisation despite evidence to the contrary. In such a way the ideas of 'free and fair elections' and 'inter-Tajik dialogue' live on; they are rescued in international peacebuilding which serves to justify the disbursement of substantial donor assistance and the employment of international programme staff and consultants.

Conclusions

In this chapter I have considered how the International Community objectives for democratic reform have not only been thwarted but have served to add symbolic and material resources to this increasing authoritarianism. A regime whose authoritarian rule, at the beginning of the century, was quite accurately described in one influential volume as 'ineffective' (Atkin 2001), being heavily dependent on Russia, and was said to possess 'neither authority nor power' (Cummings 2001b: 6), has emerged as barely more effective, yet significantly less dependent on Russia and considerably more authoritative by 2008.

By classical political science definitions the political system of contemporary Tajikistan should perhaps be understood as a post-Soviet hegemonised system, albeit one that has acquired these characteristics much later than its neighbours, rather than a fully authoritarian regime (Linz *et al.* 1988; Olimova 2004). Yet the differences between a hegemonised and a harder authoritarian system are negligible in their form of legitimate order and discursive practices. 'Authoritarian legitimation must not be seen', March contends with respect to Uzbekistan, 'as primarily a set of explicit arguments against democracy, but rather a consistent rejection of the existence of conceivable ideological alternatives to the substantive orientation of the regime' (2003: 210). Similarly, the discursive environment of contemporary Tajikistan, for want of plausible alternatives, supports myths of authority, stability, statehood and modernisation. Authority in such settings remains based on what Alexander calls 'formless political culture' where political practice is legitimated in terms of the residual markers of the Soviet era rather than being based on a new symbolic order of legitimation (2000: 40–41). Tajikistan's civil war and international peacebuilding have exacerbated this formlessness and its neo-Soviet aspect. The reasons why the discourse adapts and survives in international practice, and how it contributes to the emergence of legitimate order, will be explored further in Chapter 6 in terms of security and sovereignty.

6   Security and sovereignty

The subject of security is the *subject* of security.

(Walker 1997: 78)

[A state] depends not only on political representation but also upon symbolic representation.

(Weber 1995: 124–125)

Security is the second category of interventions pursued under the name of peacebuilding and for the end of peace in Tajikistan. In Chapter 2, I explored the discursive invocation of security in the International Community's peacebuilding, particularly its statebuilding discourse, and specifically with respect to the dangers ascribed to Tajikistan. Security practices in post-accord peacebuilding most often involve 'leftover' tasks under the rubric of Disarmament, Demobilisation and Reintegration (DDR) as well as a new agenda of tasks under the title of Security Sector Reform (SSR). Yet as discursively constructed practices their exercise is contingent on other strategies at play in global politics. SSR initiatives are frequently pursued not only in terms of peacebuilding but merge with the maxims of counter-terrorism and international security cooperation. However, this chapter will tell quite a different story of DDR and SSR in Tajikistan than that envisioned in these international objectives – be they for peacebuilding or counter-terrorism. It explores the re-establishment of 'security' in terms of processes of securitisation and the simulation of sovereignty. As representations and simulacra of sovereignty emerge or collapse so too, by extension, does the legitimate order of which they are central properties. Thus, before addressing the empirical work of this chapter, I will explore what it is about the nature of security that makes its subject, the sovereign, often identified as 'the state', not a fixed entity but a work forever in progress.

In studying the security dimension of peacebuilding we must address questions of political community and identity. Barker reminds us that legitimacy is 'sustained to a greater or lesser degree by the depiction of enemies' (Barker 2001: 138). The Copenhagen School of security studies (Buzan *et al.* 1998) and more radical critical security studies literature both see the presence or absence of security as a product of discursive practice (Der Derian 1995; Krause and Williams 1997; Lipschultz 1995; Walker 1997). Here security is discursively practised, in Austin's terms, as a 'speech act' (Wæver 1995: 50) or, put slightly differently, as 'a performative discourse constitutive of political order' (Der Derian 1995: 78). In this way, 'security' is generated through '*processes* of securitisation and desecuritisation' (Wæver 1995: 57) as 'extreme form[s] of politicisation' where 'the state' demands the right to take extreme measures, ostensibly in the name of protecting its citizens (Buzan *et al.* 1998: 241). The invocation of 'national security' and the specifications of 'threat' and 'enemy' serve a political purpose for the accumulation of authority locally or 'internally' with the regime and to the state.

Adopting this securitisation approach, this chapter explores two areas of security that have been of considerable interest to elite and international actors: the reintegration of warlords (the latter stage of DDR), and the reform of border management (one aspect of post-conflict SSR). The first section looks at the reintegration of commanders alongside the resecuritisation of renegade commanders as 'external' threats and the desecuritisation of the 'internal' public spaces of Tajikistan. The second section turns our attention to an increasingly securitised aspect of the security sector in Tajikistan: the state border. It dwells on the contrasting nature of three performances (securitisations) of sovereignty – national, regional and international – during the handover of the Tajik–Afghan border from regional to national responsibility from 2004–2005. The third section extends this argument to consider attempts to reform border management. It show how the state border, and by extension sovereignty, as a property of legitimate order, seems at once both ever-present, as an idea in contending discourse and representations, and strangely absent, in the rent-seeking actions of 'state' actors and the struggles of daily life. This paradox can only be resolved analytically through the acceptance of this contrariety. Ontologically, sovereignty is neither present nor absent, but in a constant process of construction and deconstruction. More accurately, it is concomitantly simulated and dissimulated.

DDR and securitisation: from 'warlords' to 'statesmen'

The implementation of Tajikistan's peace agreement between 1997 and 2000 began a process of integrating or excluding commanders from political authority through the distribution of positions in the state; at a lower level this took the form of DDR. By August 1999 the official disarmament process was declared complete although only a minority of the weapons thought to be held by opposition forces had been handed in. UNMOT officials admitted that the number of arms held in stores fluctuated from day-to-day as weapons were removed and carried by fighters in public. However, despite the weaknesses of official DDR, security began to be re-established. A qualitative change in the balance of power between military commanders was occurring: warlords continue to exercise influence to the extent that they were 'statesmanlike'.

Some studies of Tajik warlords draw an unambiguous distinction between warlords and the state and have thus failed to grasp the nature of this change (e.g. Lezhnev 2005). The actual practice of DDR – making statesman out of warlords – departs considerably from any neat division between the two. In Tajikistan, as I have discussed elsewhere, disarmament has been usurped by rearmament: the recycling of small arms by the regime under the authority of 'the state' (Heathershaw 2005a: 28–29; Heathershaw *et al.* 2004: 15–16). Demobilisation was superseded by a policy of destroying independent, non-state military commanders (forced demobilisation). Many commanders have been killed, jailed or fled overseas, others have been incorporated within the burgeoning 'state' either formally as state officials or informally and more commonly as 'businessmen'. Furthermore, reintegration has entailed the rent-seeking and capturing of public resources by commanders incorporated into elite networks which constitute the regime and represent the state. These people could easily have become, in international peacebuilding's terms, 'spoilers' (Stedman 1997; Torjesen and MacFarlane 2007) but in fact are part of the consolidation of an authoritarian peace. The means by which independent military commanders (*komandiri*) have lost power and legitimacy in the period since 2000 warrants particular attention in this study.

Forced demobilisation and securitisation, 2000–2001

With the conclusion of the implementation of the peace agreement following its overwhelming victories in the fraudulent presidential and parliamentary elections of 1999–2000, the regime turned its attention to completing the work of establishing total military control over the country. From 2000 independent military commanders were securitised as a 'threat' which required their 'neutralisation'.[1] A number of high-profile assassinations and hostage-takings in 2000 and 2001 were represented nihilistically as 'terrorist acts'.[2] Such commanders were forced to bring their violence within 'the state' or face elimination. As the regime extended its reach, any local support commanders had for operating independently was waning as their ability to command powers of patronage and protection declined.

Mirzo Ziyoev, the MCHS and the commanders

It is difficult to categorise these remaining independent commanders as either criminal leaders or Islamic militants – by their very nature they were implicated in criminal networks and some were heavily involved in the drugs trade. But not all expressed a radical Islamic agenda and many were ardently secular. What is more important is what they did not represent: 'the state'. The regime targeted primarily those connected with the UTO, in particular those who were one-time lieutenants of the Minister of Emergency Situations (*Ministerstvo Cherezvichaynikh Del* [MCHS]), Mirzo Ziyoev, also known as Jaga. Ziyoev's involvement in these operations, as a senior representative of the state and at the request of Rahmon, highlights the growing credibility of 'the state' as a uniting force for commanders who were previously in conflict. At a representational level, the state thus constitutes much more than the elite networks centred around Rahmon and his Danghari allies.

Mullo Abdullo was one prominent commander, based in Darband, who had rejected offers of formal reintegration in 1997. It was, however, not until 2000 that the government felt able to take action against Abdullo, a move prompted by his killing of the head of Gharm regional administration (*raiyon*) in June 2000.[3] Following the assassination, Ziyoev was called on to negotiate a deal which involved the incorporation of seventy of Abdullo's followers into MCHS structures. Abdullo himself was offered the position of chairman of a Dehkon farm. It is not clear exactly how the commander responded. Despite Ziyoev's ongoing negotiations, others in the regime continued to portray Abdullo as refusing reintegration because he wanted to continue drugs trafficking and held 'the same religious convictions as the Taliban'.[4] The truth about Abdullo may never be known yet the representation of him as a 'terrorist' was a fait accompli after the group itself was destroyed by government forces. In September 2000, in an attack on his militia, twenty-eight fighters were killed and a further forty apprehended (ICG 2001a: 17). Abdullo fled to Afghanistan and was reportedly killed in fighting with American forces in February 2002 (Torjesen *et al.* 2005: 111).

Rahmon Sanginov (known as 'Hitler') was another commander in whose clash with the government Ziyoev became the key negotiator. While Sanginov had been portrayed as a criminal, he also expressed religious convictions and political interests (Nourzhanov 2005: 127). Sanginov had been briefly reintegrated into the Ministry of Defence after the war but was later dismissed for refusing to implement orders. He subsequently formed a militant group with Mansur Muaqqalov, another ex-UTO commander, and relocated to the village of Rohaty outside of Dushanbe.[5] In April 2001, a number of Sanginov and Muqqalov's men who were already integrated into the state – as part of the MCHS in Tavildara – were arrested for the assassination of the Deputy Minister of the Interior. Sanginov and Muaqqalov responded with two apparently coordinated hostage-takings, one in Teppai Samarkandi village near Dushanbe on 11 June in which several MVD officers were apprehended, and a second shortly after where fifteen workers from the NGO German Agro-Action were taken captive in the village of Sabzikharv, near Tavildara.[6] The Tavildara kidnappings had been led by the Head of the District MCHS for Tavildara, Hasan Saidmahmadov. The personal intervention of Ziyoev was required to secure their release on 18 June 2001.[7] Following this embarrassing incident, forces of the MVD under ex-warlord Suhrob Kosimov launched an assault against Sanginov's group on 22 June 2001. Over the coming days and weeks he and many of his supporters were killed or captured, as his group was destroyed.[8]

Fixing the shifting boundaries of 'terrorist' and 'state'

Military power played an important role in these cases but it is only one part of the political story here. The examples of Abdullo and Sanginov are indicative of a broader process of securitising and destroying commanders to fix 'the state' as the unchallengeable basis of political power in the country. They illustrate the fine line between state and non-state ('terrorist' or 'warlord') – where representatives of the state can be portrayed as terrorists if they do not publicly subjugate themselves to the authority of the regime. Moreover, these cases show the particular dynamics of DDR and state consolidation where, as Torjesen and MacFarlane (2007) point out, reintegration precedes demobilisation – where armed bands are formally integrated into the state *without* submitting fully to its authority. This post-DDR initiative was to eradicate those elements which refused to accept this authority. Here, the increase in the regime's authority goes hand-in-hand with an increase in state authority as regime enemies are represented as state enemies. The regime represented these crackdowns not in terms of turf wars between trafficking groups, nor as a power struggle within the state, or even a campaign against radical Islam. Rather Abdullo and Sanginov were portrayed as criminals who refused the authority of the state.[9]

These representations were largely well received among elite and subordinate audiences of post-conflict Tajikistan. They constitute specific and successful securitisations of 'the state' over non-state actors. For example, Sanginov's band was portrayed by Isamova (2001), for the national Asia-Plus news outlet, as an 'uncontrollable group' which was one of 'the forces in Tajikistan, which try to destabilise the peacebuilding process in the country, and rattle the sabre'. Such forces, she notes, cannot be negotiated with. Whilst they had been given amnesty in 1997, Isamova remarks, they continued 'committing crimes'. Thus, the idea that government actions are persecutions with political motives is 'out of the question'. The commanders can be regarded as 'criminals, who must appear to court'. This writing of commanders as criminals is a constructive act in the resecuritisation of the state. A further step is to call on others in the International Community to affirm Tajik sovereignty against non-state threats. 'Tajik power structures', Isamova notes, need the cooperation of regional neighbours who have 'signed appropriate agreements on [the] fight against terrorism, and religious extremism' (2001: no pagination).

Via such discourse, the ruling faction is imagined as 'the state', the purveyor of 'stability' and 'authority', concealing its own wartime origins in pro-government militias. Whilst securitisation of threats against 'the state' is typical in international relations, in so-called 'failed states' or conflict zones the state may be usurped as referent object of (national) security by a particular ethnos or locale. Thus, the objectification of the state as guardian constitutes a vital element of the emergence of legitimate order. This process is temporally situated as a post-war stage of development: locating the commanders in the wartime past (Usmonov 2003b). It is a security campaign, Lavrakos notes, 'aiming at preserving all past stages of the transitional period of the country's development' (2004: 22). Understood in these terms, the neutralisation of the commanders cannot simply be interpreted as renewed conflict between government and opposition – not least because errant pro-government commanders have also been neutralised since 2000. The paramilitary categorisations which are now important in Tajikistan are no longer 'pro-government' and 'opposition' commanders, but 'state' and 'terrorist'.

Reintegration and rent-seeking

Some scholars have argued that those Tajik commanders who were successfully reintegrated into state structures can still be considered independent 'warlords' (Lezhnev 2005; Nourzhanov 2005). Yet we must look more closely at the degree of independence they possess. One study includes several 'where are they now?' tables for former field commanders of both government and opposition (Torjesen *et al.* 2005: 77–85). These data indicate limited career options for ex-commanders with fourteen out of a total of twenty-five surveyed being employed by the state while the remaining eleven are either dead or incapacitated, have left Tajikistan, are imprisoned, or have abandoned military activity and their whereabouts is unknown (ibid.). Ex-commanders now hold senior positions in the military formations of the MCHS, Ministry of Interior (MVD) or the Committee for the Guarding of State Borders (KOGG). Tajikistan's most experienced and effective military forces are spread primarily across these organisations rather than in the army. This has dispersed military power between several commanders, rather than providing a single power base which might mobilise against the President. However, this 'reintegration' (being able to represent oneself as statesman) is not just about the reintegration of military and political resources, but also entails the provision of substantial rent-seeking opportunities across the regime.

The personal economic functions of 'the state'

The official reintegration process between 1997 and 2000 was accompanied by something of an unofficial process where the Committee for State Property distributed various public goods between commanders who restyled themselves as 'businessmen' (*biznezmeni*). The new business of the commanders includes both public bodies and private companies – yet the distinction between the two is blurred.[10] Hoji Akhbar Turajonzoda, for example, a former UTO leader and leading member of the Islamic clergy, acquired the cotton processing plant and department store in the town of Vakhdat, and two flats in Dushanbe.[11] Others registered their assets in the name of relatives or associates. Suhrob Kosimov, a powerful governmental warlord and commander of interior ministry troops until April 2007, is thought to control the Sadbarg shopping centre, Bordjuma factory and holiday resorts in the Varzob area.[12] However, to seek rent from these properties a cover or 'roof' (*krisha*) is required. This is where reintegration into the state, and membership of its elite networks, allows such businessmen-officials to expand their commercial interests.

Whilst this 'reintegration' may at first appear as its inversion: a simple process of disintegration or state capture – the reappropriation of the public to the private – the reality may be more complex. As 'private' business may require state protection, equally 'state' enterprises can be indirectly run as profit-making businesses. According to Torjesen and MacFarlane, this is exacerbated by 'a choice on the part of the president not to prevent corrupt practices and/or abuse of government position for personal enrichment' (2007: 322). For lower level commanders and fighters, 'business' can simply mean the extraction of fees for permits, or the issuance of fines for 'traffic violations' on the road. At the lowest level of all, fighters who would previously have shown up in bazaars at any time and used their weapons and status to demand goods without payment may now be policemen who continue to receive contributions from stall-holders to supplement their legal income. Business people who are not ex-commanders with networks of former fighters must hire MVD protection (Torjesen *et al.* 2005: 30).

The mark of state approval is vital for business and businessmen. However, the power of marking is limited with all but those at the very top around Rahmon finding their ability to bestow official approval highly circumscribed. With their formal integration into state structures, commanders, even the most powerful ones such as Ziyoev, have been unable to remain entirely independent and have had to accept strict limits on what they can do militarily, and even economically. By the middle of the decade, Ziyoev's MCHS soldiers, formerly overwhelmingly from Tavildara, were drawn from across the country by the national draft and the employment opportunities he can offer to local youngsters are thus diminished (Torjesen *et al.* 2005: 112, fn 19). While state economic resources may have been 'privatised' (outsourced to commanders), the military and political power of commanders has been 'nationalised' (brought in to the state).

The re-/deintegration of Ghaffor Mirzoyev

The story of Ghaffor Mirzoyev, head of the presidential guard and a key ally of Rahmon, demonstrates this fusion of polity and economy under the symbolic power of 'the state'. Mirzoyev, from Kulob, became head of the presidential guard in 1995 and through his position was able to acquire for himself or his family a meat processing factory, the Olimp bank, Jomi Jamshed casino and over thirty apartments in Dushanbe.[13] He was removed from his position on 26 January 2004 whilst rumours circled Dushanbe that he was planning a coup against Rahmon.[14] When usurped, Mirzoyev, unlike many lesser figures, took a stand against Rahmon. He publicly denounced the President and, for a day, at his instruction, his guardsmen refused to step down and accept their patron's dismissal (Pannier 2004). Behind the scenes he called a meeting of ex-commanders which involved ex-opposition figures as well as former Popular Front warlords.[15] Mirzoyev was soon assuaged with the position of head of the Drugs Control Agency (DCA), an organisation set up under the initiative of Western donors, to the chagrin of the International Community who saw him as especially corrupt.[16] However, this public negation of Rahmon's 'authority' – a rare rupture in the public transcript of the elite – and Mirzoyev's subsequent announcement of his intention to run for the presidency in 2006, meant that this move was only temporary. On 6 August 2004, he was removed as head of the DCA and charged with numerous offences including the 1998 murder of a police official, embezzlement and the illegal possession of arms.[17] Mirzoyev was ultimately tried behind closed doors and sentenced to life imprisonment on 11 August 2006.[18]

This application of state law to a senior state representative was clearly triggered by his public affront to Rahmon's 'authority' (Gulomov 2004; Matveeva 2005: 141). It affirms Scott's assertion that, given their 'political electricity' and potential to incite wider rebellion, challenges to the public transcript of the dominant must not remain unanswered (Scott 1990: 45). Mirzoyev is one of several ex-commanders, including ex-head of the DPT Mahmadruzi Iskandarov, from both of the formerly warring sides whose narrative illustrates the dynamics of reintegration or deintegration. All these cases involved current or former senior representatives of the state in public acts of insubordination. Together they constitute a peculiar mode of reintegration. On the one hand, it entails adherence to the state under the President via an elite transcript of national stabilisation. On the other hand, providing this hierarchy is publicly performed elites are allowed to pursue hidden practices or rent-seeking which directly contradict this discourse.

Desecuritisation and the politics of forgetting

Reintegration is symbolically constituted via the objectification of 'the state' as a bulwark against disorder. However, there is also an apparently more benign partner to this process in the desecuritisation of day-to-day routines of both elites and subordinates.

Operation Order

A presidential decree was issued in 2000 banning the public possession of weapons by all – including those with certificates and state representatives – except the security services within their military units. This included the direction to the state security services, 'to prohibit commanders and servicemen from using private guards', and was part of a move after 2000 to demilitarise the streets of the country, particularly the capital.[19] To this end, Operation Order was launched in Dushanbe by Mayor Ubaidulloyev. Weapons, uniforms and civilian cars with darkened windows were confiscated from officers of the MVD, MCHS, KOGG, Ministry of Defence and even from soldiers of Russian Federation forces.[20] In September 2000, President Rahmon issued a further order to remove illegal checkpoints from roads heading east from the capital to Jirgital and Khorog, areas formerly occupied by opposition commanders.[21]

What is most striking about these initiatives is that they place the state against the state. This is not simply a request for certain actors to target other actors, both of whom happen to be part of the state, but for the very state actors who are violating procedures in the first place to police themselves. In such circumstances where it is quite clear that the principle providers of security are also one of the principle sources of violence, it may be assumed that the image of the *leviathan* state as guardian against anarchy might be undermined. However, this is not reflected in the elite public transcript of both government and opposition. Despite several high profile assassinations in 2000 and 2001, opposition leaders and state representatives continued to speak uniformly of the threat to the state and 'stability' from 'terrorism'. For example, following the killing of a presidential advisor in July 2001, Shodi Shabdolov, head of the CPT, commented,

> those forces that committed the terrorist act evidently are not aware of [the] political and social situation in Tajikistan. It is not Tajikistan of 1990–1991, when one newspaper or slogan could bring disturbances in the country, now it is not that Tajikistan, which could be easily brought to civil confrontation. [The] self-consciousness of Tajiks, having learnt a bitter experience of a civil war, will not allow the recurrence of such events. Therefore I think that these terrorists acts are useless – no force is capable to destabilise [*sic*] the social and political situation in Tajikistan.[22]

IRPT leaders made similar statements.[23] Few people in Tajikistan may know why the advisor was killed; personal dispute, criminal rivalries, or something more directly political are all possibilities. However, this reiteration of a public transcript of *national stabilisation* indicates the discursive reconstruction of 'the state' as a solidarity group and imagined community of elites.

Everyone forgets, everything is forgotten

Not surprisingly after years of civil war and political violence, the Tajikistani people were a receptive audience for these statements and practices of desecuritisation. Often this resignation to an unjust 'peace' is labelled 'war weariness'. To those who don't take discourse seriously, war weariness is a label which serves as a simple shorthand for a subjective shift beyond their analysis. However, 'war weariness', represented differentially by elites and subordinates, is the product of the discursive environment introduced in Chapter 4. These relations foster the desecuritisation of (public) space in terms of 'unity' and provide the basis for a politics of forgetting. Elites and subordinates make frequent proclamations of the stability and calmness of Tajikistan,[24] and often object to the association of the country with conflict.[25] There is an empirical basis for these claims. Since 2002, public violence has decreased substantially, the after-dark curfew has been lifted and more people are seen to walk in the streets and travel from one part of the country to another. Public opinion surveys show both a low perception of threat from guns and an increased sense of security (Torjesen *et al.* 2005: 28, 32). Yet this sense of security does not exist a priori to discourse, but is constituted in the context of a discursive environment which mitigates against public discussion of conflict.

Forgetting has been actively encouraged by elites who are conscious of its political functions. Rahmon, for example, in 1998, asserted that Tajikistan must 'bid farewell to the past' (cited in Safarov 2003: 131). The country has not been through a process of post-conflict justice or truth and reconciliation commissions, there is no authoritative history of the war available in a local language, and anniversaries of the peace agreement are marked by choreographed displays of unity, rather than discussions of the causes and consequences of the conflict. Tajik TV shows film of the horrific events of 1992 to serve as a warning against the return to that time – a time which must be associated with the past, 'opposition' and 'political parties'. This representation, without elaboration or discussion, leaves no space to challenge the official version of events, and no room for reconciliation and/or truth-telling.

Once again then, Tajikistan proves the anti-case of peacebuilding where an elite-led maxim to forget precludes any initiative for post-conflict justice or truth and reconciliation. In a fascinating contrast, in 2005, the country, along with most of the rest of the former Soviet Union, remembered the sixtieth anniversary of 9 May Victory Day with the familiar Soviet pledge, 'no one forgets, nothing is forgotten' ('*nikto ni zabit, nichto ni zabito*'). Posters and banners with this slogan went up in many towns across the country in exhortation to remember the events and the sacrifices made by the citizens of the Soviet Union. By contrast, 27 June 2007, the tenth anniversary of the peace accords, was marked in more muted fashion with little public performance or celebration. The maxim of this anniversary might be 'everyone forgets, everything is forgotten'. A conference of parties and mediators of the agreement took place behind closed doors whilst the President's speech praised his opposite number, the now deceased Said Abdullo Nuri, as it emphasised unity. This was accompanied by solemn and uniform public pledges of 'no return' by elites, muted public ceremonies and an increase in peace memorials such as the one at the front of this book. This mantra to forget is axiomatic of elite–popular relations in Tajikistan. 'War weariness' and its political functions are reproduced by a collective discourse of silence about the war itself. Clearly 'desecuritisation' is symbiotic with resecuritisation and, to a degree, generated by the inside/outside logic of statist security discourses. Such discourses are deeply linked to the identity of the peaceful Tajik citizen – a 'nation of poets' it is often said by leaders and citizens alike. Yet this peaceful 'poet' is overshadowed by multiple representations of in/security and the guardian state.

Managing the Tajik–Afghan border: three discourses

There is no site which receives greater attention in official discourses of security than the state border. This was particularly true in Tajikistan over recent years as the border has been the object of national, regional and international attention. In fact, the southern border with Afghanistan has been objectified in at least three different ways: as the frontier of the nation, of the Central Asian region and even of the International Community. From independence until the middle of the 2000s the border was guarded by Russian troops. Yet over that time it has been breached by thousands of Tajik refugees heading to Afghanistan in 1992, by hundreds of opposition fighters heading back to Tajikistan during the 1990s, and most likely by scores of drug traffickers heading towards Europe every single day. Nowhere is the contrast between state-idea and state-system so intense yet nowhere is the production of 'state' so intrinsic to the corruption of state. For all these reasons the formal handover of this border from Russian to national control is a revealing moment in the emergence of legitimate order in Tajikistan.

In 2004, an agreement was reached with the government of the Russian Federation to transfer responsibility for, and control of, the Tajik–Afghan border to the government of Tajikistan. Following a friendship treaty signed in 1993, Russian troops had continued to patrol almost the entire length of the 1,344-kilometre frontier, with just seventy kilometres guarded by Tajik troops.[26] By 2004, Russia had approximately 11,000 troops in Tajikistan. Whilst border management was supposed to be financed jointly and equally, in 2003 Dushanbe made only 2.4 per cent of its instalment and never made more than 5 per cent in any year (Matveeva 2005: 146). Despite these unpromising circumstances the handover began in late 2004. The agreement allowed for the presence of Russian advisors and the training of Tajik officers in Russia. With the fear of a growth in narcotics trafficking and instability in Afghanistan in mind, Western governments moved fast to increase security assistance to Tajikistan, particularly in the area of border management. Yet the handover was clearly about something other than ensuring efficient border management. Many of the personnel guarding the border before 2005 were Tajik citizens; yet they wore the uniform of the Russian state. After 2005 they wore and flew the Tajik flag. The transfer was driven by security discourses which asserted the sovereignty of the Tajikistani government, its authority over its territory and people, its place in the region, and its status in the International Community.

International security/community

'International security' is the first transcript through which the Tajik–Afghan border is represented. The picture of a sovereign Tajikistan is performed in the International Community under the practices of 'statebuilding' and the 'war on terror'. Before 9/11, Tajikistan had already committed to joining NATO's Partnership for Peace programme and received a visit from the Commander of the US Central Command (CENTCOM) Tommy Franks.[27] In the months following 9/11, some confusion ensued as to whether Tajikistan would provide the US with basing rights as its neighbours had done. The US went through Russia to negotiate but in the end settled on overflight rights, perhaps partly because of the lack of appropriate facilities. Tajikistan instead hosted a small French air force detachment of around twenty men, which provided logistical support to operations in Afghanistan.[28] Although Western military involvement was limited, engagement with Tajikistan increasingly presented it as a 'frontline' in the war on terror. This is shown most strongly in the writings of a Washington-based community of security analysts who are part of, or act as consultants for, US defence establishments. International security discourse on Tajikistan thus inscribes it as a part of an orientalist 'Central Asia' and, thus, in need of Western-style statebuilding.

In Central Asia and the global war on terror

Tajikistan's significance for international security derives from spatial imagination and territorialist reasoning where Central Asia is on the 'frontline' with Afghanistan (MacFarlane 2004; Hill 2002: 17; Wishnick 2004: 1). By such accounts, it is in 'Central Asia', an especially perilous and porous region of the world. The region is described by the head of the Strategic Studies Institute of the US Army War College as a 'key theatre in the war on terror' (Lovelace 2004: iii) which according to Giragosian, 'has acquired a new strategic relevance' (2006: 133). In the US Secretary of Defense's 2002 report to Congress it was identified as part of an 'arc of instability' from the Middle East to North East Asia. Wishnick, familiarly, adds that it is part of the 'Great Game' (ibid.: 29).

   These spatial and historical tropes are constitutive of foreign policy approaches to the region. In particular, they legitimate a focus on security. According to Assistant Secretary for European and Eurasian Affairs Elizabeth Jones, 'since 9/11 US strategic interests in the region have focused on anti-terrorism, especially the elimination of terrorist and other destabilising groups.'[29] This has led to a massive increase in US strategic involvement following 9/11 in the establishment of the Ganci and Kharshi-Khanabad military bases, and over-flight rights across Tajikistan. Hill notes,

> The primary American interest is in security, in preventing the 'Afghanici-sation' of Central Asia and the spawning of more terrorist groups with trans-national reach that can threaten the stability of the interlocking regions and strike the United States.
>
> (ibid.: 18)

Such thinking has apparently contributed to an internal reorganisation of the US state department. By late 2005, Jones' department of European and Eurasian affairs had lost responsibility for the region which had been incorporated into a South and Central Asian section. In itself this bureaucratic change reflects US thinking about Central Asia as a region apart from other Former Soviet Slavic states. The move is a particularly fascinating one, foreshadowed in the 1999 shift within the Department of Defense to place Central Asia under CENTCOM. It is easier to understand why Washington-based analysts may believe Russia's role in the region is increasingly peripheral (Plater-Zyberk 2004) if they imagine Central Asian states as culturally and politically akin to Pakistan or Afghanistan. As we shall see below, however, such spatial imaginaries are vehemently opposed within the region by elites who often imagine themselves as more 'European' than 'Asian'.

In need of statebuilding and reform

Understanding Tajikistan as a part of a 'Central Asia' or 'South and Central Asia' seemingly leads to hyperbolic analyses of Tajikistan's political dynamics and, in turn, inscribes as a state which requires building. For one US diplomat in Dushanbe, there are 'shallow roots to stability' in Tajikistan and the country remains a 'tinderbox'. As such it is at risk of 'violent Islamisation' or the danger that 'narco-traffickers could take the government out'.[30] Under discourses of the 'failed state'/statebuilding, societal forces are set up as both 'strong' and in opposition to a government which is 'weak'. For Hill, Central Asian states are challenged by 'extreme domestic fragility' (2002: 19). The complexity of relations between state and society, where the former's inextricability from the latter is the basis for its hegemonic position, are rarely explored in these accounts. That organised criminals might be constitutive or supportive of many Central Asian regimes themselves is difficult to explore (ICG 2003; Marat 2006), and is rarely discussed by security analysts.

Where it is discussed it is in the form of a problem which can be solved via statebuilding. Mihalka, a US Army War College professor, laments 'state weakness' and the lack of political will in Central Asia to introduce the necessary reforms 'to counter insurgency and terrorism' (2006: 150). For Giragosian, the central problem is 'the vulnerability of illegitimate governance' (2006: 150). Such thin analyses feed into official announcements and policy statements. Richard Boucher, the Assistant Secretary of State for the new bureau of South and Central Asian Affairs, remarked in his 2006 testimony to Congress:

> Central Asia faces numerous threats to its stability, including Islamic extremism, a population that remains poor and has little economic opportunity, the post-Soviet legacy of authoritarianism, public perceptions of injustice, and high levels of corruption.
>
> (Cited in Mihalka 2006: 133)

Underwriting such testimony is the assumption that 'they' ought to be more like 'us' – that is more like who we imagine ourselves to be. Therefore, whilst the initiatives of regional governments are assumed to be ineffective, US officials and analysts furthermore imagine their own government to provide the solutions. Giragosian notes, 'what is essential for Central Asia is a continued and even greater US commitment', and specifically argues against regional coalitions such as the SCO (2006: 152).

International assistance to the security sector in Tajikistan continued to expand to pursue the goals of statebuilding following the announcement of the Russian withdrawal. One US diplomat acknowledged that the International Community was 'caught off guard' by the Russian border guards withdrawal and that it was 'not in our interests for them not to be there'.[31] Thus, these events accelerated a shift towards a statebuilding following some disappointment with democratisation initiatives (Epkenhans 2005: 3). Matveeva contends that it was Rahmon's visit to Washington in January 2002, shortly after the launching of the 'war on terror', which 'provided impetus for development of a relationship in the security field' (2005: 149). The shift was also discursively constituted in the post-9/11 global trends towards statebuilding (see Chapter 3), but it did not signal conformity with *mirostroitelstvo* discourse. International initiatives mixed, to varying degrees, a liberal-reformist plank with capacity-building. Two very large EU regional programmes, initiated by Austria, including Border Management in Central Asia (BOMCA), had been launched and funded prior to the announcement of the Russian withdrawal in March 2004.[32] Subsequent to this, the International Community found US$4 million of new funding specifically for projects at the Tajik–Afghan border.[33] European donors in particular publicly reiterated 'multilateral cooperation' and 'integrated border management' with the International Community in order to introduce 'legal and institutional reforms'.[34] Such programmes aimed not just at building the government's capacity but socialising it into better practices.

Tajikistan's national security/community

These interventions, despite their self-referential precepts, elicit enthusiastic responses from a Tajikistani government eager to be accepted into the International Community. Elites seized on the increased anti-terror discourse as an invitation to assert sovereignty and crack down on transnational dissident groups whilst representing themselves as a part of the International Community in 'the war on terror'. The government banned *Hizb-ut-Tahrir* in 2001 (before 9/11) and was quick to associate them with the 'war on terror' following the attacks. As early as October 2001, Minister of Security, Khayriddin Abdurahimov, noted that *Hizb-ut-Tahrir* was 'undoubtedly connected with those terrorist centers being prosecuted by world community'.[35] While up to 2001, Tajikistan had arrested just 120 members, far fewer than its neighbours in Uzbekistan and Kyrgyzstan, the suppression of the organisation intensified following the launch of the 'war on terror'.[36]

Such actions are frequently cited to international researchers and policymakers in terms of working together against Islamic extremism and drugs. For example, Asozoda reminded me of these 'common' problems:

> Indeed, we mustn't forget that in Tajikistan 90 per cent of the population is Muslim, and this is the only state where there is an Islamic Party. And their only aim is the creation of an Islamic state. But we say that religion is separated from the state. We accepted a unified constitution, and whoever comes to power must observe this. But we need help: from the USA, China, Russia – our strategic partners. If they support us, this will be good for them and for us. We were the first to speak at the UN and say that we need to create an anti-terrorist ring around the Talibs. Emomoli Rahmon called to everyone from the platform of the UN. But they didn't listen to us and as a result they got September 11th. Now we say that in Afghanistan 90 per cent of agriculture is narcotics. We say, 'let's create a belt [*poyaz*] around Afghanistan', so that they don't produce opium or drugs but something else. If they listen to us this time then we will do everything possible to keep out the drugs.
>
> (2005: 10)

Asozoda is quoted at length as his statement reveals how international security discourses are redeployed by national actors to serve instrumental ends in accordance with authoritarian visions of state security. Here, the definition of threat widens potentially to include legal political parties within the country, and the identification of proportionate response expands to a suggested exclusion zone around the country. This essentialisation of political Islam is a long-standing feature of elite–secularist discourse in Tajikistan (Wennberg 2001: 6).

In this manner, with its particular contrasts to international discourse, Tajikistan articulates its sovereign position in the International Community under the 'war on terror'. They explicitly represented the takeover of the southern border from 2004 as a triumph of national sovereignty. Official discourse exhibits four representational strategies which serve to inscribe 'us' and 'them' on the border:

1   The imperative of 'national security' for a unitary Tajik state-nation.
2   The specific location of authority over the border with President Rahmon.
3   A broad definition of a transnational 'terrorist' threat.
4   The specific location of the threat of drugs and terrorism in Afghanistan.

The first two of these relate to the representation of 'inside' or 'Us', while the second two concern the 'outside' or 'Them'.

'Us'

The drive to national security and stabilisation led to a strategically dubious shift to exclusively national border protection. The move was predicated in discursive trends leading up to the handover. Rahmon, for example, stated that 'the border is one of the most important symbols of a state, and its defence is [the] honourable debt of every citizen of the state'.[37] The national press provided extensive coverage of the various stages of the handover, which largely supported this version of events. Prior to 2004, it was frequently emphasised that '2,912 of 4,183 kilometres of the Tajik border is being defended by Tajik border guards' and that '80 per cent of Russian border guards are Tajik citizens'.[38] Following the 2004 decision, it was often repeated that 'from the beginning of 2006 the Tajik flag will be waving along the whole Tajik border of 4183 km', thus showing that the Tajik guards are 'ready to defend their border themselves'.[39] A report by the state newspaper, *Jumhuriyat*, of 28 May 2005, official Border Guards Day, entitled 'We are able to defend our border' [*Mo sorhadoti hudro hifz karda metavonem*], nicely summarises the official discourse on the border handover.

> The Tajik state and government is always concerned about strengthening the border. The passing of the law, 'Border Military Forces of Tajikistan' increases the responsibility of Tajik border guards. Until taking over the defence of the border with Afghanistan, the border forces of Tajikistan were second behind Russian border guards. Now they have taken the first place,

i.e. they took the defence of the state border upon them. It is right that the challenges of state border defence are plenty, but it is our motherland. Every independent state should defend its borders itself.[40]

Such understandings unite the Tajik people under the state. The Chairman of KOGG, Colonel-General Saidamir Zuhurov, noted that according to the Law on the State Border of the Republic, 'all citizens of Tajikistan are obliged to participate in border security' (UNDP 2005c).

Second, discourse highlights the personal authority of the President over the national border. President Rahmon performs his own authority over Tajikistan by making frequent speeches on and sometimes at the border.[41] In a 2000 speech, he argued that 'half-measures' and 'not enough orderliness' on the Central Asian continent are 'inadmissible'.[42] The concept of 'authority' which underlies such statements is one which suggests maximum credit to, and minimum debit from, the President's personal power. This is affirmed by Rahmon's inferiors. Zuhurov tied the integrity of the national border to the personal authority of the President. He noted at an international conference on the border in February 2005 that 'the President personally checks on the status of achievements' (UNDP 2005c). The President thus has the authority to identify those responsible for violations of the border, rather than take personal responsibility for failures of management. For example, the President has threatened to relocate forcibly border residents who are 'involved in drugs trafficking'.[43] Moreover, he will occasionally purge the Tajik border forces (KOGG) not just to distribute patronage but to illustrate his authority as head of state.[44] Such practices may not constitute an effective counter-narcotics strategy but they do serve purposes for Rahmon who is able to practice intra-elite rotations in terms of national stabilisation.

'Them'

The third representational strategy of elite discourse is the creation of a transnational terrorist other, which encompasses both criminal and political groups. The construction of the transnationalism of 'them' is the mirror image of 'us' who are peacefully united within Tajik territory. Thus, the threat is located as both foreign and refusing to abide by state boundaries which, it is implied, are natural. Commenting on joint CIS military exercises in April 2000, the President noted that, 'we must remember that international terrorism, extremism and national separatism do not recognise borders and act at their [*sic*] will. Therefore [the] armed forces must be ready to resist any threat to our security, no matter where it originates from.'[45] This invocation of 'terrorism, separatism and extremism' discursively links oppositional, criminal and militant activity. It is commonly deployed across post-Soviet Central Asia.[46] The definition is invoked particularly against *Hizb ut-Tahrir*, a militant group with no confirmed record of violence.[47] Such representational strategies once again create space between 'the state' and criminal and militant groups which in (hidden) practice are very closely linked to state officials (Marat 2006: 103–108).

Fourth, in elite discourse the threat especially emanates from Afghanistan. Tajikistan has typically been portrayed by Kyrgyzstan and Uzbekistan as the haven for the IMU;[48] in turn, Tajikistan has sought to locate that threat in Afghanistan.[49] Afghanistan was identified by Rahmon as 'the source of international terrorism' and an 'outpost of extremism'[50] both before and after 9/11.[51] Moreover, Afghanistan is inscribed as a backward and primitive place – a place which post-conflict Tajikistan must leave in the past.[52] Drugs trafficking and extremism are thus the 'Afghan problem', a problem *for* Tajikistan, the region and the International Community, rather than a problem with Tajikistan. For example, a Tajik National Security Council statement noted that 'many foreign mass media portray Tajikistan as a drug-trafficking country. However, they fail to mention that the drugs come from Afghanistan that Tajikistan has common borders with.' These drugs, the statement noted, are trafficked across the CIS and Europe. Thus, 'the International Community should not view Afghan drugs as solely a problem for Tajikistan.'[53]

Central Asia's regional community/security

A third discourse of Tajik security/sovereignty is that 'Tajikistan' is a part of 'Central Asia'. However, this Central Asia, a post-Soviet regional space which includes a leading role for Russia and an increasing role for China, is quite different from that rendered in the US State Department's 'South and Central Asia'.

A regional community of states and statesmen

Tajikistan's elite networks today are primarily understood in terms of their regional (provincial) ties. However, elite networks in the post-Soviet space extend beyond national boundaries. Soviet legacies provide a unique historical basis for Central Asia's new regionalism – networked elites across the region who share similar experiences, spaces and discourse. As an imagined rather than a territorially based community, it can be argued that Central Asia is a regional space governed by illiberal norms of 'authority' and 'stability'. The continuance of a cadre of Soviet-era elites and bureaucrats in the region, and the almost complete marginalisation of liberal reformers in all of the five new states, provides the human foundation for this.

As a space, the boundaries of the region are fluid not fixed. Adler and Barnett remark that 'regions themselves are socially constructed and susceptible to redefinition' (1996: 77). Locating 'Central Asia' provides a particular challenge. Regional leaders have often been ambivalent about Russia's role in the region, at times calling on the Kremlin for leadership, at other times resisting arrangements which create an exclusive relationship with Moscow (Allison 2004). Furthermore, Central Asia's imagined community is accompanied by apparently contradictory national independence discourses in the new republics (Prazaukas 1997; Rumer 2002; Vasiliev 2001). However, one must ask whether this contrariety must necessarily be resolved. The existence of multiple and contending identities should not be a surprise in a region where political elites are practised at playing both national and regional cards (Brill-Olcott 1996: 40–41). Such ambivalences are very much a part of neo-Soviet elite discourse and post-Soviet politics. Elsewhere, I have argued that the prevalence of multiple signifiers of regional space – from 'Middle Asia and Kazakhstan' (*Srednaya Aziya i Kazakhstan*, the term commonly used during the Soviet Union) to 'Eurasia' (*Evroaziya*, which has a particularly complex genealogy [Smith 1999b]), from 'the New Great Game' to 'the Heartland' – indicates a space-making as well as space-contesting function for 'Central Asia' (Heathershaw 2007a). Whilst territory may provide a bone of contention between elites, and border clashes remain frequent, in their similar spatial, ethical and temporal imaginaries state officials often find common ground for security cooperation.

These imaginaries are reproduced discursively, and in the formal institutions of regional international relations. Discernible post-Soviet elite discourses of *mirostroitelstvo, mirotvorchestvo* (Lynch 1999; Smith-Serrano 2003) and *konfliktologiya* (Reeves 2005) establish the norms and beliefs which divide 'Us' from 'Them' as a nation and as a region. Governments across this space seek to delegitimate clandestine or exiled opposition groups by portraying them as an external and nihilistic challenge to the legitimate authority of the state, and a threat to the prospects for economic development and social stability. In this sense it is a shared image of the importance of state territorial independence that paradoxically constitutes common regional space. In such a way, since 2000, Tajikistan has increasingly been cast less as regional bogeyman and more as a sovereign member of 'Central Asia'. Numerous CIS, SCO, Collective Security Treaty Organisation (CSTO) and Central Asian Cooperation Organisation (CACO) summit meetings often do little more than express one another's membership of an identity group of 'Central Asia'. Joint military exercises, frequently performed between Central Asian states and Russia, are usually conducted under the auspices of the CIS or CSTO.[54] They serve to demonstrate a continuing sense of 'Us' and a degree of cooperation against domestic opposition and transnational foes. The USSR's disintegration, we might argue, served to *de-territorialise* and *de-spatialise* one regional identity but *re-spatialise* imagined communities of 'Tajikistan' and 'Central Asia', at the heart of both of which is the strong state.

Regionalism in the border handover

Given this regionalist discourse, it would have been implausible for Tajikistan to present national control of the southern border without articulating a continuing and strong role for Russia whose troops have remained in the country since independence. This highlights a certain and irresolvable ambiguity in the representations of sovereignty during the handover. For example, the state newspaper *Jumhurriyat* in December 2004, tells the audience that 'we longed for many years [for the Russian border control] to come to an end', whilst simultaneously being told that Russian guards 'made a great contribution to protecting the region',[55] and in a subsequent edition that 'the beginning of activity of the Russian military base on the territory of Tajikistan provides for regional security'.[56] Moreover, testimonies of national independence in border management are habitually supplemented with the caveat that Russians will remain as advisors and trainers of Tajik guards.[57]

The shared political ethics and spatial imaginaries of Rahmon and Putin underpinned the 2004 Tajik–Russian agreement. Rahmon was quick to applaud Putin and appear alongside him in public even when state-to-state relations have been fraught with difficulties, particularly with respect to Tajik labour migrants.[58] While the beginning of the handover was announced in March, sparking local and international concern, it became clear that the exact terms were linked to other negotiations between the two presidents related to the establishment of a permanent Russian base to house the 5,000 troops of the 201st Motorised Rifle Division, the status of the Nurek space facility, Russian investment into hydropower and relief of Tajikistan's bilateral debt. After a meeting between Rahmon and Putin in Sochi on 4 July, an agreement was signed on 17 October 2004 (Arman 2004a). Moreover, following the establishment of US bases in Kyrgyzstan and Uzbekistan following 9/11, the news of the permanent Russian base in Tajikistan was greeted as an example of the renewal of Russian influence by its national press. Initially the negotiations over the base had been held up by Tajikistan's demand that the President be able to take over command of Russian troops 'under extraordinary circumstances'.[59] However, as an alternative, the agreement eventually reached included an informal security guarantee from Putin to Rahmon (Matveeva 2006: 142). Here so-called 'hard' power issues of military cooperation are interdependent with 'soft' power issues of trust, prestige and performance.

The handover of the guarding of the Tajik–Afghan border to national security forces is emblematic of the dynamics of security and sovereignty in contemporary Tajikistan. The findings above, along with those from the preceding chapter, indicate that the Tajikistani government has been remarkably successful in having its representation of 'authority' affirmed by subordinates, elites and, to a lesser extent, internationals. However, authoritarian elites generally face much more difficulty controlling representations of state *sovereignty* – the status of government to represent the people. Often the primary site for claims about sovereignty is the border. Some observers in the 1990s feared that Tajikistan might break up, perhaps losing control of the northern province of Leninabad (now Sughd) or the Pamiri autonomous region of GBAO. In fact, nascent irredentist claims failed despite only limited decentralisation. The idea of a single Tajik political community has survived and apparently strengthened since 2000 both within Tajikistan and overseas. Yet the nature of this enhanced sovereignty and its role in the emergence of legitimate order, needs unpacking.

Sovereignty

The empirical studies undertaken above should make clear the importance of sovereignty in the practice of security and statebuilding, however conceived.

Sovereignty is the supreme form of authority; in modern times it has been increasingly attributed to the state. Much like security, sovereignty entails, 'a practice of legitimation that serves to render other ways of being human, other ways of being both one and many, of relating self to other, of articulating space/ time – almost unimaginable' (Walker 1997: 321–322). This implies that, unlike authority, sovereignty cannot be divided or dispersed. It is either absent or present. If security discourses lose all plausibility among elite, subordinate or international audiences this can delegitimise the subject itself; similarly, it is via these discourses that sovereignty and authority can be reconstructed. For many established or 'strong' states these discourses can become 'sedimented' or relatively static so that largely material considerations of the balance of power seem to predominate (Buzan 1991; Wæver 1995). Thus the (re)construction of sovereignty in 'strong' states is often ignored despite being central to how foreign policy is made in these states (e.g. Campbell 1992). However, in the case of a 'weak' state such as Tajikistan, where acquisition of international legal sovereignty is a recent development and one that remained questionable for some time, clear distinctions between national and international representations of the sovereign state, and between them and hidden practices are readily apparent.

The contrasting representations of the Tajik–Afghan border outlined above indicate that this myriad of actors together negotiate exceptions. In doing so, they draw the line of Westphalian sovereignty (the state-idea in its international political aspect) and intervention (those political practices undertaken by actors representing a foreign state or international organisation). There are clear overlaps in the three performances of security/community outlined above which provide the virtual bricks in the construction of sovereignty. Yet where, (i) the gap between any one public representation and the 'hidden' experience is apparent, and (ii), the various international and national representations and practices of this sovereignty are inconsistent, we can think about sovereignty not just in terms of discursive representation but also as a product of simulation. In Tajikistan, sovereignty is not singularly represented but is ultimately *simulated*, via this playing to multiple audiences, and *dissimulated*, via the hidden transcripts and practices of these audiences which deny that such authority exists.

State versus 'the state' in border management

The Tajik–Afghan border is a site which is concomitantly manipulated by state actors (both elite, senior officers and subordinate foot soldiers) as it is represented as the frontier of national, regional and International Community/security. Yet the clandestine nature of trafficking ensures that research can rarely provide more than glimpses of its practices at the border.

Drugs trafficking and the violation of borders

Tajikistan is a key transit country for Afghan opium on its way to be processed as heroin and trafficked to the markets of Europe. Production of opiates has risen since the defeat of the Taleban in Afghanistan in 2001, with the subsequent weakening of central control, despite international intervention. Both Tajik and Afghan state representatives are deeply bound up in the trade. Much of the violence in the latter stages of the civil war and the post-war period can be linked to drugs trafficking.[60] Organised crime groupings are very powerful in Tajikistan, include high-level government officials and therefore retain significant political influence (Marat 2006: 107–108; Akiner 2001: 72–76). High-level officials like Ghaffur Mirzoyev carry immunity from prosecution until the point at which they fall out with the regime and thus there are few public examples of their complicity. One exception concerns the Tajik Ambassador to Kazakhstan, twice caught for trafficking (ICG 2001b: 15–16). Occasionally 'turf wars' between official actors simmer to the surface with recriminations and accusations of trafficking between elites.[61] There are even occasional prosecutions of businessmen-statesmen who have lost their cover after falling out with colleagues in the regime.

Whilst border management in Tajikistan is subject to the power struggles of the black economy, international programmes are premised upon the possibility of demarcating a non-corrupt or, at least, considerably less corrupt space. They assume that newly trained units of guards, or new institutions such as the Drug Control Agency (DCA) under Zuhurov, can operate relatively honestly and effectively within an extremely dishonest system. However, the sheer extent and nature of the trade suggests that this is overly optimistic. The direct profits of trafficking are so great as to make such institutionalised corruption a comfortable business cost. UNODC estimated in 2003 that drugs smuggling was worth US$2.27 billion to Central Asian gangs, the majority of which are Tajik. By these estimates, it is possible that the value of drugs trafficking to Tajik gangs exceeds the country's official GDP (UNODC 2003: 167). Unsurprisingly, interdiction rates are low. Traffickers report that it is relatively easy to pass checkpoints with bribes (Torjesen *et al.* 2005: 43). One study reports, 'it is striking how little violence is associated with the multibillion dollar drugs business in Tajikistan' (ibid.: 29). UNODC estimates that 23 per cent of Afghan heroin and morphine transit through Tajikistan, yet only 16 per cent of all seizures were made there (2003: 161, 167). In short, despite increasing international assistance, traffickers and state officials continue to transport drugs through Tajikistan on a grand scale.

The international/intertextual relations of border management

The Tajik regime pays lip-service to donor objectives but emphasises retrenchment over reform. This is reflected in the maxims that, according to a DCA official, 'Tajikistan is the main barrier to prevent [Afghan] drugs reaching markets' and 'that only joint efforts can be effective'.[62] Through the acceptance of public transcripts Tajikistan becomes an increasingly important member of the International Community for the first time in its history as an independent state. The Tajik authorities play up to this role with performances of sovereignty which feign international standards. KOGG makes monthly and annual reports on drug seizures and comments on the nature of the trafficking threat, which is widely reported in the national press.[63] Such reports create a public transcript of state border protection which denies collusion with drugs traffickers.

Yet there is dissonance between international and national approaches. In the press conference following a major international meeting in February 2005, General Zuhurov, in accordance with a public transcript of *mirostroitelstvo*, summarised the two days of talks:

> I have been talking about the projects and wishes of the country donors that are interested to equip the Tajik–Afghan border. Everybody is interested about how this border will be equipped and secured and this depends not only on the security of Tajikistan but other neighbouring countries.[64]

But in the same press conference Zuhurov departed from the international consensus in defending Tajikistan's right to fixed border outposts (*zastava*), in the face of donor calls for mobile units which would be better equipped to interdict highly mobile smuggling gangs. 'I know better the status on the border than regional reps of UNODC', he noted, adding that effective border posts in Tajikistan 'must be physical'.[65] This dispute gets to the heart of the different conceptions of Tajikistan as a barrier and the tensions between them which are left unresolved in the public transcript. While Zuhurov is widely respected in the International Community, it is also acknowledged that *zastava* are integral for institutionalised corruption as fixed outposts provide points for the collection of bribes from legal as well as illegal travellers and traders.[66]

At the time of my fieldwork it was premature and impractical to assess the impact of international assistance on border management yet for a number of reasons its prospects looked weak. Not least amongst these are the functions of such assistance for retrenchment – the very opposite of its stated reformist objectives. As argued by Matveeva, with the financing, infrastructure and training for border security and anti-drugs operations being 'outsourced to external powers', the ruling elite is able 'to concentrate on the challenges it considers important' (2005: 134). These include suppressing internal dissent. Moreover, simulating sovereignty through 'border management' and 'reintegration' allows this sovereignty to be dissimulated by state actors' complicity in trafficking and the looting of official resources. For example, the process of border guarding in Tajikistan provides a means of extraction for guards and officials:

> Presently, corrupt networks of border guards/policemen/customs officials are firmly entrenched and are interested in the preservation of a *status quo* of closed borders. They also have a lobbying capacity in the capital to argue the case for 'better security' which in reality means more barriers to the movement of goods and people, and more extraction opportunities.
>
> (Matveeva 2005: 138)

However, short of demonising Tajikistan to make a pathway for 'humanitarian war'-type intervention, there is little alternative for the International Community but to work within the local system. 'People who are corrupt are experienced in dealing with border management', one international representative working on BOMCA privately noted. 'If we remove them there will be none left.'[67] Publicly, the solution (reformed border management) is found in the problem (corrupt border management). 'Hidden transcripts' reverse this logic: the problem is found in the solution. Thus, it seems a matter of audience as to whether 'the state' should be seen as part of the problem or part of the solution for 'porous' borders in Tajikistan. Moreover, this conclusion indicates the limited power and political imagination of the International Community if international actors cannot find alternative allies in combating trafficking in Tajikistan to the very people who are benefiting from the illegal trade. It furthermore illustrates the inauthentic character of such SSR programmes; they are often practised not because of real belief that they will work but because of the absence of widely accepted alternatives and the presence of an institutional interest in seeing it through for its own sake.

Simulating sovereignty

To understand this puzzle one must reflect theoretically on this interplay of discourse and practice in international security assistance. In addition to these counterproductive effects, there is a symbolic function of SSR which is in accordance with the interests of international powers. The international relations of border management serve to inscribe internationally the government as responsible authority. In doing so, these relations simulate Tajik sovereignty. This sovereignty is contingent upon wider regional and international acceptance of the government's performance in terms of anti-terrorism and drugs control, however ineffective this is in everyday practice. To this extent, rather than sovereignty being cooperatively shared (singly represented) or competed for (contradictorily represented), contrasting representations are, to a limited extent, complementary as they allow different representations and, by extension, different communities to co-exist. Sovereignty carries different meanings nationally (where it supposes self-sufficiency) compared with regionally and internationally (where, in different ways, it requires intervention).

Cynthia Weber's notion of 'simulating sovereignty' sheds some light on this complex puzzle. The idea of the simulation of sovereignty is developed from the work of Jean Baudrillard. Weber (1995) argues that it is no longer possible to fix sovereignty according to a single representation of the nation-state. Sovereignty and intervention, she argues, are frequently invoked in the same sentence. Weber contends,

> If in the same discursive locale where one finds a 'legitimate' claim to sovereignty, one finds a 'legitimate' example of intervention, sovereignty and intervention cannot be opposed to one another. Rather they can be substituted for one another. Sovereignty is intervention, and intervention is sovereignty.
>
> (1995: 121)

The world has simply become so complex that the principles of international law that may have made it easier to 'fix' or 'mark' the sovereign state are no longer widely accepted. Moreover, when 'sovereignty' and 'intervention' are used interchangeably, a state loses control of its claim to legitimacy. Weber argues that such competing and co-existing representations of sovereignty displace a 'logic or representation' with a 'logic of simulation' (ibid.: xi–xii). In cases of simulation, discourses constantly shift in their use of referent objects, where any of *inter alia* 'the people', 'the state', 'the region' or 'the International Community' may be inscribed as sovereign. These shifting sets of norms and symbols comprise a 'code' (ibid.: 127) for statesmen to adopt in their representations to various audiences. Yet despite this lack, James Der Derian argues that such simulations are affective: they 'produce real symptoms, hyper-real effects' (2001: 214). It is an 'order of simulation' which 'marks the legitimate range of [the state's] legitimate powers and competencies' (Weber 1995: 129).

Simulation allows the elite to manipulate international assistance for their own ends, such as in the case of border assistance under the 'war on terror'. Often agents are able to avoid the functional fulfilment of agreements, but simultaneously adhere to contrasting 'codes' of sovereignty and intervention. Tajik elites are well practised in this, having signed dozens of international agreements which remain unfulfilled (Lavrakas: 2004: 18). However, state actors will increasingly seek to gain control for themselves of these representations of sovereign authority, seeking to manage the 'hyper-real effects'. Der Derian, in the context of US national security, considers the ability to manage hyper-reality makes wars virtuous through a Military-Industrial Media-Entertainment Network (2001). Less technologically advanced states, or at least those places without a large entertainment industry and (the need for) sophisticated strategies of media management, seek to manage the 'unreality' of peace and security through more prosaic strategies. Yet, in similar ways, the ability to shape these representations and make them conform to one's own sense of 'self' is for the leaders of a state intrinsic to their agency and their authority, locally and globally. Indeed, it relates to the very ability to control what is local ('domestic', 'internal', 'national', 'inside') and what is global ('foreign', 'external', 'international', 'outside').

In recent years, as shown in terms of reintegration of ex-commanders and border management, Tajikistan has regained some ability to perform a sovereignty/ intervention boundary to determine how the country is represented nationally, regionally and internationally. The regime seeks to maintain favourable relations across the International Community through a foreign policy of 'open doors' (*otkritiyie dveri*). One senior diplomat puts it this way: 'In our foreign policy we don't swing from the US to China and then to Russia – we keep relations with all.'[68] Significant credit and investment in infrastructure by China, including a US$600 million loan awarded in 2006, have engendered a sense of optimism amongst Tajik foreign policy-makers. Tajikistan's increasing acceptance as an equal by regional partners and the increased emphasis on statebuilding by the International Community allows it to justify, to a national audience, the use of state violence by one group (the regime representing 'the state') over everyone else

(the 'citizens'). Threats to the state are identified and demonised as 'external' and
– to a certain extent – suppressed. The 'logic of simulation' in Tajikistan has
remained relatively consistent since the handover of the border to Tajik forces
from 2004. In neighbouring Kyrgyzstan, by contrast, representations of the border
have been the subject of significant political dispute as powerful opposition discourses have emerged against the government (Megoran 2002). Whereas in Kyrgyzstan 'the border' became a hotly contested site of controversy in newspapers
and an issue which contributed to the popular putsch of March 2005, in Tajikistan
articles in the infrequently published opposition paper *Ruzi Nav* did not impact
public discourse.[69] This comparative lack of dissent illustrates the powerful effects
of the simulacra of sovereignty.

Dissimulating sovereignty

Discussion at the representational level of analysis inevitably raises questions
which go beyond the discursive environment: about the reception of discourse
and how and when simulacra are dissimulated. Whilst public practices are intrinsic to the emergence of legitimate order, they are negated by hidden practices
which serve to show the very precariousness of this order. In other words, as
sovereignty is simulated it is concomitantly dissimulated by elite and popular
practices. We must go beyond simulation to dissimulation.

Dissimulation is concomitant to simulation. In Baudrillard's terms, cited by
Der Derian, 'dissimulation is to feign not to have what one has' (1991: 214).
Public transcripts profess state sovereignty and claim the rights and responsibili-
ties that this entails; hidden transcripts deny these rights and responsibilities.
Sovereignty becomes a thin simplification. Its unreality can at times give it an
Orwellian character: a trope used to convey its very antonym. Elites claim official rights and responsibilities but deny them in their actions, in effect saying:
we are sovereign but powerless to prevent trafficking. The people have greater
security but deny this, in effect saying: we are at peace but subject to violence.
Elite practices entail illegality and corruption (as discussed above). Popular practices challenge state sovereignty by highlighting the continual failure of the elite
to represent national or public interests (as discussed below).

Daily life at the border

Everyday life at the border serves to dissimulate state sovereignty and challenges
the meaning of peace itself. Consequent to the high volumes of drugs trafficked
through the country, drug abuse in Tajikistan is on the rise, although exact
figures are hard to determine.[70] Hidden transcripts of life at the border represent
this murky picture in terms of poverty, the reappropriation of the state for personal enrichment, and accounts of state violence against communities.

The reaction in borderlands to the Russian withdrawal was couched primarily
in terms of livelihoods, both the wages that Tajik contract soldiers received
directly from their Russian paymasters, and the benefits to the economy of the

extra consumption of soldiers. In 2004, most 'Russian' troops were contract soldiers (*kontraktniki*) recruited locally. Whilst the head of the Tajik border forces officially earned US$42 a month, *kontraktniki* typically earned US$200–300 per month. 'Where can you find a salary like that in Tajikistan?' one *kontraktnik* complained. 'Tajik soldiers get 30 somoni [US$10], which is laughable – one person can't even live on this money, let alone feed five children.'[71] Among soldiers themselves, it is widely believed that poverty wages, poor quality equipment and training will mean that Tajik soldiers are even less likely to interdict drugs than Russian troops were.[72] Thus, a further concern was that the handover to Tajik control would increase the flow of drugs across the border. 'If the Russian border guards leave for good, it's hard to imagine the amount of drugs that will arrive here', commented one villager from Buni, near Khorog. 'A lot of young people here have become addicts, and it's terrible to think of what will happen. Our politicians should think about this when making decisions.'[73]

State violence in Tajikistan can be physical but it is often economic or 'structural'. With contract soldiers unlikely to sign up to vastly reduced salaries, the Tajik government has relied on rounding up conscripts to patrol the border. However, those recruited into the armed forces are not necessarily bound to be used exclusively in public service. Families complain that their sons are being used as free labour by officers to renovate houses and other construction jobs.[74] These proceeds go straight into the pockets of senior officers. Travelling along the remote Badakhshoni stretch of the border in 2005, I talked to numerous conscripts, mainly teenagers from Khatlon province, who were walking along the road with weapons but no radios or supplies. They complained of not having enough to eat and asked for food and cigarettes from us. Poor food and living conditions and widespread bullying are reported and lead to resistance or evasion by families during government conscription campaigns.[75] Such practices, where acts of state violence against its own people continue without redress, indicate that the boundary between security providers and 'threats' is an entirely constructed and barely justifiable one.[76] Such practices dissimulate sovereignty and make the divide between 'state' and 'terrorist', which state actors are seeking to re-inscribe, extremely thin indeed.

Practices of dissimulation are begotten by the 'logic of simulation' but, in this case, have not superseded it. As Baudrillard notes, to dissimulate something 'implies a presence' (cited in Der Derian 1991: 213) and thus one dynamic of the practices of dissimulation is inherently conservative: the reproduction of the (artificial) reality – state sovereignty. As Reeves (2006) has perceptively claimed, it is this intrinsic ambiguity of (Central Asian) post-colonial state formation which produces paradoxes such as 'strong-weak' states. 'These paradoxes and puzzles arise', Reeves argues, 'from an initial assumption that *the* state "ought", in both a normative and descriptive sense, to be a singular rather than multiple entity' (2006: 11, emphasis added). However, Reeves goes further, via ethnographic study and notes that these multiplicitous acts – or practices of dissimulation – are themselves reproductive of state sovereignty. 'What initially appears', she notes, 'as a violation of a pre-existing boundary between "state" and "society", "legal" and "illegal" can rather be understood as *constitutive* acts' (ibid.: 12). They constitute the state but not one that exists in an ideal form. Thus, both simulation (of its 'presence') and dissimulation (in its 'absence') make the state appear as if it is real, in *both* the daily life of subordinates and discursive and representational practices of elites and internationals. This, once again, points to the inherently ambiguous and precarious nature of statehood and peacefulness in post-conflict Tajikistan.

Conclusions

Sovereignty is the second property of emergent order in post-conflict Tajikistan. However, whilst in Chapter 5 performances of authority were seen to be highly successful at determining spatial boundaries 'inside' Tajikistan (demarcating the elite in terms of the state), this chapter shows the limits of this success in the face of contrasting representations and practices of state sovereignty at the margins of Tajik space. Rather than being *either* absent or present, sovereignty is *both* simulated *and* dissimulated.

This chapter has sought to take the argument beyond the contradiction of state-idea versus state-system in its elite, subordinate and international dimensions. Simulation is a very different process from those of institutionalisation and representation. If we see security and sovereignty as established rules or as singly constructed discourses, we lose the ability to see how their seeking constitutes the very things themselves. The practices of international security assistance (in terms of sovereignty) are more significant than any cosmetic changes that may be achieved in border management. Yet this sovereignty and this emergent order remain limited and contingent in that they are denied by the practices, often hidden, of elite self-enrichment and popular avoidance. I have introduced the Baudrillardian idea of simulation to convey this unreality. Together multiple discursive practices of sovereignty constitute a process of simulation and beget practices of dissimulation. (Dis)simulation is concomitant with material relations of exchange. Yet this invites a question of the significance of the materialisations and political economy networks which sustain and are sustained by these discursive practices. This question is considered in the final empirical chapter, on community development and livelihoods, which explores how practices of physical and structural violence, and acts of departing from Tajikistan, constitute a third dimension of the practical realities of peace.

7 Development and livelihoods

Anything that people do in life may cause conflict, but as I was saying things are going in such a way that if you point this out to someone it means that you are against national unity and accord (*natsionalnovo edinstva i soglasiya*). That's how everyone holds each other in check. Well, look, there's no work, however no one demands work, because if 3 million people demand work then we may go off our heads. [...] That's why everyone knows that you shouldn't demand work but you need to go to Russia, Kazakhstan, and it's not important if [there] they kill you or they don't.

(Dinkayev 2005: 10)

It has been established that public discourses of peacebuilding are challenged by hidden discourses and practices of international technocracy, elite patron–client relations, and subordinate conflict avoidance and even radical dissent. In this sense, peacebuilding can be understood intertextually: a process which emerges in the relations amongst discursively constituted subjects and between their public and hidden transcripts. Authority is performed in the public spaces of politico-administrative spaces and sovereignty is simulated at the site of the border of regional and international communities. Performances of authority and simulacra of sovereignty are productive in a negative sense, in that they delegitimise alternative modes of governance and intervention. However, public discursive formations, in their performative and simulative functions, do not create widespread order beyond their national, regional and international sites and moments such as those explored in Chapters 5 and 6 (the higher offices of state, the state border, international conferences and seminars, parliamentary elections). As modes of governance they are contingent on the vagaries of everyday subsistence and economic life. It is this contingency – the continuing differentiation of subordinate, elite and international spaces and the moments of discursive mediation between them – which is the first concern of this chapter.

The second concern is with the politics of international development and the emergence of new forms of livelihood in post-conflict Tajikistan. The chapter considers the efforts of the International Community to facilitate community development and civil society peacebuilding, particularly by means of establishing community-based organisations (CBOs). It moves the debate on from the elite levels of national and international politics to politico-economic relationships in local spaces. Furthermore, it seeks to emphasise the extra-representational (economic and physical) dimensions of elite, subordinate and international practices which create an interest in territory and livelihoods as well as those acts which undermine this ideal. I show how *livelihoods* are *re-/de-territorialised*, where elite networks are increasingly regaining dominance of the land and subordinate actors are increasingly relying on labour migration.

Livelihoods must be examined in the context of authority and sovereignty but at the level of quotidian. The re-centring of authority is most visible in the everyday informal and performative dimensions and administrative and economic functions. State laws determining the expenditures and administrative functions of local government, including staffing levels and wages, are set by Dushanbe (Urban Institute 2003). One of the most obvious powers is the President's power summarily to dismiss and appoint heads of oblasts and raiyons. This constitutionally enshrined function of the presidential office was used frequently throughout the period from 2000 to 2005.[1] Regular turnovers keep appointees strictly loyal to their patrons and prevent too much power from being accumulated by any particular local fief (Weigman 2004: 14–16). Both appointments and dismissals are enacted on national television with each act of dismissal and appointment followed by the speaking of the name of the President, embodying the power of the state (see Burke 2005a). One of the main commodities traded is cotton. Production targets, as during Soviet times, are set centrally, but it is localised coalitions of future companies and local authorities which lock local farmers into producing cotton at below market rates and bolsters control of elite networks over cotton production. New raiyon and oblast heads quickly gain a piece of the pie as state structures are deeply intertwined with the cotton business in the south and parts of the north of the country (ICG 2004: 14).

It was this re-centring (increasing authoritarianism) and de-centring (corruption and patronage relations) which the International Community sought to address via community development and decentralisation programmes. In 2004 and 2005 I conducted research on behalf of international organisations in communities and centres located in three of Tajikistan's four administrative regions (see Table 7.1): Sughd oblast (*Veloyati Sughd*, formerly *Veloyati Leninabad*),[2] in both Asht and Panjikent raiyons; Khatlon oblast (*Veloyati Khatlon*), particularly districts around the south-western town of Sharituz;[3] and in the centrally controlled raiyons (*Nohyiahoi Tobei Jumhuri*), including the Rasht Valley districts of Nurabad, Gharm and Jirgital.[4] I worked in a total of nineteen 'communities'.[5]

The chapter is divided into three sections. The first investigates the practical impact of the International Community peacebuilding programmes of Mercy Corps in this wider context. It explores the resilience of local spaces, the avoidance and accommodation strategies of subordinates, and the hybrid forms of local governance that, ironically, have strengthened the discursive and informal institutional structures of an authoritarian elite. The second section of the chapter looks at how 'community development' and 'self-government' are simulated by

Table 7.1 Sites of field research, 2004–2007

Organisation (programme: donor)	CBO concepts	Region	Districts	Villages/towns
Mercy Corps (CAIP: USAID)	Community Action Group (CAG)	DRC	Nurabad	Humdon
			Garm	Bedak, Shule Garm
			Jirgital	Jailghan Dombrachi
		Khatlon	Sharituz	Sharituz
			Beshkent	Komsomol, Kizil Ketmen
			Kabodiyon	Pakala
Mercy Corps (PCI-2: USAID)	Community Initiative Group (CIG)	Sughd	Asht	Navbuned, Tajikokjar
			Panjakent	Novabad, Koshonar, Margedar
Aga Khan Foundation (MSDSP: GTZ)	Village Organisation (VO); Water Usage Association (WUA)	DRC	Garm	Rasht Sovkhoz

the (mis)representations of INGOs and the discursive mediation of their local staff and subcontractors. The final section outlines the importance of livelihoods in the actual practising of building peace, looking specifically at the case of Rasht state farm, showing how livelihoods are being de-/re-territorialised.

Community development and peacebuilding

On the face of it, Tajikistan seems ripe for community peacebuilding. As the country lacks an abundance of natural resources, it has not succumbed to the resource conflicts that have beset other developing states and complicate decentralisation initiatives. Furthermore local self-governance seems necessary to attenuate the country's regional divisions. The concept of the CBO has emerged partly as an antidote to the centralising demands of the post-conflict state and the corruption of elites (Ball 2002: 37). Community peacebuilding[6] is one strategy emanating from the discourse of civil society peacebuilding which demands the distribution of decision-making and budgetary control from central government to local governmental actors and/or CBOs. As shown in Chapter 3, promoting community-based development was a priority goal of the International Community in Tajikistan in the early 2000s (De Martino 2004). Abdullaev and Freizer's 'peacebuilding framework' for Tajikistan, for example, targeted citizens' opportunities to 'participate in local decision making and policy formulation through reform of local self governance bodies and the development of more efficient community development institutions' (2003: 53). However, Tajik communities relate to elite and international practices in their own communities in light of the discourse of *tinji* and the economic practices of survival.

Donors, contractors and CBO concepts

Major western donors including USAID and GTZ led the way in community peacebuilding. By Spring 2004 the rapid expansion in the volume of 'peacebuilding' programmes conducted in Tajikistan via the capacity-building of CBOs encouraged the UNDP to bring the various agencies together to share information about 'community-linked development' and coordinate activities to 'promote decentralisation and provide a stronger framework for governance at the municipal level' (UNDP 2004). CBOs, as idealised in the programme proposals and 'success stories' of international organisations, represent the first steps of a nascent democracy. Indeed, in rural Central Asia, they seem to offer unparalleled opportunities for devolving power whilst respecting local customs.

USAID is the largest donor in support of local self-government and has several major INGO contractors in Tajikistan. Its Community Action Investment Program (CAIP) is the largest ever community-based programme in Tajikistan and is imbued with specific peacebuilding objectives.[7] CAIP's stated goal was to 'help prevent conflicts and promote broad based-citizen dialogue and participation', to achieve 'improved standards of living, more active and engaged citizens and more open, accountable local government' (MCCAR 2005: 1). The methodology of CAIP, as implemented by Mercy Corps, entailed 'the democratic election of Community Action Groups (CAG), transparent, sustainable, and accountable management of projects, and advocacy for support from local government and community residents'.[8] USAID was also one of the financiers of the Village Organisation (VO). Aga Khan Foundation's Mountain Societies Development Support Programme (MSDSP),[9] which set up and oversees VOs defines them as, 'a body of representatives from households in a given rural geographic locality', which is 'transparent', 'autonomous' and 'self-directed' (MSDSP 2001: 4).

The vital link between the INGO and the CBO in all these programmes is the local NGO contracting partner (LNGO). With multiple organisations and models working in Tajik communities in recent years, numerous partnerships and collaborations have been launched. Scores of LNGOs have sprung up to work as subcontractors for international NGOs in implementing donor-funded programmes. They undertake training in conflict resolution, project management and a myriad of other general and specialist areas of community mobilisation. *Ittifok*, for example, in Sughd province, was one of the largest and gained significant business from Mercy Corps and UNDP amongst others before it was forced to close down in the mid-2000s, not long after funding for these programmes expired. Over time, these institutions develop off-the-shelf packages which they can adapt to offer what is essentially the same product for ostensibly distinct programmes. Thus, while their relationship with donors and INGOs is subservient they are able to operate as efficient businesses based on economies of scale.

Despite conceptual and operational similarities among different international programmes, each INGO is keen to develop and protect its own distinctive approach. In Tajikistan such rivalries have primarily been played out with regard to 'level' of engagement. The UNDP alone has sought to work at the Jamoat-level[10] with their Jamoat Development Committee (JDC).[11] The Presidential Administration has supported the JDC drive and directed heads of Khukumats to facilitate the UNDP's efforts. Similarly, the UNDP emphasises that JDCs must support government and not be an alternative to it. In some cases funding goes straight to Jamoats and there is deemed to be no need to set up a JDC.[12] By contrast, INGOs, given their mandates and identities as representatives of 'civil society', have taken a different tack, preferring to work directly in villages. They practise civil society peacebuilding with its emphasis on the 'grassroots'. Freizer articulates the idealised image of the mahalla which is widely shared by many humanitarian agencies in Tajikistan:

> Mahallas brought people living on the same territory together on a voluntary basis, along interest lines based on profession or good neighbourliness. They created a forum where local values, rules of behaviour, and common interests were defined, through which group interests were protected and joint actions organized.
>
> (2004: 18)

This notion of the benign and voluntary nature of action under the mahalla is strikingly depoliticised in that it does not question where power lies in 'group interests' and 'joint actions'. In such a way, this ideal mahalla is represented as in need of rescuing from its post-conflict, post-Soviet predicament, with Freizer arguing that 'they are increasingly passive and risk withering away' (ibid: 19).

This raises a much greater issue which will be explored through the rest of this chapter: how the boundary between 'state' and 'society' gets lost in this representation 'community'. On the one hand, this is an unavoidable product of the dual societal and state roles of local elites. This is evidenced in the ambiguous nature of the mahalla committee which was surprisingly absent from Tajikistan's foundational local government legislation of 1994. On the other hand, international NGOs explicitly blur the boundary in their discourses in order to express positive engagement between 'state' and 'civil society' – the dual subjects of peacebuilding. Mercy Corps, for example, includes civilian institutions of the state (presumably including the Presidential Administration) in its definition of civil society. Country Director for Mercy Corps Tajikistan Gary Burniske remarked, 'you may ask "well, what isn't civil society?" Well, I'd answer that the military isn't civil society and, in some countries, they are a large part of the state.'[13] In reality both the merging and dividing of 'civil society' and 'state' are problematic. When the same individual represents both the 'state', as a district (raiyon) official, and 'civil society', as a member of a CAG, we have to question to what extent state and civil society are actually institutionally separable in the first place. At the same time their inscribed separation is vital for the practice of International Community peacebuilding, and the exercise of elite authority.

The practice of community peacebuilding demands further analysis. In the case of Mercy Corps' CAIP, intervention took the form of three principal phases: establishing and training the CBO; community decision-making; and conducting social and infrastructure projects. Below I contrast the claims of the official Mercy Corps (MCCAR 2005) evaluation of the programme (of which I was part) with local practices, which contradicted these claims. This raises an interesting question of evaluation – how did we get it so wrong? – that I will discuss in the next section of this chapter.

Establishing CBOs: the re-formation of hegemony

The methodology of CAIP called for the establishment of the CAG via an election and its continued capacity-building throughout the three-year programme. Towards the end of the programme the CAG was encouraged to continue its activities by continuing to act and seek registration as an NGO. The final evaluation argued that CAIP was 'moderately successful in institutionalising the organisational arrangements' of the CAG'.[14]

However, underlying both the programme methodology and the evaluation is a particular approach to community development which considers context to be a matter of secondary consideration. As Giffen and Earle note, 'while rhetorical recognition of "local culture" is standard, assumptions about post-war and traditional society mean that in practice a methodological assumption of *carte blanche* is dominant' (2005: 37).[15] The problem with this analytical step is that one cannot necessarily expect it to be shared by community members whose habitual practices provide a pre-existing institutional context. This is confirmed by the private testimonies of programme staff. One CAIP manager reflected after the end of the programme,

> Is it really sustainable to create new groups rather than work with existing structures, like these elders committees? The problem is that the relationship between the two was not planned for in the programme.[16]

Thus, in effect, Mercy Corps tried to introduce formal institutions into Tajik communities in which informal institutions of self-governance were already quite well established. This meant that the processes of forming CBOs were distorted by those institutions and ideas to the extent that Mercy Corps' intervention served to *re-form* pre-existing institutions.

In the ten CAIP communities which I studied in some depth the CAG was in fact the re-formation of the local mahalla committee or groups of elders (*aksakals*). For example, in the village of Shule, CAG members noted that 'the *raisi mahalla* is the head of the CAG. When he wants to do something for the village he can go through the CAG to achieve it.' While they cited that they were 'elected', when asked about term limits and future elections they noted, 'for now there's no need for change'. Moreover, they added they were selected on the basis of ability and that, while they didn't have formal rules, they had 'mutual understanding'.[17] The CAIP women's committee in the village of Dombrachi, Jirgital district, shed more light on how the process of re-forming takes place. 'In a general meeting', one woman noted, 'the community voted on previously nominated candidates. We nominated each other ourselves.' Another commented that 'we have an informal selection process and are accepting new members'.[18]

In addition to such pre-existing local institutions, international interventions were often faced with numerous pre-existing donor-supported formations. This was especially true in the Rasht valley which is sparsely populated with people yet densely populated with international agencies. Consequently, within communities the practice of 'double-hatting' is common. Under double-hatting the same group of people serve as the members of several 'institutions', the VO and the CAG, and perhaps also the JDC. In the town of Gharm, 'CAG members', for example, noted that the VO predated the CAG, so that the group simply took on the institutional identity of the CAG as well. They deal with VO and CAG business in the same meetings and see no difference between the two organisations. When asked how they decide through which institutional identity they do projects the group replied that, 'we go to whichever will support what we want to do: if Aga Khan [MSDSP] says no then we go to Mercy Corps'.[19] In these cases of double-hatting the process of intervention is reversed: rather than the utilisation of a particular donor-supported methodology into numerous communities, there is the use of a single community methodology in relationship to multiple donor-funded projects.

Thus, the formation of CBOs over the course of 2002–2005 was often conducted on top of both pre-existing local and international structures. But while local pre-existing discursive institutions and relationships remained salient, a direct translation of the mahalla committee en masse to the CAG is rare. The key qualification for membership of the group is less the formal membership of another group but the qualities of being 'respected' and having 'authority' in the community. The CAG in Bedak, for example, was formed out of a collaboration of six mahallas which were present in the 'community' which Mercy Corps had selected. Members of the group were quite open about their institutional ambiguities and how they sought to manage them. Bedak hosted a CAG, VO and JDC – although the CAG had arrived first – from which they had formed a single committee. The head of the village (*raisi kishlak*) was made leader because he is 'our leader'. While, in principle, the committee could be re-elected this had yet to happen. 'Every two years we could have an election for the one committee', they noted. 'If people are not happy we will do this.' Under this arrangement the rais 'works directly' with Mercy Corps and the other international organisations.[20] Such a harmonisation and consolidation of the CAG chimes with subordinate ethics of 'unity' and 'cohesion', and with elite discourses (the 'necessity to have a uniform situation (*tipovoye polozheniye*) in order to define the status of mahalla committees' [UNTOP/NAPST, 2002a: 2] and 'unification of these territorial organs of self-government' [ibid.: 23]).

Community decision-making: mahalla rules

The imperative to subjugate the CAG form to the mahalla leadership derives from patriarchal discourses of authority as well as interests in capturing resources. These processes of becoming more patriarchal and patrimonial have been common across Tajik regions in the 2000s and have been inadvertently advanced by international assistance. In Bedak, for example, attendees at formal CAG meetings are generally male heads of households; occasionally a small group of women would come and sit apart from the men in their own group. The rais, emboldened by his access to foreign funding, receives requests for support direct from heads of households and then discusses it within the group of patriarchs.[21]

This kind of re-formation in communities challenges the idea that interventions can institutionalise new procedures of decision-making in communities. CAIP's methodology entailed conducting social and infrastructure projects using 'participatory cycles of problem identification, project selection, planning, and implementation' (MCU 2005: 3). Hence, the process of decision-making was deemed to be more important than the conducting of projects itself. Programme managers repeatedly referred to the maxim that 'the means are more important than the ends' and 'it's not so much what is achieved but how'. In particular, communities were to gain new beliefs and rules via a training process, 'using a curriculum including modules on development principles, transparency and accountability, the value of public meetings, community participation and mobilisation, conflict resolution skills, creating sustainable communities, project management and related topics depending on circumstances' (MCU 2005: 3). Overall, the programme evaluation gave a positive conclusion regarding the inculcation of new decision-making rules. CAIP was, it argued, 'highly successful in engaging the local population in participatory and democratic change processes at the community level', but was 'less successful in transferring a "CAIP methodology" and ensuring the sustainability of program approaches and processes' (ibid.: 26). Yet my academic research indicates that this cautious optimism obfuscates actual practices of governance.

CAIP decision-making ostensibly begins with community meetings to identify problems and select projects. However, participation in these meetings is not at all equitable; from my own observation of such meetings it is clear that some voices are dominant whilst others are unheard. Meetings are often directed by a head who makes proposals to the community to receive their approval. Moreover, such a formal setting may be superseded by prior informal agreements made in the community meeting place or choihona. Groups of men informally discuss community and family matters. As one CAG member in the village of Humdon noted, when asked how they receive requests from the community, 'of course since we live in the village and talk to people, and meet in the choihona every evening we know what the problems are'. Another said, 'we meet each other five times a day for prayers (*namaz*) – people know'.[22] In such conditions the formal meetings can simply serve to validate pre-ordained, informal decisions. '[The meetings]', one group member in Sharituz admitted, 'are for the purpose of asking in the community for contribution and mobilising them for voluntary work (*subbotnik*)'.[23] Sometimes this leads to resentment from those who feel excluded from the process, and are thus not willing to take part in the meetings. In the village of Jailghan one group member explained that in one case, 'the poor did not want to make community contributions. Some did not want to come to community meetings. We told them it was obligatory to be at the meeting for the sake of the project.'[24] This was told as a positive example where 'participation' in formal meetings had been achieved against the odds after intervention from the leadership.

The inequities of community 'participation' are evident from the responses of community members during the survey that was conducted as part of the CAIP evaluation. Ninety-two people were interviewed to form a statistically valid sample.[25] Of sixty interviewees, thirty-five had heard of the 'CAG' and eight were able to describe one of the projects. This poor level of knowledge is extraordinary given that most of the communities are extremely poor, very small (less than 1,000 residents) and close-knit and that CAIP represented the largest state or international intervention conducted in these villages in their history (an investment of up to US$75,000 in material and in-kind resources per community). However, knowledge is mediated by power relations. Gender differences indicate that level of awareness is quite closely correlated to one's influence on re-formed power structures. Table 7.2 shows the answers of respondents to a question about how the CAG was formed. While the most popular answer for women was that they did not know (twenty or two-thirds of respondents), less than one-fifth of men (six respondents) said this. This indicates both actual levels of knowledge and gender roles which were inscribed in local discourses and inadvertently re-inscribed by international intervention.

Conducting projects: performing consent

Whilst the processes of forming and decision-making were superseded by the re-forming process and pre-existing beliefs and rules, the conducting of projects made a powerful impact on the physical infrastructure of communities, at least in the short term. The thirty-five CAIP communities in Tajikistan conducted 231 infrastructure and twenty-three social projects during the three years of the programme and contributed an average of 45 per cent of the costs of these projects

Table 7.2 'How was the CAG formed?' – responses by gender

	Don't know	Through an election	Mercy Corps selected community leaders	Other	Grand total
Female	20	9	2	0	31
Male	6	10	12	1	29
Grand total	26	19	13	1	60

through the in-kind provision of labour. They conducted far more projects (especially in infrastructure) and made greater community contribution (mostly in-kind in the form of labour) than the communities in the more urbanised Ferghana valley of Uzbekistan which also underwent the CAIP programme (MCU 2005: 16). However, for international peacebuilding the preponderance of project implementation over processes is understood as a real difficulty. One programme manager noted that it is 'very difficult to separate the idea of a complete infrastructure project from the process it takes to get there'.[26]

Local elites, by contrast, were instrumental with respect to infrastructure projects. Elite-led projects serve purposes beyond whatever social and economic legacy they may or may not bring. It is argued by local INGO and LNGO staff and CBO members alike that getting things done requires the support of local informal authorities. One representative of a subcontracted LNGO working on Mercy Corps' PCI programme in Sughd province noted that it was crucial to find leaders with 'their own authority (*sobstvennyi avtoritet*)'. 'In principle', she noted,

> when such people come with us and begin to work with us it's not difficult [to conduct projects]. But there were also naturally such incidents when we weren't able to find such people. These were difficult incidents. [These leaders have] this authority from the population. They respect and trust these people and are attentive to the opinions of these people.
>
> (Safarova 2005: 3)

When local elites are brought on side they can organise *khashar* – a 'traditional' institution of community mobilisation – in order to provide a labour force. However, two quite contradictory misunderstandings of *khashar* are often held by foreign observers.

First, whilst *khashar* can be romanticised as an entirely voluntary, kinship-based institution which can simply be 'harnessed' by NGOs, my findings indicate it is led by those with 'authority'. In the town of Gharm, CAG leaders explained how they mobilise the people for non-CAIP social projects using Mercy Corps methodology: 'for example, we say we are having a wrestling match and tell people they must come to *khashar*'.[27] The deputy chair of the Jamoat in the same community noted that the aim of the programme was to 'direct (*napravit*) the young people for the development of the community' and that the role of the chair of the CAG is as the 'main organiser of people'.[28] Such conceptions belie the idea of consensus-based mobilisation found in international discourses. Giffen and Earle have characterised this as a form of 'obligatory voluntarism' found commonly in *khashar* across Central Asia (2005: 85).

Second, and somewhat in tension with the first assumption, it is often assumed that it is exclusively led by 'traditional' leaders – those possessing charismatic authority (such as a mullah) or age (an *aksakal*). Yet my research indicated that 'authority' is not exclusively 'charismatic' or traditional but can be very modern, understood in terms of the control and administration of resources. In the village of Margedar, where a PCI group had recently been established, the group noted the importance of having the head of the local farm on the group. While the explanation of the leader of the group as to why the group is listened to began in traditional terms, it quickly evolved to link this authority to resources. 'They respect us because we are respected', one man noted,

> but they don't listen often because they know we have no financial means to build a new sportsground or new classrooms. It depends on what we can provide. If, for example, a donor buys pipes for a water system all the people will listen to us as they will see we've been able to do this.[29]

From statements like this it is clear that in this emergent order INGOs are not neutral actors. In practice the mobilisation of communities through CAIP meant that hegemonic local elites, whatever their precise sources of authority, were handed an opportunity to perform.

While economic power often accords with social status, particularly with respect to land ownership, Tajik society is fluid and contingent as wealth is accumulated by a small minority of the country's many labour migrants (usually in their twenties and thirties). One NGO representative described how he hit a dead-end in a community where they could not get the local leadership on side and explained how the problem was resolved with the help of a relatively wealthy returnee:

> When we decided that we will conduct a meeting behind closed doors, that we would no longer work here, and would make this known to people. But there was one person who participated [in that meeting], who had for a long time been working in Russia. He said: 'guys, I am sitting over here listening and am not able to understand what's been going on here.' And when we told him he said: 'okay, so here there's such people.' Everyone still closed their eyes and didn't understand this but in the course of literally two weeks this person organised everything. He organised everything and in the course of a year they were outstripping other communities. All depends on the authorities (*avtoritetov*) and the person who takes responsibility for others (*vedyot za soboi drugikh*).
>
> (Safarova 2005: 3)

In this sense, through *khashar*'s renaissance, international interventions reproduce power relations in post-conflict communities. In the village of Dombrachi, this was evident in numerous statements and stories. The secretary of the local Jamoat remarked that through CAIP, 'we realise how *khashar* can be combined with international funding to complete a project'.[30] This conception of CAIP by leaders who now felt themselves more authoritative in their communities was common across communities.

These testimonies support my general findings that elite hegemony and patriarchal leadership were re-formed and reinforced under international interventions. Figure 7.1 nicely illustrates these findings. It compares communities at the beginning of PCI with those at the end of CAIP and shows two main response categories to the open question 'How are decisions made in the community?' The first category, 'together', includes those answers which emphasise the community as a whole, or the community with its leaders making decisions (in accordance with *tinji* discourse). One would expect that this would be the default answer given to an international researcher. The second category of answer, 'by leaders', includes those answers which emphasise an independent decision being made by leaders (including 'by the mahalla committee', 'by the men', 'by aksakals', 'by local authorities', or some combination of these groups, in accordance with *mirostroitelstvo*). Research conducted at the beginning of the PCI programme showed an overwhelming majority of villagers (forty-seven out of sixty) answering 'together' and affirming the maxim of 'unity' of the *tinji* discourse. Research conducted at the end of the CAIP programme, however, showed many fewer respondents giving this response (31 out of 60) and many more saying they were taken by 'leaders' (25 out of 60). The outcome of community peacebuilding in Tajikistan may then be the very reverse of its intent. These and other findings indicate a significant shift in perceptions of authority from the norms of *tinji* towards the renewal of elite hegemony and the acceptance of *mirostroitelstvo*. The role of international peacebuilders here has been to shift the balance in the community towards greater patriarchal domination and patrimonial economic relationships.

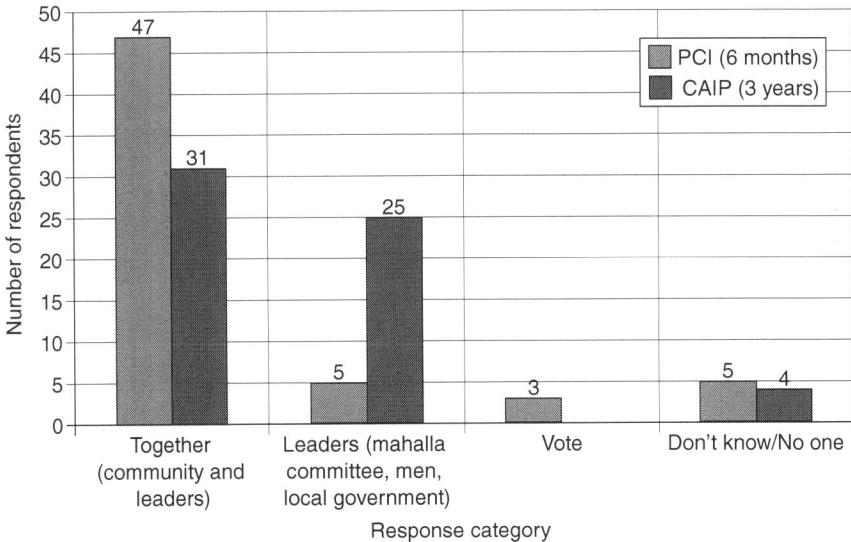

Figure 7.1 'How are decisions taken in the community? – A comparison between the beginning and end of international programmes.[1]

Note
1 CAIP findings from a survey of sixty villages in April/May 2005, at the end of the three-year programme. See footnote 25; PCI findings from a survey of the same number of respondents across five villages in Asht and Panjakent raiyons in June 2005, six months into the programme.

Mediating community in monitoring and evaluation

We have seen how international discursive performances of 'community self-government' (this chapter), 'border management' (Chapter 6) and 'elections' (Chapter 5) contrast with realities for elites and subordinates. These contrasts raise questions about how multiple contrasting representations are sustained and not subsumed into a single transcript, despite claims made to the contrary in specific in-between spaces and at intertextual moments. Such differentiation is tremendously important. To speculate somewhat, community peacebuilding programmes such as CAIP would not get funded if they were believed to be part of the re-constitution of elite domination and manipulated by elites in the ways argued here. These discursive performances are apparently self-legitimating. It would be tempting to argue that some privileged agent, a grand master of discourse, must be consciously reproducing such representations. This would be an overly agential explanation and lacks evidence. In reality there are multiple agents of discourses, from within and without the International Community, complicit in the reproduction of these contrasting transcripts. In my explanation, agency remains, but it is produced intersubjectively. To remain discursively differentiated international representations must be discursively mediated. This section looks at the nature of programme evaluation, the role of discursive mediators and how they both act to simulate 'community'.

Quantifying success

Monitoring and evaluation (M&E) is an integral component of any major, donor-funded programme. International staff spend a considerable proportion of their time producing various images and texts to represent their programme in terms which will be appreciated by an audience in Washington, London or Berlin. It is these practices which explain how an intervention which has had very little impact on the pre-existing practices of communities can plausibly be considered to have transformed a community and be worth millions of dollars of assistance. This also gets to the heart of differentiation and discursive mediation: how multiple, contrasting representations of the same object can co-exist.

I was part of the final evaluation of the multi-million dollar CAIP programme which assessed a sample of sixteen communities (from a total of seventy-five) across three countries[31] in terms of the specific and measurable objectives of the programme.[32] The final report which we produced inscribed CAIP as a qualified success. 'Among the most significant changes brought about by CAIP', it argues, 'are increased trust and cooperation in the communities, changed outlook and increased capacity to solve problems' (MCCAR 2005: 14). The report acknowledges that impact on Tajik communities was less than anticipated. However, the reasons for the lack of complete success in this area were deemed to be internal programmatic issues where Mercy Corps had not paid sufficient heed to institutionalising the CBO after it was up and running. Thus it argues a 'much higher level of achievement' could have been reached by 'a clearer articulation of the process of capacity building' (ibid.: 39).

In such a way a considerable degree of success was rescued for the programme and, more importantly, for the idea of the CBO and the legitimacy of the 'third-party' self-identification of the International Community. Interventionism, we are told, largely works and, where it fails to achieve its objectives, it can be improved through solvable factors such as 'articulation of the process' by international actors. The report does not even consider contextual and non-instrumental factors. Community development, as discussed at the beginning of this chapter, is thus written as something which can be made, driven and controlled by the International Community. In this sense, and in keeping with international discourse, the report depoliticises and objectifies the highly political and relational processes of change taking place in Tajik communities. In cases where international agencies are using consultants to examine themselves – as was the case with CAIP[33] – 'independent' research is all the more subjective. How is such knowledge produced? I argue that three processes of power-knowledge are at work here: quantification, narration and visualisation.

The reductions and distortions of local practice which are found in reports such as the study I worked on are particularly acute in quantitative analyses. In accordance with the principles of new public management (NPM) thinking common to the International Community, CAIP was designed with SMART objectives.[34] SMART objectives are the foundational act of reducing a complex social and political environment to a set of quantifiable indicators in order to demonstrate objectivity, transparency and accountability. In the final evaluation we conducted a survey according to a statistically valid sample of respondents as well as focus groups and elite interviews using a standardised interview form. Many of the questions asked required closed answers which could be numerically represented. The evaluation was designed this way in order to make our data quantifiable according to the requirements of the donor, USAID, who wished to rank communities across the region according to their degree of success in terms of programme objectives. Quantification seemingly provides standardisation where the same attributes can be measured across the world. Moreover, it demands a method and model which is universal and can be applied in any context. An M&E consultancy business has mushroomed to meet this demand, where individuals who know a model can 'parachute' in to conduct a programme in a region which they have never visited before. This was the case in our evaluation where the lead consultant had not previously visited Central Asia and did not visit Tajikistan – where 60 per cent of the programme resources were invested – at all during the exercise.

The problem with such a standard or 'objective' approach is that it requires numerous 'subjective' judgements by the researcher. As a member of the evaluation team I was very much a participant in this process of categorising and re-categorising data in terms of types, and then into larger categories. There are many degrees of separation from the original collection of data. Quantitative analysis requires that meaning be transposed across several media:

1   translated question by researcher or interpreter;[35]
2   original speech in vernacular by respondent;
3   written record of respondent (written questionnaires) or researcher (oral survey);
4   English translation of original by translator;
5   classification into data type by researchers; and
6   aggregation into data category by researchers.

Clearly, at all stages, there is a great deal of interpretation. Data can be shaped by considerations such as how the respondent views the researcher (and vice versa). Questions asked reflect certain international assumptions about local people. Equally respondents testify in support of the international programme in line with what they think is expected by both their peers and the researchers.

For example, 'how have you changed during the programme?' assumed that the respondent would interpret 'you' as 'I' the individual (rarely the case) and that they would accept 'change' as a good (often not the case). In the case of written questionnaires, demanding a written answer to such a question also assumed that (often semi-literate) respondents would be comfortable answering alone without consulting their peers. This was never the case.

Questions often received collective and defensive answers. A closer look at original completed questionnaires indicates an interesting usage of the maxims of both the discourse of subordinate *tinji* (among all respondents) and that of elite *mirostroitelstvo* (more common among older men). The categorisation of data was also shaped by how the reader viewed the data. I observed in numerous meetings of the research team and programme staff how those who worked on the programme would understandably interpret local practices as culturally appropriate variations on universal international principles of participation and representation. To a certain extent this intersubjectivity of findings is a feature common to all social research, but it is a particular problem with quantitative M&E exercises.

An illustration of these intersubjectivities is shown in two attempts to classify data on community 'change' shown in Figures 7.2 and 7.3.[36] Version one (Figure 7.2) of that chart shows a version done by my colleague, according to the instructions of the lead consultant. It finds 39 per cent of respondents say 'I' am 'committed to work with community using democratic principles'. Version two (Figure 7.3) shows my version, composed – in a more discretionary and less 'scientific' manner – having seen chart one and found it to be a distortion of what I had heard from community members. It finds 42 per cent of respondents saying 'we' are 'more united [in our] approach to development in the community'. It is not clear how we judge which of these representations is more valid. Both charts necessarily reduce a huge range of data, gathered in and translated from four languages, to just five categories. For example, my category of 'Increased ability to manage projects' (Figure 7.3) was around three times more common among (overwhelmingly male) local government leaders than women's group members. Problematically, it includes both statements

Community Action Group members

Category	Percentage
Commitment to work with community using democratic principles	39%
Improved outlook/wellbeing	17%
Improved living conditions/infrastructure	14%
Gained skills in problem-solving/conflict prevention/resolution	10%
Better understanding and application of project cycle	9%
Improved communication/public relations skills	5%
Acquired leadership/organisational skills	5%

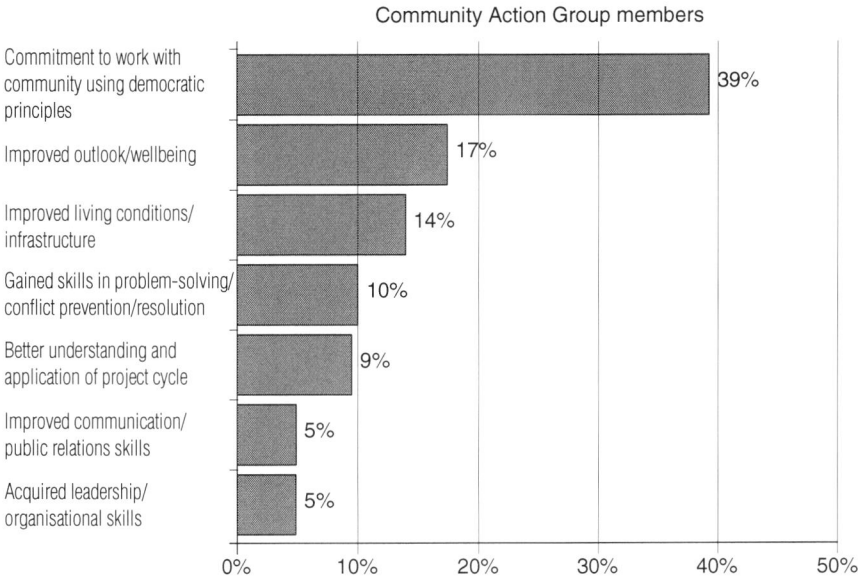

Figure 7.2 'How have you changed?' – chart version one.

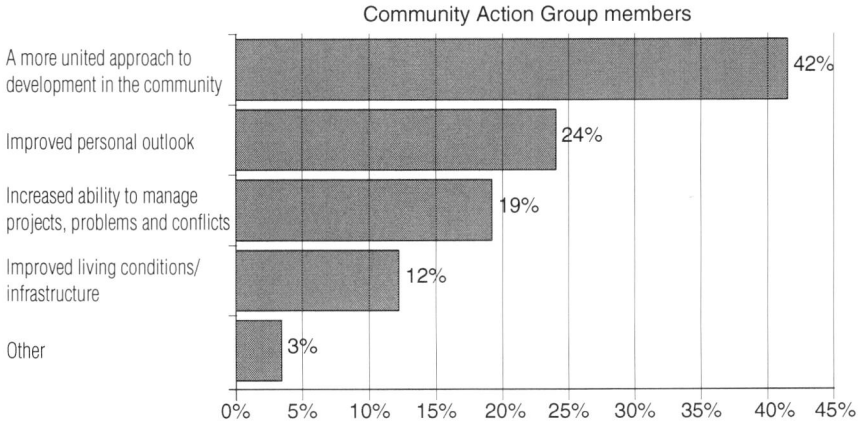

Community Action Group members

Category	Percentage
A more united approach to development in the community	42%
Improved personal outlook	24%
Increased ability to manage projects, problems and conflicts	19%
Improved living conditions/infrastructure	12%
Other	3%

Figure 7.3 'How have you changed?' – chart version two.

about authority (e.g. 'I think that my authority has been increased among people') and those implying acquired skills (e.g. 'project selection'). While our research sought to account for these validity questions by conducting several exercises of classification and re-classification, the social fact of intersubjectivity can never be circumvented.[37] Moreover, while the two charts give very different pictures, neither shed much light on what actually happened in communities and why. In short, much is left to the eye of the beholder at the stage of report writing and reading – the seventh and eighth stages of interpretation in addition to the six above. Writers and readers may discern from Figure 7.2 that 39 per cent of community leaders in CAIP communities have become more 'democratic'. I witnessed some international officers making just such claims. It is via this kind of intersubjectivity and intertextuality that (mis)representative international norms and symbols are reproduced.

Narrating and visualising 'success stories'

Reproducing 'community development' in the discourse of international peace-building involves more than just numbers. Stories and images from CAIP communities were a hugely important part of Mercy Corps' narration of the programme. Photographs and 'success stories' were crucial accompaniments of quarterly reports to donors. They are particularly important as the decision-makers of donor agencies are unlikely to spend much time reading formal M&E reports. Photos and anecdotes then make a significant contribution to perceptions of the programme. Success stories are told in such a way which inscribes a clear distinction between state and civil society. One 'success story' from the village of Jailghan in the Rasht valley (MCT 2005) recounted the case of the covering of an open-top, fast-running irrigation canal which had been responsible for the drowning of several children in recent years. 'During the project's implementation', the Mercy Corps version notes, 'Jailghan's Community Action Group mobilised extensive support from the local government and community members' (MCT 2005, no pagination). Yet Jailghan was one of those communities where government employees and representatives served on the CAG. This discursive separation of 'government' from 'community' reinforces a state–society dichotomy which does not exist in Tajikistan. This is justifiable only when one considers that by Mercy Corps' definition the civilian organs of the state are part of civil society. With such moves, the dual subject, which is integral to the justification for a community development programme, is inscribed even if, paradoxically, the 'state' must be subsumed into 'civil society'.

During my fieldwork I had personal experience of this phenomenon. In June of 2005, I was asked by Mercy Corps to study one of the cases considered most successful from the thirty-five CAIP communities in order to provide a success story for the programme's final report to USAID. I chose the community of Kizil Ketmen, near Sharituz, close to the Afghan border, and opted to spend a week there conducting research and living with the head of the CAG.[38] Compared with previous CAIP communities where I had conducted research, Kizil Ketmen was indeed a flagship case where a large number of projects had been completed over the course of the programme.[39] Thus, I wrote and photographed a story of success, 'The village of Kizil Ketmen on an upward trend' (Heathershaw 2005b). In the account I tried to explore this story of success with quotes and examples which showed how local leaders had to work amid a corrupt government and exploitative economy. Nevertheless I wrote for an audience in terms such as 'progress', 'challenges' and 'change', and illustrated my account with pleasing photographs.

My analysis was built upon the foundational step of community peacebuilding success stories – that the CAG is an independent institution that functioned as an agent of change. I profiled the CAG deputy chair – also the Director of the School where the group met – who worked busily for the community. I picked out the members of the women's group and recounted their public testimonies: 'We have our rights and we know them. When we have different meetings we find that we have the ability to analyse and solve problems.' I explained the CAG's flagship project of clearing out an irrigation canal. The case study concluded:

> Like many other grassroots leaders and community members, they have begun to see that change for the better can really impact their own lives and that of their fellow community members. Hope, like water, is beginning to flow through Kizil Ketmen again.
>
> (Heathershaw 2005b: 11)

The point here is not that I deliberately misrepresented the village. Rather, I did not tell the whole story. Indeed it is not possible to tell the whole story. Knowledge is not produced in laboratory conditions but a social space.

As a consequence, M&E might tell us more about us, the evaluators, than about them, the evaluated. As an evaluator I was in a certain sense 'trapped' by peacebuilding discourse. This 'entrapment' took place owing to the broader context of the International Community: I understood that I was paid to produce a story which would showcase the successes of CAIP to an audience of paymasters; I was part of a team of dedicated international and local staff, many of whom believed in the programme (albeit for different reasons); I myself had developed a personal perspective that CAIP had achieved some socio-economic good for poor communities (despite failing to achieve its peacebuilding objectives) and did not want to denigrate its positive achievements.

In this sense, M&E tells us a considerable amount about the social and political relationships between evaluator and evaluated. In this sense, as a form of (mis)representation, it serves a very important function: it keeps international cash coming for community development in the sincere hope that such programmes are benefiting communities. Whilst the discursive practices of M&E do not necessarily constitute direct manipulation or fabrication (although at times they can), programme coordinators are often quite ambivalent about their work in private. One Mercy Corps programme coordinator complained several weeks after the programme had finished that the CAGs had already ceased to exist. I remarked in response that such programmes might work better if they had aims which were more consistent with local expectations. The coordinator responded: 'if you wrote a realistic proposal the donors are not interested – so you have to write something that interests them and then you end up with a programme which is really hard to implement'.[40] Such testimonies exhibit a certain amount of cynicism and scepticism in private, but not do not constitute the widespread public disclosure that would challenge the whole idea of 'community peacebuilding'. More importantly, they indicate that local and international readings of community peacebuilding are irreconcilable. This in itself witnesses to the power of discourse to shape how 'community' is written, imagined and read.

Discursive mediation

The way that monitoring and evaluation is practised reveals a great deal about the character of international interventions: the unquestioned superiority of their external models leads interveners to disregard or downplay those local practices which may be inconsistent with their model. This happens, despite stated claims of capacity building and methods of facilitation. How are these parallel universes maintained? In many contexts where governance is based on broadly authoritarian practices, international organisations can find their intervention is not welcome as it seeks to challenge directly the authority of the government. However, in Tajikistan the International Community has maintained good relations with the government and has continued to put substantial resources into communities. I argue that this requires discursive mediation and, moreover, agents which function as discursive mediators.

In the context of community development and decentralisation programmes the local staff and subcontractors of INGOs fulfil the role of discursive mediators. They work for the International Community but grew up and exist in a Tajikistani social and political context. During 2005 I spent considerable time with local staff of INGOs, working together and getting to know several individuals quite well. I noticed that local staff discourses shift around much more than those of other agents. Moreover, these people behave quite differently depending on whether they are interacting with internationals, officials or villagers. Yet not all were conscious of this triune role and none wittingly shifted from one mode to another. Consequently, these shifting discourses became an important part of two mini-evaluation exercises I led (Heathershaw 2005c, 2005d). I became gradually aware of how elite practices of domination and subordinate practices of avoidance and accommodation are often explained in different terms to ex-pat INGO officers as positive aspects for the completion of projects. Equally, local INGO officers typically represent international peacebuilding amongst themselves and in villages in terms which draw upon precepts of both *mirostroitlestvo* and *tinji* discourses. I noticed three discursive strategies which bring 'peacebuilding' into local–subordinate spaces; the process, it should be remembered, also works in reverse.

First, the risk of conflict is reduced to an absolute lack of resources. Democratisation, conflict resolution and other transformational interventions are transposed into economic development initiatives. Mercy Corps local staff in Sughd oblast cited the stated conflict resolution aims of the programme when communicating with community leaders, whilst at the same time, like community leaders, denying that conflicts exist and citing economic 'threats' such as unemployment. This dual role was repeated in the SWOT analysis I conducted with local staff where they both raised issues which were of concern to internationals (at least partially for my benefit) whilst also repeating elite assumptions about conflict. One noted that tension comes from 'the lack of general resources'. Another staff member remarked that lack of finances is the most important weakness of communities (see Table 7.3). Thus, here local staff represented community problems in terms similar to local elites. Unlike ex-pat programme managers, they did not acknowledge an inequality of access to resources (either between villages or between groups within a village) as part of the problem, but rather cited an absolute insufficiency. This is an important difference as it de-politicises the nature of resource conflict.

Second, interventions are represented to local audiences largely in terms of conducting infrastructure projects. The following conversation between local Mercy Corps officers in Asht is revealing:

Officer 1: What are we doing setting up women's groups, youth groups, mixed-sex groups or whatever? We should just set up one good group with the power to get things done in the community. After the projects are finished the groups just close down. They're only there when the projects are going. I think we should set up one group with one fund to keep working after the programme – some contribution would come from the community, some from Mercy Corps.

Officer 2: But we have different groups because different groups have different views. There are various views. Some may want to renovate the water system, others may want to do the school – that's why we need different groups.[41]

While one officer is apparently more aware of social diversity than the other, as the conversation continued they both failed to acknowledge that certain sections of the community may be marginalised, partly due to the actions of the others.

Third, the unquestionable authority of elites is explicitly affirmed, particularly amongst those elites themselves. According to one member of the Asht

Table 7.3 SWOT analysis, Mercy Corps local staff, Panjakent, June 2005

Strengths	*Weaknesses*
• Hard-workingness	• Distrust and misunderstandings
• Work experience	• Lack of skills
• Desire to work	• Absence of financial means – the main
• Tolerance to each other	thing
• Ability to work in a team	• Absence of work places
	• Absence of technical equipment
Opportunities	*Threats*
• Knowledge which they received in	• Labour migration (*zarabotka*)
trainings	• Drug addiction
• To mobilise to address needs	• Extreme poverty
• An improvement in the conditions for	• Increase in various diseases
living and welfare	• Illiteracy of youth

team, the CIG is a group of 'respected people who are heeded'. While programme staff share managers' concerns regarding cross-border problems, they were very positive about the permission-granting role of local government. One told me that, 'the role of local government is positive. Without the permission of local government it's not possible to work in communities. They are the masters of their territory [*hozayeva svoikh territori*].' Moreover, 'we coordinate our work together'.[42] Following from this representation of 'authority', women and youth were re-interpreted as passive, needing to be led. One member of the Asht team disagreed that the lack of female participation was a real concern in the communities. For another – the only woman on the team – the problem was 'inactivity', for which 'training of women' was needed to attract and mobilise them. A male team member added that the problem was that local women conform to stereotypes. In response to the question of what's best about the programme, the Asht team replied: 'what's best about the programme is the coming together of the team with the community, to become kindred spirits (*rodstvenni dushi*) and one family'.[43] By contrast, it is often argued by international staff that if development is about change, some tension in communities is desirable and inevitable.

In summary, local staff discourse translates peacebuilding programmes through the precepts of *mirostroitelstvo* and *tinji* to elite and subordinate audiences, indicating the relational and inconsistent articulation of subject roles as the context shifts. The local staff SWOT analysis (Table 7.3) bears a family resemblance to that shown in Table 4.3 for the discourses of village leaders. This interpellation of discourses has far-reaching consequences for international assistance. Regardless of what is written in programme documents, it is local staff with local knowledge and relevant languages who represent what the programme means to the target community.[44] In reverse, skilful staff can explain local practices in ways which make international staff modify their expectations of what constitutes 'peacebuilding' and 'success' in context. They thus stabilise the basic discourses, minimising or avoiding the points of conflict between them. With such *discursive mediation* the intertextual relations between basic, contrasting discourses are reduced and parallel realities are maintained. This has the overall effect of moderating international programmes and gutting them of their 'otherness' – which for international peacebuilding represents their transformative quality.

Livelihoods

As the mediation of multiple discursive orders shapes the politics of peacebuilding it also shapes the emergence of legitimate order. Yet in order to grasp how this works we need to shift our attention away from the international object of community development to a more ordinary pursuit of the poor to scratch out a living. Local economic strategies are a product of the wider politico-economic environment. Livelihoods, as a property of peacebuilding, are products of 'everyday economies' rather than any specific mode of accumulation (Humphrey

2002). Discursively, the primacy of livelihoods is expressed in public demands for modernisation, agro-industrialisation and employment and often hidden laments of poverty and destitution (see Chapter 4). Yet discourse analysis alone is insufficient here. In the post-conflict era the link between livelihoods and territory is at once being re-established (among the rural peasantry) and disestablished (through the making of 'translocal' spaces of labour migration). This can be understood in terms of the dialectical processes of *re-territorialisation* and *de-territorialisation*.

Re-territorialisation: water and 'the state' in Abdulhanon

The livelihoods of rural Tajiks have suffered at the hands of inequitable land reform and an exploitative cotton industry. As interventions are made through local authorities they serve to embolden forms of domination and exploitation. Zürcher finds particular cause for concern in the Rasht valley where, 'a rural elite that consists of an amalgam of former fighters, religious leaders and state officials has emerged' (2004: iv). This elite has captured land using informal control mechanisms and the distortion of internationally supported privatisation processes. In bringing material and symbolic resources to this context international actors are in specific ways facilitating such processes.

The example of the new water usage association (WUA) of Abdulhanon in the Rasht valley witnesses to the formal and informal re-territorialisation of livelihoods under the state, and how this process is resourced by international assistance.[45] WUAs are an increasingly important aspect of community development and local-level peacebuilding by the International Community. MSDSP and GTZ in the Abdulhanon area of Rasht valley followed a model similar to that found in GTZ interventions elsewhere as they established their pilot WUAs in 2005.[46] Their vision was for WUAs to serve as an NGO to lobby for the interests of community members against the state, and seek to redress some of the inequities of post-Soviet privatisation and land reform.[47] However, the WUA is in no sense independent of the informal and patriarchal governance of the community. Therefore conflicts over water are typically resolved by informal agreements between neighbours, and even villages, according to public principles of 'authority' and 'stability' and hidden practices of patronage and preference.[48] Much like in the case of other CBOs, the leadership of the community regards the WUA as a tool to undertake projects which require outside funding. For example, in Kalanak an aksakal described how they would meet in the choihona and decide who they would approach to solve their water problems, the Jamoat or, more often, the VO.[49]

What's interesting here is the specific way in which the state is supplanted by the international organisation in service provision, but in terms of political authority. WUA members do not expect the state to assist in the provision and maintenance of water systems, but they do require its permission. This is very much reflective of the post-conflict and post-Soviet agriculture of Tajikistan's mountain valleys. During the Soviet Union, the authorities pumped water up the hillside at considerable expense in order to irrigate the state farm. Today communities are criss-crossed by a dilapidated water infrastructure which has been ineffectual since the end of the Soviet Union – a powerful symbol of state economic weakness and public squalor. However, in another sense 'the state' is deemed essential to the management of livelihoods and the suppression of economic disputes. The role of local government is thus largely confined to watching over, approving and granting permission for the activities of both international organisations and subordinates. If water disputes escalate, authoritative figures linked to the state will intervene. According to one farmer, the aksakals can solve the problem and 'even kick this person out of the village'.[50] For example, the head of the sovkhoz (state farm) in Abdulhanon solved a dispute over the rights to pastureland between two villages by declaring it owned by the *sovkhoz* and whoever wanted to use it must pay rent.[51] Thus, re-territorialisation occurs as international economic resources are utilised by elites who personify or impersonate the state and thus have the political resources to veto subordinate and international actions.

'The state' here is again the legitimating idea for the re-territorialisation of political and economic space. The question of the registration of WUAs illustrates this role of the state-idea. While communities do not pay local government directly for the provision of water – and the government does nothing to provide it – members must pay a $US300 registration fee to the Ministry of Justice in Dushanbe in order legally to establish a WUA with the power to collect revenue. It is highly likely that 'additional payments' will be required to facilitate registration.[52] Hegemonic domination requires that WUAs become part of the elite/'state' if they are to acquire a proper place in water management. It is necessary to have official recognition to be accepted by local government, to demand compliance from community members and 'punish' those who do not pay. The head of an unregistered WUA in Shulonak noted:

> Now, I am the head, but not according to the law. Anyone in the village can reject me if we are not legally established.... In such a case we would have power to punish people who do not pay and even cut them off. If the association is voluntary they can just ignore us.[53]

Here 'the law' and 'the state' become the essential signifiers of 'authority'. Moreover, they are made more legitimate by international programmes as this move to official registration has been backed by GTZ's local partner in their attempts at developing 'civil society'. It is MSDSP practice to recommend that WUAs attain such status to achieve legal backing for their rules and procedures, and in order for them to undertake some of the functions of the Soviet-era water committee (*vodkhoz*).[54]

MSDSP is aware of some of these difficulties and claims to support WUAs only in areas where land reform is taking place.[55] However, reform has been extremely weak: territories are not privately owned, nor are they truly independently managed, as 'privatisation' has involved the leasing of land and the cut-price selling off of equipment to individuals who are connected to state-based elite networks (Porteous 2003; Zürcher 2004: 16–24; Gomart 2003: 62–63). Abdulhanon sovkhoz is a state-owned collective farm. In other areas a smaller, quasi-state collective *dekon* ('peasant') farm has been established, alongside several 'private' *dekon* farms (of several hectares each). Private *dekon* farm plots were sold off in a late 1990s land reform when few could afford land. These buyers had connections and influence. Thus, even private farmers manage rather than own their land and thus their degree of control varies according to local factors.[56] The elite impersonating 'the state' (the state-system) plays a largely opportunistic, rent-seeking role in terms of water management in the Rasht valley. Elite practices – strengthened by international programmes – act to re-territorialise Tajik livelihoods under 'the state'.

These findings confirm earlier research which has shown that there has been a demand for more state from farmers in the Rasht valley in the post-conflict period (Zürcher 2004: iii). But this demand needs unpacking. It is clear that WUAs feel they are unable to influence local government on water issues, or solve problems completely alone, without becoming part of the state itself. However, Humphrey's judgement of Soviet-era Siberian collective farms (kolkhoz), that 'the private is not as "private" as it may seem, nor is the "public" as public' (1998: 1), holds true for contemporary Tajikistan. Those who impersonate the state trade in 'manipulable resources' of products (including access to irrigation water and land) and money (ibid.: 435). Although these resources are greatly diminished, it is to be expected that both elites and subordinates would seek to ape a hierarchical and kinship-based model of the rural economy which, to a degree, 'worked' for both. As Humphrey notes with respect to post-Soviet Siberia, returning to the region twenty years after her original research, 'the collective often still acts as the substitute for the state, and where it does not, it is felt that it should do' (ibid.: 503). Similarly in Tajikistan, 'the state' is the essential public marker of a hegemonic process of re-territorialisation which unites local elites who might otherwise, as they did during the state breakdown of the early and mid-1990s, have fought for resources.

De-territorialisation: translocal migration

Of particular importance in the everyday economies of post-socialist spaces is the creation of new 'localities' which challenge territorial notions of community (Humphrey and Mandel 2002). Thus, one cannot fully comprehend re-territorialisation without grasping how Tajik livelihoods are undergoing de-territorialisation. This takes the form of labour migration which breaks the link between livelihoods and the land. It constitutes the re-location of livelihoods to the 'shadow' or 'hidden' spaces of the grey economy. There has been a huge rise in migration since the late 1990s to the extent that, between 2000 and 2003, 18 per cent of the adult population had been or were currently labour migrants (Olimova and Bosc 2003: 20). With demographics indicating that almost 50 per cent of the population is under eighteen, and the vast majority of migrants being male, this may mean that around a half of working (and, potentially, fighting) age men spent at least part of this time working overseas, largely in Russia.

Migration is an economic practice which is socially and discursively constituted. International and popular discourses affirm the importance of migration for work (*zarabotka*). It is a 'safety valve' which delays a return to civil war, according to international peacebuilders (Malekzade 2005: 7), and is simply a consequence of the lack of employment opportunities, in *tinji* (Rahmonova 2005: 7). However, migrants themselves are located on the margins of local spaces. Their transcripts often express a mixture of hope and lament, dissenting from the public transcript of harmony (see Chapter 4). In such a way, the practical realities of scratching out a living and avoiding domination practised by many Tajiks undermine the efforts of central authority to re-territorialise the economy, to discipline it to become a system which can be controlled by government and a wealthy network of elites. New, cross-border spaces are reproduced in everyday life through migration, shuttle-trading and other business links which provide connections, typically, between a Tajik village and a district of Moscow or Russian provincial city.

These new spaces of labour migration should be understood as *translocal* rather than transnational. Kaiser defines translocalism in terms of the linking of local spaces across borders that provides an alternative community to that provided by the territory and identity of the nation-state. He argues that,

> new nationalist endeavours have to coexist, if not compete, with the trans-border, translocal patterns of sociation. There are undeniable tensions: on the one hand, social reality contradicts the efforts at national separation, and on the other, the organisation of the national state is constantly influenced by (translocally structured) groups in the national state context that operate successfully across borders.
>
> (Kaiser 2003: 317)

He remarks that 'a common world beyond borders and differences is being created' which represents a 'removing of the spatial component from the social' (ibid.: 327, 315). However, I would argue that it represents not a 'despatialisation' but a de-territorialisation of identity. Identity is thus increasingly complex and differentiated – where multiple translocal spaces may constitute local, national and regional identities.

These translocal spaces are emergent. Despite the increased personal opportunities and challenges which labour migration offers, the practice is nevertheless governed by translocal authority structures extending from home village to destination workplace. Olimova and Bosc note that familial *avlod* structures determine who will migrate and when as it is these connections which provide a space to stay and work whilst in Russia. A foreman of a work brigade in Russia – a senior member of the *avlod* – may 'play the role' of head of the *avlod* in Russia and thus 'exercises undisputed authority over the brigade' (Olimova and Bosc 2003: 58). These discourses and networks have normalising effects. 'You know', one NGO worker in Sughd noted, 'people used to say that all the men are at the front fighting, now they say that all the men are "in town" (*v gorode*) – they mean Russia, but they say it as if it's just nearby' (Kurbonkhojayev 2005: 10). Labour migration is thus 'part of the normal life of society' and thus a product of ethnoregional solidarity (Olimova and Bosc 2003: 100, 58). However, what's interesting here is how labour migration discursively and spatially reproduces avoidance and apartness, from the state and from other regions, as opposed to the form of regionalism prevalent in the war which led to violent competition. By such social processes, regionalism in Tajikistan has been reconstituted in a non-violent and, to the extent that it has been translocalised, largely non-competitive manner. In this sense, processes of de-territorialisation are dialectically produced by re-territorialisation and are intrinsic to the Tajik peace.

The interdependence of territory and space

The consequences of the above analysis for legitimate order in Tajikistan need unpacking further. It is difficult to find either consent or resistance to this process of de-/re-territorialisation. Rather strategies of avoidance and accommodation are necessary for everyday economies. Both localised (re-territorialised) peasants and translocalised (de-territorialised) migrants remain preoccupied with survival strategies which accommodate the territorialising demands of the elite and avoid them through de-territorialising practices of migration. It is tempting to view these two sets of practices in dichotomous terms: that an individual is forced to choose between accommodating local hegemons or avoiding them and subjecting oneself to the forms of hegemony and exploitation constructed at state borders. However, as individuals whose potential choices are socially constituted by their situation in groups, peasants and migrants find that their role is determined relationally. A migrant's income-generating potential is strongly connected to his support from the relatives who finance the journey, provide accommodation and a first job. Moreover, the 'choice' to be a migrant is often out of the hands of young men and women; each *avlod* unit exists both in local and translocal spaces, and it is often its patriarchs who send migrants (Olimova and Bosc 2003: 58–61). Labour migration is thus a vital part of the Tajik peace. Moreover, if it were inhibited or prevented by the elite, this might jeopardise the precarious legitimacy which they have garnered. This is not to say that it is controlled by either family or state. In hidden translocal spaces migrants can undermine the family unit (by absconding) and elite hegemony (by acquiring capital extra-territorially).

The importance of practices of labour migration to the constitution of peace is increasingly acknowledged by international actors in Tajikistan who consequently attempt to reconcile and manage these economic processes through international programmes aimed at agricultural reform locally (often unsuccessfully, as shown above) and migration management transnationally and translocally. There is considerable consensus regarding the need to incorporate both a reformed agriculture and managed migration to facilitate Tajikistan's transition into the world economy

(EBRD 2005: 23–27; Porteous 2003; UNDP 2003: 60–61). Such programmes attempt to resolve the dialectic of re-/de-territorialisation generated by the Tajik peace. The IOM argues against official efforts to curtail the export of manpower and for a proactive government policy of assisting migrants through information provision, consular service and the introduction of a system of guarantees for money transfers of remittances (Olimova and Bosc 2003: 125). There is some evidence to suggest that the Tajikistani government is aware of the importance of labour migration and thus lobbies the Russian government on migrants behalf. Neo-liberal peacebuilding, however, would go further and suggest that such marketisation is natural and might lead to poverty alleviation locally as migrants can invest remittances in agriculture back home.

However, there are at least two problems with such thinking. First, the nature of hegemony and authority in Tajikistan precludes the realisation of a law-based free market. Research on the Rasht valley indicates that future distribution of land is likely to remain highly 'politicised' in that it depends on connections to local networks and on having the means to work through them (Zürcher 2004: 16–25). The wealthier rent a few hectares of land from the sovkhoz or collective *dekon* farm. All those who rent, 'own' or manage (in the case of the sovkhoz)[57] such 'irrigated' land must pay an expensive 'unified tax' of around 120 *somoni* (US$38) per hectare, per year.[58] Second, the International Community, whilst idealised as a cooperative and coordinated group of actors, in fact acts extremely inconsistently and competitively. Statebuilding can often undermine humanitarian projects. Anti-drugs projects and anti-terror initiatives advocate and fund a stiffening of defences against informal economic activity, and thus embolden elite-state actors who control borders and take a part in the illegal economy. Even humanitarian projects, as shown above, may be co-opted by local patrons. Under these dynamics of national and international hegemony it is difficult to see how de-territorialised migrants can become re-territorialised agricultural entrepreneurs. Today, the overwhelming majority of both migrants and peasants remain in poverty, maintaining a precarious existence where they are subject to exploitation and domination by elites within and beyond the borders of Tajikistan.

These conclusions have evident implications for 'peace' understood as legitimate order. In a relationship of landlords and peasants, Beetham notes, where the latter depend on the former, 'it is the failure to guarantee subsistence and the *means of livelihood* that is destructive to legitimacy, rather than the extent of any exactions made, since it infringes the basic interests that are presupposed in the relationship' (1991: 84). Scott, similarly argues that it is, 'when [a worsening balance of exchange] stretches existing subsistence patterns to breaking point, that we expect explosions of rage or anger' (1976: 177). Similarly, in Tajikistan, while many remain impoverished, across Tajikistan peasants testify that post-conflict order and increased opportunities for migration have improved their livelihoods. Livelihoods have emerged despite the oligarchic state. They have done so in terms of de-/re-territorialisation. Thus is a peace reliant on precarious sources of off-shore capital.

Conclusions

Some critical analyses of peacebuilding have argued that international interventions impose 'democracy' and the 'free market' on post-conflict politics, and then 'fake' their practical existence (Chandler 1999). This may be true in some cases, such as Bosnia, where international intervention has been more intrusive. In Tajikistan, it is the parallel existence of multiple orders of discourse which characterises peacebuilding. International discourses continue apart from local practice as they are affirmed through discursive mediation and the simulation of success in M&E. Moreover, via public and hidden transcripts of *tinji* and the translocal spaces of migration, subordinate actors avoid and accommodate both elite and international interventions. Yet in doing so, they relinquish the opportunity to shape their political environment. In Tsing's terms they reinforce their 'marginality'; they 'respond, reinterpret, and challenge even as they accept and are shaped by these forms of knowledge' (1993: 8). In the Central Asian context, Morgan Liu argues that international 'attempts to encourage "grassroots" initiatives may end up reinforcing such illiberal institutions as patriarchy and clientelism' (2003: 3–4). Community peacebuilding programmes then do not fail like 'oil on water' but themselves contribute to the remaking of hegemony and legitimacy in local spaces.

In such a way, as argued in this chapter, the simulation of 'community' has consequences for the re-/de-territorialising of livelihoods. As long as 'community development' still seems a plausible goal or endpoint, international assistance to local spaces in this form will keep coming. Such assistance creates momentary meeting points of international, elite and popular discourse through which legitimacy is remade. Whilst international peacebuilders have sought to form new groups and introduce new norms, in practice their interventions have served to re-form pre-existing institutions, renew evolving local norms and perform the power of hegemonic local elites. As statespeople have sought to increase central control over local governments using administrative resources, donor interventions have facilitated this by providing the resources for greater material interaction between elites and subordinates. Together they have recrafted local political space, reinforced patriarchal rule and legitimated a new elite. To consider the complex properties of livelihoods, sovereignty and authority, in their global and local and public and hidden aspects, is to look radically at what 'peace' means in a post-conflict environment.

8 Conclusions

Politics, economics and global structures have become so inauthentic that few of us truly believe in them. We live in this paradox: the things most omnipresent that govern our lives are the very things from which we feel distant. We hold fast to myths that what we have created to govern our lives is responsive to whom we are as human beings and to our communities. Yet at the same time these creations seem to have lives of their own independent of us, foreign to us, and distant from us. An inquiry that seeks to understand how cycles of violence can be broken and transcended is precisely one that must infuse politics, political discourse and governing structures with a capacity for responsiveness to our human community.

(Lederach 2005: 28–29)

Official elite accounts of Tajikistan's peace seek to present a government which is not just legitimate, but predestined to determine national progress (Fatoev 2001: 104). International discourses, by contrast, increasingly losing hope in Tajikistan, present a government which is 'weak', illegitimate and maintained largely by the 'war weariness' of the population. In this vein one long-term observer of Tajikistan argued at the beginning of this decade that the regime would remain illegitimate until certain substantive and procedural sources had been established.

Until a full range of political parties can operate legally and unhindered in Tajikistan, until there are free and fair elections for the legislature and the presidency, and until those in power use that power to improve the standard of living for most of the inhabitants, neither [the President] nor his rivals will be able to claim political legitimacy.

(Atkin 2001: 111)

Yet, as this book has attempted to show, a legitimate authoritarian order has emerged over the 2000s without the democratic transformation described above, nor necessarily any objective procedural or institutional basis. This is not to say that material and institutional dimensions are not important but that they are made meaningful in terms of the representations, performances and simulacra of the discursive environment. Order has emerged because it has been deemed legitimate by an International Community ready to tolerate retrenchment whilst representing it as progress, by an opposition which is unable to find political space for alternative discourse, and by a people who lack hope of an alternative and thus resign to the status quo. This order is not coercive but is weakly and contingently legitimate.

The puzzle of peacebuilding without democratic transformation with which we started is not a paradox if we avoid the temptation to discipline peace to a single strategy, account, representation or even a single logic of simulation. It can at times appear that the public transcript of the power-holders is being endorsed without reservation or re-presentation. Indeed, it can appear to subordinates and internationals that their understandings too are being validated by events. However, this book has refuted such a univocal and unequivocal story. Tajikistan's peace is neither an objective condition of order, nor the subjective self-image of an elite which imagines itself as the bastion of 'authority' and 'stability'. Rather, it is built on an intersubjective process of complex legitimacy. This process produces hybrid forms where order is never total, and multiple transcripts and diverse practices constitute a complex peace. The post-conflict order is legitimate but its legitimacy is differentiated – it emerges from the contrasting public and hidden discursive practices of elites, subordinates and internationals. Its properties of authority, sovereignty and livelihoods do not derive directly from one hegemonic discourse, much less an all-power actor, but are constituted via intertextual relations and discursive mediation. This has produced something variously called 'peace' which we can understand as the emergence of legitimate political order

The case of Tajikistan has implications for how we understand international development interventions across Central Asia and post-conflict peacebuilding more broadly. Here I speak primarily to the policy-oriented field of peace research which, as Lederach (2005) and others (Jutila *et al.* 2008) have claimed, is in critical need of renewal. This book does not afford the space to situate my findings within broader comparative and theoretical contexts. In lieu of this, I consider below some possible objections and qualifications to my reinterpretation of the international peacebuilding in Tajikistan and clarify the contributions of this book to conceptual debates in peacebuilding scholarship.

Tajikistan's peacebuilding: objections and qualifications

In this book I have argued that the ascriptions and prescriptions of international post-conflict peacebuilding posit a representation of Tajikistan which is refuted by the messy cases of peacebuilding. From this point I could have dismissed peacebuilding as mere normative theory (*the ought*) and picked out better tools of analysis (*the is*). Yet interests are never entirely free of ideals, and vice versa. Peacebuilding must be analysed discursively (as relatively stable, ideologically informed formations by which communities interpret the world), politically (how power is acquired, legitimated, deployed and challenged in these discursively constituted communities) and spatially (how power and authority are differentiated across different scales and sites). These three principles of analysis drove this investigation of the historical and discursive emergence of international, elite and subordinate orders of peacebuilding in Tajikistan (Chapters 2–4). I then furthered this argument through detailed contextualised discussion of the dynamics of discourse and practice in the politics of peacebuilding in this emergent order (Chapters 5–7). I argued that legitimate order (peace) emerges intertextually, inter-spatially and politically in properties of authority, sovereignty and livelihoods.

As these examples have shown, international peacebuilding in Tajikistan has cushioned the blow of poverty for many, trained thousands of Tajiks in new skills, transferred millions of dollars of equipment and infrastructure to the regime and local communities, and provided fleeting glimpses of a more open society. It has also been complicit in the development of authoritarian governance over democracy, the simulation of state sovereignty rather than popular sovereignty, and the growth of economic networks of exploitation as opposed to broad-based rural development. In this sense its successes are perhaps overshadowed by its failures. However, the categories of 'success' and 'failure', commonly deployed by practitioners and analysts alike, provide a woefully inadequate framework through which to make political sense of international assistance. Peacebuilding may do more symbolically and materially for the builders than it does for the recipients; it legitimates international intervention into new fields of operation and justifies the burgeoning global political economy of international development. Moreover, most of its contribution to the local context – in supporting the reformation of authoritarian governance – is indirect and inadvertent.

This critical approach to peacebuilding is likely to face objections from those pragmatists and reformers who eschew radical critiques in favour of incremental reform and 'lessons learned'. Whilst these representations are challenged in hidden sites and moments, the weakness of public dissent serves to reproduce peacebuilding in the International Community – a thin representation of reality but a very real influence on donor decisions and practices. In the following paragraphs I will consider some of the objections to my argument that might emanate from scholars and practitioners in peace studies.

One standard refrain from practitioners is that we are merely at the beginning of a long-term process of democratisation and the limited 'progress' which can be seen represents a 'first step'. The idea of a 'first step' is based upon illusory teleological notions of progressive enlightenment found in liberal peacebuilding discourse. If this point seems overly abstract, let us put it more plainly: there's only very partial and fragmentary evidence in the specific case of Tajikistan to support the idea that it is going in this 'direction'. One variation on the 'first steps' argument contends that if peacebuilders had committed more money and resources to Tajikistan, and if the International Community had been more united in its approach, the country's reform might take place more quickly and more substantively. A former deputy head of UNTOP, Jan Malekzade, argues credibly that resource deficiencies undermined UNTOP and international peace-building as a whole, remarking that intervention was insufficiently 'comprehensive' (Malekzade 2005: 3). The relative lack of resources for peacebuilding in Tajikistan is not an unimportant consideration. But the bigger point here relates to the formal, technocratic and external nature of international peacebuilding interventions, however well resourced. 'First steps', when placed in a broad political context, as I have attempted to do here, can be seen to be mere simulacra of liberal peacebuilding. 'Formal order', Scott reminds us, 'is always and to some considerable degree parasitic on informal processes, which the formal scheme does not recognise, without which it could not exist, and which it alone cannot create or maintain' (1998: 310).

A second and more serious objection may relate to the post-positivist methodological approach adopted in this study. In short, the correlations that I have described do not provide a causal explanation. That was by design. But there are indeed weaknesses to my methodology and things I have been simply unable or unprepared to do. Had I been able to live in the country for several years and develop the language better, I may have had access to a hidden world of radical discourses which reveal a militant and [ripe] Islamic 'threat' to the state, which some claim (Karagiannis 2006) but I consider overblown. Moreover, while migration and drug-trafficking, in particular, seem to be dynamics potentially corrosive to public transcripts of central authority, state sovereignty and territorial livelihoods, I was unable to undertake substantial original research in these areas. One of these factors may be overwhelmingly important in constructing legitimate order, or undermining it. If, we might wonder counterfactually, Tajikistan's borders were 'sealed' – although it is difficult to imagine the circumstances under which this would be possible – the whole symbolic and material order of authority, sovereignty and livelihoods might quickly transform. It is one of the key conclusions of this study that Tajikistan's peace and polity are constituted across multiple scales, including translocal spaces of labour migration.

A final caveat placed on this analysis by many may be whether such weak legitimacy is sustainable, and if not whether it counts as legitimacy at all. The Tajik political analyst Abdullaev, for example, provides a plausible portrayal of why peace will not hold:

> Born in crisis and chaos, the current system assimilated deep seated traditional political loyalties, Soviet standards and recent rational-legal requirements. Beyond the façade of Western patterned legal arrangements in Tajikistan hides a remarkable blend of secular and traditional features that can poorly connect civil and political society, promote the perceived interests of individuals and different solidarity groups. Quasi-democratic rule is being built on a highly fragmented society with yet declared, but unabled [sic.] protection of civil liberties. This foundation feeds growing violence, and corruption in society and government.
>
> (2004: 8)

These concerns are important. I have argued that while legitimate order has emerged in Tajikistan, this order is contingent and differentiated. Tajiks resign to authoritarian government not because they value it but because there are no plausible alternatives. Some analysts speculate that as the new generation which does not remember the war grows up, they will be less 'war weary', less bound to what I call *tinji* discourse. Moreover, the country is dependent on international assistance and, should that be withdrawn, social and political order would break down.

However, if new violent political conflict were to come to Tajikistan it is highly likely that this would centre on a different range of issues and be drawn along different lines. At the time of completing this manuscript (September 2008), Tajikistan had recently experienced a horrific winter of extreme cold and high fuel prices, followed by a summer of higher food prices, and was expecting yet another winter of deprivation ahead. There is much anecdotal evidence that the desperate humanitarian situation for the poor is leading to rising discontent. In the spring and summer of 2008 there were a number of small public protests in the country. What's interesting for this analysis is that these protests apparently focus on issues of livelihoods and contemporary governance rather than the ideological and inter-regional questions which animated the conflict before the civil war. This is the post-colonial and post-conflict context of Tajikistan today. The contentions of contemporary Tajikistan are quite different to those of fifteen to twenty years ago. That being said, subordinate discourses contain powerful ethical, spatial and temporal markers which mitigate against future violence. These discourses and their associated practices seem to be relatively stable for the time being, yet they are not static and over time they will transform according to the wider political conditions which sustain them. The shift from a military conflict to political order, which began in 1993 and went through significant moments of crystallisation between 1996 and 2000, has matured from 2000 to 2007. But it has neither been linear nor consistent. It is a contingent process of the differentiated legitimation of power and the recreation of authority, livelihoods and sovereignty.

Emergent and legitimate order: Tajikistan's contribution to theory

This study of a particular Central Asian case has strayed into epistemological and disciplinary terrain unfamiliar to conflict studies in order to develop a new approach to thinking about post-conflict peace(building). David Beetham's reading of legitimacy as an intersubjective and emergent order provided the inspiration for this approach to peacebuilding. Inspired by Scott's public and hidden transcripts, I became increasingly sensitive to the irresolvable ambiguities and contingencies of Tajikistan's discursively constituted legitimate order. In investigating the Tajik case in some depth, I sought not just to apply the concepts of Beetham and Scott but to develop an understanding of peacebuilding in terms of its emergent processes and properties. Specifically, I have drawn attention to (i) dialectical and productive *processes* and, (ii) constitutive *properties* of building peace. Peace can be understood as legitimacy in terms of the re-/de-centring of authority (Chapter 5), the di/simulation of sovereignty (Chapter 6), and the re-/de-territorialisation of livelihoods (Chapter 7). The identification of these processes and properties is an attempt to answer the two conceptual puzzles that inspired this research.

The first of these puzzles concerned the impact of international peacebuilding, its failure (to meet its ostensible objectives) and its wider functions. International interventions, such as those described in Chapters 5 to 7, do not directly determine the processes taking place in post-conflict societies but rather are one dynamic of the emergence of legitimate order. Simulated 'elections' and an 'opposition', 'border management' and 'community self-government' feign the existence of a sovereign and democratising state to the International Community. In Tajikistan, where the international peacebuilding resources deployed were very modest, they seemingly play a secondary factor in that emergence. Yet, it is a mug's game to quantify the relative importance of the global, national and local scales. International intervention is important however much material assistance is dispersed, but can only be understood in the interdependent terms of the bigger picture. In Tajikistan's case, there would not be the particular extent and form of labour migration without the exploitation of land and water by a small elite, which in turn would not have occurred to the same extent without international assistance for community development and, earlier, privatisation. Tajikistan would not have corruption the way it is today without simulated sovereignty and internationally assisted border management. It would not have the particular de-centred patronage system which it has today without the dominant conception of 'authority' that exists in Tajik politics or without internationally supported 'political parties' and 'elections'. In the chapters above, I explicitly linked political party building and election monitoring to the authority, community development to livelihoods, and SSR to sovereignty. Yet, in practice, the processes associated with all three properties shape and reshape all international interventions, and vice versa (Table 8.1). This study makes a modest empirical contribution to a growing body of scholarship on post-conflict interventions which gets beyond the shackles of the 'third party' assumption (Chandler 1999, Richmond 2005, 2006; MacGinty 2006; Nordstrom 2004; Debrix 1999; Hansen 2006).

The second puzzle which I faced was the nature of this illiberal peace which is typically dismissed as negative in peace research. Part of the purpose of this thesis is to challenge the dichotomous portrayal of peace as *either* positive *or* negative. Whilst this neat division may be normatively appealing it does not get us very far in understanding the very messy nature of actually existing 'peace'. Tajikistan may be one of the most stable and legitimate post-conflict spaces found anywhere in the world today. Yet this is not much of a claim. In cases where large-scale physical violence has been vastly reduced, yet structural and cultural violence continues, some form of order has emerged. Yet negative peace over the longer term is never just 'peace as order'. Rather it requires that authorities are being legitimated. Peace as legitimacy entails the quantitative reduction of physical violence, and qualitative shifts in cultural and structural violence. It

Table 8.1 The emergence of legitimate order in Tajikistan

Elements[1] and dimensions[2] of international peacebuilding	Properties of peace (legitimate order)	Public processes of peacebuilding	Hidden processes of peacebuilding
Representation *Political*	**Authority**	**Re-centred** by public discourses and practices of state authority	**De-centred** by hidden discourses and practices of clientelism
Security *Military*	**Sovereignty**	**Simulated** by public discourses and practices representing a single sovereign state as security guarantor	**Dissimulated** by hidden discourses and practices denying a single sovereign state as security guarantor
Welfare *Economic and Psycho-Social*	**Livelihoods**	**Re-territorialised** by public discourses and practices of land reform and privatisation	**De-territorialised** by hidden discourses and practices of labour migration

Notes
1 Schwarz 2005.
2 Ball 1996.

involves the reconstitution of authority, sovereignty and livelihoods yet it is never completed and the form it takes varies from case to case.

Finally, as a post-Soviet Central Asian case, Tajikistan contributes to post-conflict theory in demanding that the post-conflict be evaluated in light of the post-colonial (see Adams 2008). The emergent discourses and practices of legitimate order are laden with tropes, literary references and vital questions emanating from the Soviet era. The changing relationship between Tajikistan and Russia, however much the dependency on the former colonial power has been reduced, must also be seen in this light. Western NGOs and foreign diplomats at times deploy sovietological readings of Central Asia which originated in the Cold War era. Furthermore in their extant hopes for transition they remain embedded in a discourse of post-colonial progress. Equally, elites and subordinates derive many of their contemporary markers from reference points originating in the Soviet era. Most of all, it is in the hybridity of post-conflict spaces such as Tajikistan that their post-colonial character comes to the fore. These questions of the post-coloniality of peacebuilding must however be left for another study.

Final remarks

It has been argued that understanding peace in terms of the emergence of legitimate order sheds light on Tajikistan's international peacebuilding and its so-called 'negative peace'. To dismiss Tajikistan's peace as negative is on the one hand laudable but on the other it is a political and ethical defeat. Not only does it risk making peace studies irrelevant to the kind of peace we get in practice but it alludes to a privileging of 'us' (our idealised self-image as third-party peacemakers) over 'them' (to whose ideals and interests we pay lip-service but often don't really accept or even comprehend).

Studying and practising peace thus requires a critical orientation, as well as a commitment to a value (peace, justice, love). There is a moral imperative to retain the practice of building peace alongside the study of building peace. Amidst the distortions and deceptions of peacebuilding discourse, emancipative peacebuilding practice must begin with a critique of the status quo of international peacebuilding. This project is situated in that broader quest to challenge the forms of domination which elite and international discourses and popular accommodations to them together reproduce. The results of international peacebuilding are an increasingly familiar mix of 'community development' with corruption and patriarchy, 'multiparty elections' and authoritarian government, and 'border management' accompanied by state violence. These representations of 'peace' and practices of violence are related. In other words, legitimate order has emerged in Tajikistan *neither* despite peacebuilding *nor* because of it. Both of these alternatives imply a causal relationship where an identifiable set of factors can be said to have caused peace. Searching for the causes of peace is fanciful. Discovering its constituent properties is a potentially more fruitful and long-standing line of academic inquiry.

Thus, this book ends with a call to humility on the part of those of us who in some small form represent the International Community. As the events of 2008 in Afghanistan, Georgia, Tajikistan and countless other cases of peacekeeping and peacebuilding show, the International Community is highly reliant on *others* in its ability to support livelihoods, rebuild authority and reconstitute sovereignty, let alone achieve the fantastic goals of peace operations. Failing to grasp the limitations of discourse, politics and space, we *ourselves* are often seduced by flattering self-images and think of local dynamics as mere responses to our actions. This book has sought to expose the reductions, seductions and deceptions of elite and international discourses, and how such discourses are affirmed and resisted in practice. The better we comprehend how international peacebuilding is grounded in contemporary global and local order, the better we can imagine the limits of international intervention and the prospects for alternative ways of peace.

Appendix

Press sources

Asia-Plus Blitz [APB], electronic archive, Dushanbe, 1998–2004.

Asia-Plus newspaper, various issues, Dushanbe, 2004–2005, in Russian.

Eurasianet, Daily News, web-based archive, www.eurasianet.org/resource/tajikistan/hypermail/news/index.shtml, 2000–2005.

Institute for War and Peace Reporting, Reporting Central Asia [IWPR, RCA], by email, www.iwpr.net/, 2000–2006.

Jumhurriyat (The Republic), sampled newspapers, Dushanbe, 2000–2005, in Tajik [transl. Otabek Sindarov].

Radio Free Europe/Radio Liberty, Central Asia Report [RFE/RL, CAR], by email, http://rfe.rferl.org/reports/centralasia/, 2000–2005.

Radio Free Europe/Radio Liberty, Newsline, [RFE/RL, Newsline], by email, www.rferl.org/newsline/, 2003–2006.

UN *Integrated Regional Information Network* [IRIN], available at www.irinnews.org, 2000–2005.

Vecherni Dushnabe (Evening Dushnabe), various issues, 2004–2005, in Russian.

Glossary

Aksakal	lit. 'white beard', term used for village chief or elder
Avlod	patriarchal extended family
avtoritet	'authority'
brigadir	foreman, brigade-leader of collective farm
choihona	lit. 'teahouse', often also functions as a mosque and community centre in Tajik villages
dekon	peasant, farmer
edinstvo	'unity'
goschinovnik	'state servant', civil servant
gosstruktura	'state structures', state administration
khashar	communal labour
Hizb-ut Tahrir	Party of Liberation
Khukumat	Executive organ, local administration of district or province
khukumati rais	head of the local administration
Jamoat	first level of local administration, literally 'community'
jangsollor	'commanders', 'warlords'
kishlak	village, settlement
kolkhoz	collective farm, originating in the Soviet era
kommandiri	'commanders', used to refer to the military commanders of the civil war period
kompromat	'compromising materials', material held against another person for purposes of blackmail
krisha	lit. 'roof', used to denote cover or protection against punishment
mahalgera'y	'regionalism', in Tajiki; *mestnichestvo* in Russian
mahalla	neighbourhood
mahallinski komitet	neighbourhood committee of elders and other community leaders
Majlisi Oli	Tajikistan's parliament
mirostroitelstvo	'peacebuilding' (used to denote an elite discourse of peacebuilding)
mirotvorchestvo	peacekeeping

mullo	mullah, clergyman or graduate of *madrassa*, usually head of mosque
nomenklatura	the soviet-era elite
oblast	'province', in Russian; in Tajiki *veloyat*
pluralizm	'pluralism'
rais	'head', 'boss'
raiyon	administrative district, in Russian; in Tajiki *nohiya*
raznoglasiye	'discord'
tinji	'peacefulness'/'wellness' (used to denote a popular discourse of peacebuilding)
sovkhoz	state farm
splochonnost	'cohesion'
spokoystvo	'peacefulness', 'calmness'
stabilnost	'stability'
vlast	'power', 'government'
zastava	border command post

Notes

1 Introduction

1 President Rahmon was known by his russified surname Rahmonov until 2007 when he announced he would drop the suffix. He will be referred to throughout as Rahmon.
2 I will continue to use 'international peacebuilding' without quotes to denote international *discourse* and ideal-type models. I will continue to use 'peacebuilding' without quotes to indicate the *process* of bringing order and ending violence as a product of contending discourse and practices.
3 In fact, Galtung explicitly stated he wished to avoid a preference of positive over negative peace, or vice versa, noting that '*both* values, *both* goals are significant, and it is probably a disservice to man to try, in an abstract way, to say that one is more important than the other' (1969: 185).
4 Beetham is thus led to suggest that Weber's equating of legitimacy to belief is 'almost an unqualified disaster' for the social sciences (1991: 8). Barker argues that this failure is Weberian (made by his intellectual followers) rather than Weber's (Barker 2001: 17–19).
5 A decision was made to avoid the strategy of analysis via *LexisNexis*. Such search engines can be useful but tend to over-represent the Moscow and English-language presses and audiences. These are important ones for Tajikistani elites but they are by no means the only ones.
6 I continue to use 'Tajik' as shorthand for Tajikistani stateness and citizenship except in cases where clear reference is being made to ethnic Tajiks.

2 War and peace in post-Soviet Central Asia

1 The lack of histories of the conflict and war within Tajikistan is particularly marked. One multi-volume study provides a 'chronicle of events' of the war in Russian and is inaccessible to the vast majority of Tajiks (Nazriev and Sattorov 2005).
2 See in particular the works of Akiner (2001), Atkin (1997, 2001), Dudoignan (1998), Jawad and Tadjbaksh (1995), Mullojanov (2001a), Nourzhanov (2005) and Rubin (1998).
3 See Kosachi (1995: 125–130) for an overview of the different ideological positions of the parties.
4 *Rastokhez* was founded by Tohir Abdujabbor from Asht in Leninabad province and the DPT by Shodmon Yusuf from Darvaz in Gorno-Badakhshon.
5 This dichotomy is a simplification. Mullojanov distinguishes four basic groups of Islamic clergy in Tajikistan including Sufis of the Naqshbandi order and anti-establishment figures who had been students of Domla Hindustani. It was these latter members of the clergy who formed the IRP (Mullojanov 2001b: 226–228).

6 A widely quoted yet clearly questionable figure is that 97 per cent of people across the Central Asian republics voted for the continuation of the USSR (Soucek 2000: 262).
7 Khudonazarov was, by most accounts, a genuine reformer of the late Soviet period who had sided with Andrei Sakaharov in the Soviet Congress of People's Deputies. Atkin (1997: 287) compares him to Kyrgyzstan's Askar Akayev.
8 Safarov was convicted of offences including vehicular homicide and attempted murder and spent 23 years in jail (Atkin 2001: 102).
9 'Governmental' rather than 'state' breakdown is used to capture the removal of one regime without its replacement by another. 'State breakdown' is also a relevant description but this occurred over a much longer period beginning, at least, from the very recognition of independent statehood. See also Markowitz (2005, ch. 4).
10 Rahmon is from the same mahalla in Danghara as Safarov. He rose from being director of a sovkhoz to Chairman of the Kulob Soviet and governor of the province in October 1992, after the previous incumbent in the post was killed by Safarov on 28 October (Atkin 2001: 102; Nourzhanov 2005: 117).
11 The Rasht valley, including the town of Karategin (now Gharm), became a case in itself of the complexity of the Tajik conflict. As 'Gharmi' commanders relocated their troops to the valley, they were often greeted with suspicion by local inhabitants. Local Gharmis – seen as harbouring the opposition forces – became subject to incursions and abuses by government forces including the bombing and shelling of the valley, the laying of landmines, the destruction of homes and the mass rape of women. They organised self-defence forces which gathered in the mountains to resist these incursions. As discussed below, it was not until the early 2000s that the government began properly to retake control of the region. Personal communications with residents of the Rasht valley, 2003–2005.
12 For a comprehensive review see the edited volume of Barnes and Abdullaev (2001).
13 UNMOT's mandate was renewed successively until the winding up of the mission in April 2000 and its replacement by UNTOP.
14 The Russian government made several unsuccessful attempts to have that force recognised by the UN. Lynch argues that, having become an active party to the conflict, their involvement had 'nothing in common with traditional or contemporary international practice' (1999: 171).
15 Almost all participants in post-conflict dialogues consistently refer to the peace accords as the benchmark for compromise (Seifert and Kraikemayer 2003).
16 In 2006, following the Presidential elections, the last remaining senior former oppositionist, Mirzo Ziyoev, was removed from his post as Minister of Emergency Situations.

3 International peacebuilding in Tajikistan

1 I will continue to capitalise International Community to denote the identity group of international peacebuilders.
2 IRIN, 27 November 2002, accessed: 22 May 2004.
3 Eurasianet, 'US envoy calls for changes to Tajik laws on election, media', Dushanbe, in Russian 0830 gmt, 3 March 2004.
4 Interview, Abubakr Inomov, Ministry of Justice, 27 June 2007. This estimate is broadly supported by well placed figures in the NGO sector. Atabaeva reckons that of 450 NGOs registered in Khujand about 100 are still functioning to some degree. Saidaliev estimates that of around 100 working in the 'Kulob zone' of Hatlon around 50 per cent are inactive and 80 per cent are unsustainable. Interviews: Diloram Atabaeva, Khujand, 28 June 2007; Dodorbek Saidaliev, Kulob, 2 July 2007.
5 Interview, Diloram Atabaeva, Khujand, 28 June 2007.
6 Interview, Yusuf Kurbonkhojayev, Executive Director, Public Association 'Ittifok', Khujand, 22 June 2005; Interview, Diloram Atabaeva, CSSC, Khujand, 28 June 2007.

7 Working with and for international NGOs between 2003 and 2007, I was relayed confidentially numerous accounts of corruption involving major local and international NGOs and UN agencies including project-based corruption within or between international and local NGOs, where expenditures are forged or tenders won on the basis of informal payments. More systematically, the local NGO may have to pay staff of the international NGO a certain proportion of the total budget they receive for the programme.

8 Under a 2007 law on public associations, all NGOs were expected to re-register by the end of the year, and face tighter *de jure* controls on their work. The Tajikistani Ministry of Justice (MJ) expected a significant contraction in the size of the sector from 3,000 to an estimated 600, with fewer than that constituting sustainable organisations. Interview, Abubakr Inomov, Ministry of Justice, 27 June 2007.

9 Interview, international programme coordinator A, Khujand, July 2004.

10 Interview, international programme coordinator B, Khujand, July 2004.

11 Interview, international official, Kulob, June 2005.

12 Whilst UNTOP left a number of projects to be finished off, many in the International Community felt that the office could have been wound up at least two years previously. Around 60 per cent of its US$900,000 budget for 2007, already somewhat reduced from previous years, remained to be expended on projects. Interviews with international officials, June–July 2007, Dushanbe.

13 Interview, Vladimir Sotirov, 22 June 2007.

4 Elite and subordinate discourses of peace

1 Cited in IWPR, RCA, #347, 8 February 2005.

2 The 'ruling class', for Harris (2004: 35), are mature males.

3 APB #742, 27 April 2001.

4 APB #1223, 7 April 2003.

5 It is used also to indicate the girth of a man of some rotundity.

6 APB, #903, 20 December 2001; #1067, 20 August 2002.

7 (Tajik: '*hudshinosi pastu, ehtirom baland*'; Russian: '*nizkoye samosoznaniye, visokoye uvazheniye*'). This phrase communicates a stereotype but one which has purchase in contemporary Tajikistan. See UNTOP/NAPST (2002a: 26).

8 Donish was a Jadidist, part of a group of Muslim cultural reformers who were typically condemned as bourgeoise in early Soviet discourse. However, after the death of Stalin, Donish was rediscovered as an enlightener (*prosvetiteli*) and early proponent of 'democracy'. See the discussions of Donish in Rakowska-Harmstone (1970: 239–240) and Harris (2004: 136–137).

9 These features are discussed in joint work with the Tajik political scientist Parviz Mullojanov (Heathershaw and Mullojanov 2007).

10 The Somonid-controlled region centred on Bukhara and included much of current Uzbekistan and Afghanistan. It peaked in size in the ninth century. See Soucek (2000: 73–76).

11 'Tajik president addresses joint parliament session: full version', Tajik Radio first programme, Dushanbe, in Tajik, 0525 gmt, 27 April 2000.

12 The communities selected were Navbuned and Tojikokjar (in Asht raiyon) with Koshonar, Margedar and Novabad (all in Panjakent).

13 That he was the head of the OSCE in Tajikistan between 1995 and 1997 illustrates something of the limits of peacebuilding discourse (Roy 2000).

14 *Spokoystvo* (peace/calmness) was used more than the formal and far-reaching *mir* (peace); equally *raznogalsiye* (discord) was more often deployed than the neologism *konflikt* (conflict) which was frequently used by international officers when they spoke in Russian with locals.

15 Interview, mahalla head, Koshenar, 26 June 2005.

16 Interview, aksakal, Margedar, 27 June 2005.
17 This was an interesting departure from the discourse of the international programme managers which is extremely important to questions of the politics of peacebuilding and will be returned to in Chapter 6.
18 Group interview, CIG, Koshenar, 26 June 2005.
19 Sometimes the term *mahallinski komitet* (community committee) is used to denote the leadership of the community, at other times simply *raisi mahalla* or *raisi kishlok* (head of the community or head of the village).
20 Group interview, community action group (CAG), Komsomol, 15 April 2005.
21 Ibid.
22 Group interview, CIG, Margedar, 27 June 2005.
23 We later discovered that the three political parties represented in the village are the President's own National Democratic Party of Tajikistan, as well as the Communist Party of Tajikistan and the Socialist Party of Tajikistan – neither of which are effectively oppositional.
24 The distinction between state-idea and state-system is a classical one made by Abrams (1977) and adopted by Migdal in his definition: '(1) *the image of a coherent, controlling organisation in a territory, which is a representation of the people bounded by that territory*, and (2) *the actual practices of its multiple parts*'. (2001: 17–18).
25 Street interviews, Panjakent and Asht raiyons, June 2005.
26 Interview with villager, Sharinav, 11 August 2005.
27 Street interviews, Sharituz, June 2005.
28 It is in policy-analytical accounts where the threat of extremist Islam is emphasised, although often without a great deal of empirical evidence (Crosston 2007).
29 For a discussion of Žižek and Sloterdijk's reworking of Marx's formula for ideology, see Myers (2003: 63–77).

5 Democracy and authority

1 This group included most parties who were not formally part of the UTO nor strongly linked to the government: Party of Political and Economic Revival (suspended in April 1999), *Jumbish* – National Movement of Tajikstan (denied registration, April 1999), *Ittikhod* – Civil Patriotic Party of Tajikistan Unity (banned, April 1999), Agrarian Party (suspended in April 1999, banned in September 1999), Party of Justice and Progress (registration cancelled, September 1999), Democratic Party/Tehran Platform (deregistered, November 1999, due to having a name similar to another party). See OSCE 2000: 3–4.
2 Parliament consists of an upper house, the National Assembly (*Majlisi Milli*), and a lower house, the Assembly of Representatives (*Majlisi Namoyandagon*). The upper house is composed of eight presidential appointees and twenty five elected by secret voting in each of the four oblast assemblies and the Dushanbe city assembly. The lower house is elected on a mixed system with forty-one single-mandate seats elected by a simple majority system and twenty-two proportionally elected party seats with a 5 per cent threshold.
3 It is widely assumed by Tajikistani political analysts that the deal further guaranteed some representation in parliament for the IRPT in return for acquiescence to the results of the presidential elections.
4 For most of the campaign there was only one candidate. Two of the three opposition party candidates – Saifiddin Turaev and Sulton Quvvatov from the Democratic Party (Tehran platform) – were denied registration by the Supreme Court. Davlat Usmon from the Islamic Renaissance Party was granted last minute registration, allowing him very little time to launch a campaign.
5 A good overview of the development of political parties during the war and peace process can be found in Olimova (2004).

6 Interview, Kadirah Jurayev, Deputy Head, PDPT, Gharm, 11 August 2005.

7 APB #1218, 31 March 2003.

8 IWPR #433, 4 February 2006.

9 The registration of a presidential candidate requires the collection of 100,000 signatures.

10 *Adolathoh* emanated from the Northern district of Konibodom in 1995. After its unsuccessful moving of Turaev's candidature against Rahmon, its registration was suspended in February 2001 and banned in August 2001, ostensibly due to 'administrative violations'. APB #787, 4 July 2001; #811, 7 August 2001.

11 *Jumhuriyat*, 20 August 2004.

12 The following material is based on a narrative of the progress of this attempt recounted to me by a senior OSCE official in Dushanbe, July 2004.

13 APB #1222, 4 April 2003.

14 Eurasianet, 'US envoy calls for changes to Tajik laws on election, media', Dushanbe, in Russian 0830 gmt, 3 March 2004.

15 APB #944, 19 February 2002.

16 Interview, Stephanie Wheeler, IREX, Dushanbe, 23 February 2005.

17 Ibid.

18 Ibid.

19 Ibid.

20 The International Community provided around $US3 million in assistance prior to the elections. Grants were distributed to the CCER to train officials ($0.125 million), to political parties to train and facilitate polling observation ($0.88 million), to NGOs for civic and voter education ($0.61 million), and for media training ($0.31 million). The major donor was the US government with the State Department providing 1.1 million directly and another 0.5 million funnelled through USAID-contracting NGOs: IFES, IREX and NDI. A further $US900,000 was provided by the OSCE and its member states in in-kind assistance for the monitoring of elections. See UNTOP (2004).

21 Power was further consolidated with the PDPT of President Rahmon (who won fifty-two seats compared with thirty-six in 2000) with a decline in the number of 'independent' (from ten to five) and CPT deputies (from thirteen to four). The IRPT again achieved two seats on the party list with a slightly increased proportion of the vote (8.9 per cent compared with 7.3 per cent in 2000). See OSCE (2005g).

22 Whilst each opposition party was allowed thirty minutes free TV airtime under the 2004 amendments to the election law, state TV refused to air a number of paid advertisements by opposition parties and censored or altered some opposition party broadcasts (OSCE 2005g: 13–14).

23 Reported directly to author by DPT in Dushanbe and CPT in Gharm.

24 RFE/RL, CAR, Vol. 5, No. 6, 16 February 2005.

25 Personal observation, 20 February 2005.

26 The electoral district was one of the largest. In winter it is almost impossible to travel on side roads. We met groups who had taken twenty-four hours to travel from Jirgital to Rasht, about half the length of the district.

27 Personal communications, 27 February 2005.

28 Personal communication, 3 March 2005.

29 See also RFE/RL, CAR, Vol. 5, No. 7, 23 February 2005.

30 Personal communication of leading opposition candidate, 3 March 2005.

31 RFE/RL, CAR, Vol. 5, No. 7, 23 February 2005.

32 Themes included: 'The peace-building process in Tajikistan: problems and ways to resolve them' (2001); 'The cooperation of local self government, local authorities, NGOs, the mass media, political parties and private businesses in the development of democracy and the free market in Tajikistan' (2002); 'The broadening of pluralism in Tajikistan: political parties, elections and the national parliament' (2003). See

UNTOP/NAPST 2001a, 2002a, 2003. In 2003 there were eleven meetings and 1,350 participants (UNTOP 2003: 58).

33 The meetings involved a local dish of pillau alongside the discussions.

34 Interview, political party leader, Dushanbe, August 2005.

35 Eurasianet, Interview with Said Abdullo Nuri, Voice of the Islamic Republic of Iran, Mashhad, in Persian 0100 gmt, 7 April 2000, accessed: 10 February 2005.

36 Ibid.

37 IWPR, RCA, No. 437, 24 February 2006.

38 Ibid.

39 Interview, Dilovar Ishonov, CPT, Gharm raiyon, 9 August 2005.

40 Accounts of OSCE, UNTOP and party representatives, June 2005.

41 RFE/RL, CAR, 9 June 2000; APB #930, 30 January 2002, #931, 31 January 2002, #960, 15 March 2002.

42 APB #1131, 20 November 2002.

43 APB #1207, 12 March 2003.

44 Literal translation. Figurative sense: 'it's as if everyone carries on regardless'.

45 Nasimjon Shukurov (candidate to local assembly) and Nizomiddin Begmatov (candidate to the national parliament) were jailed for terms of eighteen and twelve months by a court in Sughd on 22 June 2005.

46 Interview, Mukhibullo Zubaidulloev, UK Embassy, Dushanbe, 6 August 2005. The Coalition for Free and Fair Elections included the SDPT, DPT and IRPT. It was set up in May 2004 as a tactical alliance. The SDPT initially included Sulton Quvatov and five other Tarraqiyot members on their list of candidates in December 2004 before they were forced to withdraw his name by the security ministry because he was suspected of committing the crime of 'insulting the honour and dignity of the President', see IWPR, RCA, No. 342, 21 February 2005.

47 Unnamed senior government official quoted in, IWPR, RCA, No. 333, 10 December 2004.

48 Personal observation, 20 February 2005.

49 Some of these are direct. For example, the NDI trip to Poland, according to ex-head of the SPT Mirhusseino Narziev, served as the catalyst for the formation with other parties of the Coalition for Free and Fair Elections to fight the 2005 parliamentary ballot (Narziev 2005: 7).

6 Security and sovereignty

1 APB #625, 7 November 2000.

2 APB #833, 10 September 2001.

3 APB #545, 14 July 2000.

4 Ibid.

5 APB #780, 22 June 2001.

6 APB, #776, 18 June 2001.

7 Personal communication, former hostage, Khujand, July 2004.

8 APB #780, 22 June 2001, #788, 6 July 2001, #790, 9 July 2001, #807, 1 August 2001, #821, 21 August 2001.

9 APB #821, 21 August 2001.

10 Such information is not publicly available and is difficult to obtain. The following details comes from confidential information made available by a local confidant.

11 Interview, political analyst, Dushanbe, July 2004.

12 Ibid.

13 *Asia Plus* newspaper, no. 17, 18 August 2005.

14 Rahmon's action may have been prompted by Mirzoyev's close ties with Ubaidulloyev, the mayor of Dushanbe and second most powerful figure in the Tajikistani government (Arman 2004b).

15 IWPR, RCA, No. 262, 3 February 2004.
16 Ibid.
17 The latter included a cache of 3,000 heavy weapons discovered in the basement of the DCA, and two government helicopters leased privately to contractors in Afghanistan. See IWPR, RCA, No. 306 (amended story), 11 August 2004; RFE/RL CAR, Vol. 4, No. 31, 17 August 2004.
18 RFE/RL, Newsline, 14 August 2006.
19 The presidential decree was preceded by a joint UTO–Government protocol on 17 June 1999. Eurasianet, 'Tajik president decree banning carrying of arms outside units', 18 May 2000, [Text of report by the Tajik news agency *Khovar* on 16th May].
20 APB #466, 20 March 2000.
21 APB #593, 21 September 2000.
22 APB #797, 18 July 2001.
23 Ibid.
24 'Nothing poses threat to security of Tajikistan', APB #841, 20 September 2001.
25 Tajikistan's Foreign Ministry noted that the association of Tajikistan with civil strife is 'politically incorrect'. See RFE/RL, CAR, Vol. 5, No. 17, 10 May 2005.
26 Whilst article 9 of the 1993 agreement had always envisioned a gradual handover to local control, this had never been seen as feasible given the weakness of the Tajik state. IWPR, RCA, No. 284, 15 March 2004.
27 APB #754, 17 May 2001.
28 Personal communication with French military officer, Dushanbe, July 2003.
29 A paraphrasing of the testimony in Wishnick (2004: 4).
30 Interview, Amanda Cranmer, 2nd Secretary, US Embassy, Dushanbe, 1 March 2005.
31 Ibid.
32 The latter was worth €23.5 million, five million of which was earmarked for Tajikistan, 2003–2008. BOMCA worked in legal assistance, staff development, infrastructure and social integration with the following objectives: to increase effectiveness of border management systems; to improve cross-border cooperation; to facilitate the movement of people and goods; to ensure border protection while easing border tension (UNDP 2005a).
33 Hoagland, US Ambassador to Tajikistan, noted that the US was interested in establishing air surveillance of the border and even salary support to Tajik border guards, although this would require 'anticorruption programmes'. This included an increase from US$6.87 to 9.5 million in funding from 2004 to 2005, the majority of which was for 'strengthening border posts'. Financed primarily by new US funding, UNODC added the project AD/TAJ/E24, 'Strengthening Control along the Tajik–Afghan Border' to BOMCA in April 2004 (EC 2005).
34 Comments by Pierre Cleostrate (European Commission), Stephen Lysaght (UK) and Harold Loeschner (Germany) in, EC 2005. See also, Odyssey Migration Control 2005.
35 APB #850, 3 October 2001.
36 IWPR, RCA, #271, 17 March 2004.
37 *Jumhuriyat* 53, 14 May 2005.
38 *Jumhuriyat*, 113, 5 May 2004.
39 See *Jumhuriyat* 136, 2 December 2004.
40 *Jumhuriyat* 59, 28 May 2005.
41 APB #585, 8 September 2000.
42 APB #583, 6 September 2000.
43 See *Jumhuriyat* 99, 21 August 2002.
44 One such purge of KOGG occurred in January–February 2002. APB #923, 21 January 2002; APB #948, 26 February 2002.
45 See APB #474, 3 April 2000.

46 See for example, SCO statement on first anniversary of 9/11. See APB #1083, 12 September 2002.
47 See for example, APB #850, 3 October 2001.
48 Eurasianet, 'Tajik minister tells Iranian radio Uzbek militants agreed to leave Tajikistan', Source: Voice of the Islamic Republic of Iran, Mashhad, in Persian 1600 gmt, 25 April 2000; APB #498, 6 May 2000.
49 At times the government has also sought to portray the threat as emanating from Uzbekistan. See APB #562, 8 August 2000, #1013, 4 June 2002; RFE/RL, CAR, 24 January 2004.
50 See, APB #440, 9 February 2000, #583, 6 September 2000.
51 Rahmon, interview with *Rossiyskaya Gazeta*, in APB #764, 31 May 2001.
52 See APB #431, 27 January 2000, #1079, 5 September 2002.
53 *Jumhuriyat* 20, 25 February 2000.
54 Initially cooperation took place under the auspices of the CIS' collective security treaty and later, after it was set up in 2002, independently under the Collective Security Treaty Organisation (CSTO).
55 *Jumhuriyat* 138, 7 December 2004.
56 *Jumhuriyat* 121, 2 October 2004.
57 *Jumhuriyat* 126, 3 December 2005.
58 Rahmon and Putin appear together in a photograph inside the front cover of *The Tajiks in the Mirror of History* volume one, leaving little doubt as to the sub-text of what is ostensibly a work of ancient history.
59 IWPR, RCA, No. 270, 12 March 2004.
60 For example, incursions into Khujand in November 1998 were allegedly linked to a failed drugs deal. See Akiner (2001: 72–74).
61 For example, in 2005, in Moskovskiy district, Tajik and Russian guards publicly accused each other of drugs trafficking. Interview, international official, Kulob, 2 June 2005.
62 See speech by Faizullo Abdulloev, First Deputy Director, Drug Control Agency of Tajikistan (EC 2005).
63 All copies of the state newspaper *Jumhuriyat* which I reviewed from 2002 to 2003 contained one account of the arrest or killing of border violators. See *Jumhuriyat*: 21, 18 February 2002; 56, 18 May 2002; 99, 21 August 2002; 20, 18 May 2003; 54, 17 May 2003.
64 Transcript of speech by Col-Gen. Saidamir Zuhurov, Director, Drug Control Agency of Tajikistan, in EC (2005), no pagination.
65 Ibid.
66 Interview, Suhrob Kaharov, UNDP, Dushanbe, 2 August 2005.
67 Interview, international programme officer, Dushanbe, March 2005.
68 Interview, Ismatullo Nasriddinov, Ministry of Foreign Affairs, Republic of Tajikistan, Dushanbe, 26 June 2007.
69 Even opposition party representatives were unsure of the details of what had happened and whether the government had 'sold' land to China. SDPT representative Samadova comments that people did not believe the news: 'You know that last year in the newspaper *Ruzi Nav* they printed about our parliament selling a portion of land to China. But when we were speaking about this to the common folk (*prostomu narodu*), no one believed us! Is there actually that policy?' (2005: 5).
70 UNODC cites 1.1 per cent of Central Asia aged fifteen and above as 'problem users' (2003: 168).
71 IWPR, RCA, No. 316, 28 September 2004.
72 Cited in, IWPR, RCA, No. 374, 7 May 2005.
73 Ibid.
74 Cited in, IWPR, RCA, No. 374, 7 May 2005.

75 See, IWPR, RCA, No. 324, 5 November 2004.
76 Locals report that IMU fighters camping in the Tavildara region between 1999 and 2001 were well behaved and even paid for goods, unlike some government troops stationed nearby in Gharm (Matveeva 2005: 141).

7 Development and livelihoods

1 See, for example, APB #601, 3 October 2000; Burke 2005b.
2 Sughd oblast includes the Zerafshon and Ferghana valley areas, including Tajikistan's second city of Khujand, and contains around two million people.
3 Khatlon oblast was created in 1992 when the regions of Kurghonteppa and Kulob were merged to form a giant region with just over two million people under the control of Kulobi elites.
4 The fourth is the eastern Gorno-Badakhshon Autonomous Oblast (GBAO), the largest and most sparsely populated region, populated primarily by Pamiri peoples and Kyrgyz.
5 International organisations refer to their target locations as 'communities'. Tajik people do not define the boundaries of their community unambiguously. 'Community' can denote a single neighbourhood (mahalla), the area served by a particular mosque/teahouse (choihona), or a village (*kishlak*). In Gharm which has one Jamoat and several mahalla committees, Mercy Corps created two 'communities', Gharm-1 and Gharm-2. The division created two clusters of mahallas with no basis in local practice. Local government officials had requested the two 'communities'.
6 In international discourse, 'community peacebuilding' is also denoted as 'community development', 'local self-government' and 'decentralisation'. All of these labels were used in Tajikistan in the early 2000s in terms consistent with the humanitarian principles of civil society peacebuilding (see Chapter 2). For the sake of consistency I will continue to use 'community peacebuilding' to denote the practice of civil society peacebuilding through CBOs.
7 CAIP, running from 2002–2005 was a three-year, US$27 million regional reconstruction programme which also worked in the 'conflict-prone' Ferghana valley of Kyrgyzstan and Uzbekistan.
8 Mercy Corps established community action groups (CAG) in thirty-five communities in Khatlon and Rasht regions. The CAG model was based on the community initiative group (CIG) employed by Mercy Corps under another USAID programme, the Peaceful Communities Initiative (PCI) in Sughd oblast from 2001 to 2006.
9 The Aga Khan Foundation (AKF) is the charitable movement of His Highness the Aga Khan, the leader of the Ismaili Shia Muslims. As an autonomous entity of AKF, MSDSP is the largest International NGO in Tajikistan with a staff of 450 nationwide. In 2004, MSDSP had a US$6 million budget and oversaw 800 VOs.
10 A total of 401 Jamoats, each representing approximately 10,000–15,000 citizens, constitute the foundational level of government in Tajikistan (Ilolov and Khudoiyev 2002: 608–609).
11 The Jamoat Development Committee (JDC; in 2005 renamed Jamoat Resource Centre, JRC) was launched in 2002 as a public association involving governmental and non-governmental representatives elected indirectly, by representatives of communities, to select and administer projects using revolving funds. In 2004 there were ninety JDCs (covering approximately 23 per cent of Jamoats) and it was hoped there would be 300 by 2007 (with 75 per cent coverage). Interview, Igor Bosc, Programme Manager, Communities Programme, UNDP, 13 July 2004.
12 Interview, Mia Seppo, UNDP, 13 July 2004.
13 Interview, Gary Burniske, Country Director, Mercy Corps, Dushanbe, April 2005.
14 The Final Evaluation noted that the level of awareness of the CAG – as measured by

a survey conducted in CAIP communities – was 'much lower' in Tajikistan than in Uzbekistan and Kyrgyzstan (where the programme also operated), and, in terms of 'sustainability', only about half of the CAGs had clear plans to continue their work (MCU 2005: 15–16, 26–27).

15 This type of approach is common among NGOs and sometimes even publicly acknowledged. MSDSP, which also administered the CAIP programme, prides itself on its ability to 'indigenise' the VO and argues that '[our] analysis of the institutional framework at the village level showed that there was a "vacuum"'. MSDSP argues that pre-existing institutions could be disregarded given that they 'were not particularly development oriented and were not what could be called "participatory"' (Tetlay 2001: 3).

16 Interview, Programme Officer, Mercy Corps, 31 May 2005.

17 Group interview, CAG, Shule, 27 April 2005.

18 Group interview, Women's Committee, Dombrachi, 21 April 2005.

19 Group Interview, CAG, Gharm, 26 April 2005.

20 Group interview, CAG, Bedak, 28 April 2005.

21 Ibid.

22 Group interview, CAG, Humdon, 27/04/05.

23 In Soviet times *subotnik* was mass voluntary service on Saturdays which mobilised many workers and students.

24 Group interview, CAG, Humdon, 19 April 2005.

25 Results are based on sixty respondents in eight communities across the Rasht valley and south-western areas of the country. Answers were open and have been grouped into categories by the author.

26 Interview, Kevin Grubb, Programme Manager PCI, Mercy Corps, Khujand, June 2005.

27 Group interview, CAG, Gharm, 26 April 2005.

28 Interview, Jamoat Deputy Head, Gharm, 26 April 2005.

29 Group interview, CIG, Margedar, 27 June 2005.

30 Interview, Jamoat Secretary, Dombrachi, 22 April 2005.

31 Nine of these communities were in Tajikistan. The other seven were in Uzbekistan and Tajikistan. This reflected the overall distribution of the sixty-five CAIP communities managed by Mercy Corps. I led the research team which studied the nine Tajik cases.

32 The evaluation looked at six 'perspectives' of community mobilisation: (i) Awareness by the community at large, and (ii) Level of community contribution to the projects; (iii) Level of training and human resource development; (iv) Level of activity; (v) Level of collaboration with cluster communities, and (vi) Perceptions of government officials (MCCAR 2005: 12–27).

33 All three 'external' evaluators, including myself, became Mercy Corps employees and over the course of the evaluation worked very closely with Mercy Corps staff.

34 SMART objectives are those which are Specific, Measurable, Achievable, Realistic, Timed.

35 In the evaluation we collected data in four foreign languages: Tajik, Uzbek, Russian and Kyrgyz.

36 Data were based on 331 completed questionnaires filled out by CAG, Youth and Womens' group members in Tajikistan, Uzbekistan and Kyrgyzstan. Around 60 per cent of the data are from Tajikistan (MCU 2005: 7).

37 Following my involvement in this evaluation I worked to try and develop my own methodology to M&E using the qualitative techniques of participant-observation and discourse analysis similar to what has been used throughout this research. See Heathershaw (2005c, 2005d).

38 My living arrangements in the community were somewhat unavoidable as living with

a poorer family would have bemused and offended the local leadership. My experience of the village was partly shaped by the CAG head. However, my position offered me privileged insights into how authority was exercised in the village.

39 In particular, a major project to clear out an irrigation canal had allowed villagers to grow fruit and vegetables in their gardens and land plots around the village for the first time in several years, making a substantial difference to their livelihoods. Overproduction of cotton had previously ruined the quality of the soil and demanded the redirection of irrigation water to the cotton fields.

40 Interview, programme officer, Mercy Corps, Dushanbe, 31 May 2005.

41 Personal communication, Mercy Corps staff, Asht, 22 June 2005.

42 Ibid.

43 Group interview, Mercy Corps staff, Panjakent, 28 June 2005.

44 This is not true in all cases. I have worked with russified, urbanised NGO staff who struggle to speak the vernacular and, as I was, were received as outsiders in the villages where we were working.

45 For an overview of water management in Rasht valley, see Heathershaw (2005c) and Zürcher (2004).

46 In the case of the Abdulhanon association, the WUA was built on a pre-existing informal group set up to manage the canal after its redevelopment and collect money from users whenever further maintenance was needed. The association manages irrigation water for five villages (including the villages of Kadara and Kalai Surkh) with around 400 households and 3,000 people. For each village there is a water users group, which consists of members of the VO and a *mirob* (water manager) who is responsible for basic maintenance and collecting fees from users. After around one year of the programme US$800 has been collected and invested with a local businessman. The WUA collected 0.3 *somoni* (ten US cents) per month per *sotka* (0.01 hectare) of irrigated land, as established by law, for the five months of the irrigation season, roughly April–August.

47 Interview, Hukumatsho Sharipov, MSDSP, Dushanbe, 4 August 2005.

48 Street interviews, Abdulhanon sovkhoz, August 2005.

49 Interview, Kalanak, 11 August 2005.

50 Interview, Shahrinav, 10 August 2005.

51 Ownership was actually unclear and neither party had previously paid any rent.

52 Interview, *mirob*, Kadara, 12 August 2005.

53 Interview, WUA, Shulonak, 10 August 2005.

54 Email exchanges between author, Hukumasho Sharipov (MSDSP) and Daniel Passon (GTZ), September 2005.

55 Ibid.

56 'Private' *dekon* farmers do not own their land but rather have it on a long-term lease from the state. This is complicated by unclear leasehold rights to land. Many farmers say that they discuss with the Jamoat or VO head what they should grow, which can lead to collective village decisions about which crops should be grown where. See also, Zürcher 2004: 16–25.

57 Like tenants and 'private' *dekon* farmers, the sovkhoz – although a state institution – must also pay the 'unified tax' to local government.

58 Interviews with farmers, Abdulhanon, August 2005.

Bibliography

Abbas, N. 'Dimensions and dynamics of Tajikistan's civil society discourse', paper presented at the fifth CESS Annual Conference, Indiana University, Bloomington, 14–17 October 2004.

Abdullaev, E. (2002) 'The Central Asian nexus: Islam and politics', in Rumer, B. (ed.) *Central Asia: A Gathering Storm?* New York: M.E. Sharpe: 245–298.

Abdullaev, K. (2004) 'Current local government policy situation in Tajikistan', in De Martino (ed.) *Tajikistan at a Crossroad: the Politics of Decentralization*, CIMERA: Geneva: 7–15.

Abdullaev, K. and Barnes, C. (eds) (2001) *Politics of Compromise: the Tajikistan Peace Process*, Conciliation Resources: Accord: An International Review of Peace Initiatives, Issue 10. Available online at: www.c-r.org/our-ork/accord/tajikistan/contents.php (accessed 23 October 2003).

Abdullaev, K. and Freizer, S. (2003) *What Peace Five Years After the Signing of the Tajik Peace Agreement? Strategic Conflict Assessment Tajikistan*, study commissioned by the Department of International Development (DFID) for the UK Global Conflict Prevention Pool. Brussels: published privately.

Abdullo, R. (2001) 'Implementation of the 1997 General Agreement: successes, dilemmas and challenges', in Barnes, C. and Abdullaev, K. (eds) *Politics of Compromise: the Tajikistan Peace Process*, Conciliation Resources: Accord: An International Review of Peace Initiatives, Issue 10. Available online at: www.c-r.org/our-ork/accord/tajikistan/contents.php (accessed 23 October 2003).

Abrams, P. (1998 [1977]) 'Notes on the difficulty of studying the state', *Journal of Historical Sociology* 1(1): 58–89.

Adams, L. (2008). 'Can we apply postcolonial theory to Central Eurasia?' *Central Eurasion Studies Review* 7(1): 2–7.

Adler, E. (1997) 'Imagined (security) communities: cognitive regions in international relations', *Millennium: Journal of International Studies* 26(2): 249–278.

Adler, E. and Barnett, M. (1996) 'Governing anarchy: a research agenda for the study of security communities', *Ethics and International Affairs* 10: 63–98.

Akhmedov, S. (1998) 'Tajikistan II: the regional conflict in confessional and international context', in Waller, M., Coppieters, B. and Malashenko, A. (eds) *Conflicting Loyalties and the State in Post-Soviet Russia and Eurasia*, London: Frank Cass: 171–186.

Akiner, S. (2001) 'Prospects for civil society in Tajikistan', in Sajoo, A.B. (ed.) *Civil Society in the Muslim World: Contemporary Perspectives*, London: I.B. Tauris Publishers, in association with the Institute of Ismaili Studies: 149–195.

—— (2001) *Tajikistan: Disintegration or Reconciliation?* London: RIIA.

Akiner, S. and Barnes, C. (2002) 'The Tajik Civil War: causes and dynamics', in Barnes, C. and Abdullaev, K. (eds) *Politics of Compromise: the Tajikistan Peace Process*, Conciliation Resources: Accord: An International Review of Peace Initiatives, Issue 10. Available online at: www.c-r.org/our-ork/accord/tajikistan/contents.php (accessed 23 October 2003).

Aklaev, A.R. (1999) *Democratization and Ethnic Peace*, Aldershot: Ashgate.

Alexander, J. (2000) *Political Culture in Post-Communist Russia: Formlessness and Recreation in Traumatic Transition*, London: Macmillan.

Alimi, J. (2005) Interview with the author, Kulob, 2 June.

Allison, R. (2004) 'Regionalism, regional structures and security management in Central Asia', *International Affairs* 80(3): 463–483.

Anderson, B. (1991) *Imagined Communities: Reflections on the Origins and Spread of Nationalism*, Verso: London.

Anon. (2005) Representative of Communist Party (CPT), interview with the author, Hujond, 20 June.

Arman, K. (2004a) 'Russia and Tajikistan: friends again', *Eurasia Insight*, 28 October 2004.

—— (2004b) 'Government shake up in Tajikistan courts conflict', *Eurasia Insight*, 2 November 2004.

Asadullaev, I. (2004) 'Tajikistan Parliamentary Elections, expert appraisal', in Tomas Lavrakas (ed.) *Tajikistan: A Guide to the 2005 Parliamentary Elections*, Geneva: CIMERA, December 2004: 3–46.

Asozoda, M. (2005) Interview with the author, Dushanbe, 17 August.

Atkin, M. (2001) 'Tajikistan: a president and his rivals', in Sally N. Cummings (ed.) *Power and Change in Central Asia*, London: Routledge: 97–114.

—— (1997) 'Thwarted democratization in Tajikistan', in Dawisha, K. and Parrott, B. (eds) *Conflict, Cleavage, and Change in Central Asia and the Caucasus*, Cambridge: Cambridge University Press: 277–311.

—— (1995) 'Islam as faith, politics and bogeyman', in Michael Bourdeaux (ed.) *The Politics of Religion in Russia and the New States of Eurasia*, London: Sharpe: 247–272.

—— (1989) *The Subtlest Battle: Islam in Soviet Tajikistan*, Philadelphia: Foreign Policy Research Institute.

Austin, J.L. (1970 [1956]) *Philosophical Papers*, Oxford: Clarendon Press.

—— (1962) *How to do Things with Words*, Ormson, J.O. and Shisa, M. (eds) Oxford: Clarendon Press.

Auten, B. (1996) 'Tajikistan Today', *Studies in Conflict and Terrorism* 19: 199–212.

Avezov, A. (2004) 'Economic aspects of the interrelation between centre and regions in Tajikistan', in De Martino (ed.) *Tajikistan at a Crossroad: the Politics of Decentralization*, CIMERA: Geneva: 32–45.

Babajanian, B.V. (2004) *Poverty and Social Exclusion in Tajikistan*, prepared for the World Bank, Europe and Central Asia Region. December 2004.

Ball, N. (2002) 'The reconstruction of war-torn societies and state institutions: how can external actors contribute?' in Debiel, T. with Klein, A. (eds) *Fragile Peace: State Failure, Violence and Development in Crisis Regions*, London: Zed: 35–55.

—— (1996) 'Rebuilding war-torn societies', in Crocker, C., Osler Hampson, F. and Aall, P. (eds) *Managing Global Chaos: Sources and Responses to International Conflict*, Washington, Dc: The United States Institute of Peace: 607–622.

Barber, B. (1997) 'Feeding refugees, or war? The dilemma of humanitarian aid', *Foreign Affairs* 76(4): 8–14.

Barker, R. (2001) *Legitimating Identities: the Self-presentations of Rulers and Subjects*, Cambridge: Cambridge University Press.

Baron, I.Z. (2004) *The Importance of Politics: Rethinking the Neutral/Political Divide*, Rubikon, August. Available online at: http://venus.ci.uw.edu.pl/~rubikon/forum/neutrality.htm (accessed 15 November 2005).

Bartelson, J. (2001) *The Critique of the State*, Cambridge: Cambridge University Press.

Beetham, D. (1991) *The Legitimation of Power*, London: Macmillan.

—— (1985) *Max Weber and the Theory of Modern Politics*, Cambridge: Polity, 2nd edn.

Beissinger, M.R. and Young, C. (eds) (2002) *Beyond State Crisis: Post-colonial Africa and Post-Soviet Eurasia in Comparative Perspective*, Baltimore: John Hopkins University Press.

Berdal, M. (2005) 'Beyond greed and grievance – and not too soon...', *Review of International Studies* 31: 687–698.

Berdal, M. and Malone, D.M. (eds) (2000) *Greed and Grievance: Economic Agendas in Civil Wars*, Ottawa: International Development Research Centre.

Berger, P. and Luckmann, T. (1967) *The Social Construction of Reality*, Anchor Books: New York.

Bergne, P. (2006) *The Birth of Tajikistan*, London: I.B. Tauris.

Bertram, E. (1995) 'Reinventing governments: the promises and perils of United Nations peace building', *Journal of Conflict Resolution* 39(3): 387–418.

Bichsel, C. (2005) 'In search of harmony: repairing infrastructure and social relations in the Ferghana Valle', *Central Asian Survey* 24(1): 53–66.

Bitter, J.N., Huerin, F., Seifert, A.C. and Rahmonova-Schwarz, D. (eds) (2004) *Postroennie Doveriya Mezhdu Islamistami I Sekularistami – Tadzhikski Eksperiment* [*Building Trust Between Islamists and Secularists: the Tajik Experiment*], Dushanbe: Devashtich.

Blank, S. (2005) *After Two Wars: Reflections on the American Strategic Revolution in Central Asia*, Carlise Barracks, Pennsylvania: Strategic Studies Institute, US Army War College, July.

Boulding, K. (1964) 'Toward a theory of peace', in Fisher, R. (ed.) *International Conflict and Behavioural Science*, New York: Basic Books: 70–87.

Bourdieu, P. (1977) *Outline of a Theory of Practice, translated by Richard Nice*, Cambridge: Cambridge University Press.

Boutros-Ghali, B. (1996) *An Agenda for Democratisation*, New York: UN.

—— (1992) *An Agenda for Peace*, New York: UN.

Brennikmeijer, O.A.J. (1998) 'International concern for Tajikistan', in Djalili, M.R., Grare, F. and Akiner, S. (eds) *Tajikistan: the Trials of Independence*, Richmond, England: Curzon Press: 180–215.

Brill-Olcott, M. (1996) *Central Asia's New States: Independence, Foreign Policy and Regional Security*, Washington: USIP.

Brzezinski, Z. (1997) *The Grand Chessboard: American Primacy and its Geostrategic Imperatives*, New York: Basic Books.

Burke, J. (2005a) 'Tajik officials replaced in major power struggle', *Tajik Television first channel*, Dushanbe, in Russian, 1400 gmt, 29 January 2005. Available online at: www.eurasianet.org/resource/tajikistan/hypermail/200501/0025.shtml (accessed 12 December 2005).

—— (2005b) 'Tajik president reshuffles border chief, other officials', *Tajik Television first channel*, Dushanbe, in Tajik, 1300 gmt, 10 January 2005. Available online at: www.eurasianet.org/resource/tajikistan/hypermail/200501/0012.shtml (accessed 12 December 2005).

Buzan, B. (1991) *People, States and Fear: an Agenda for International Security Studies in the Post-Cold War*, Boulder, Colorado: Lynne Rienner.

—— (1984) 'Peace, power and security: contending concepts in the study of international relations', *Journal of Peace Research* 21(2): 109–125.

Buzan, B., Wæver, O. and de Wilde, J. (1998) *Security: a New Framework for Analysis*, Boulder, Colorado: Lynne Rienner.

Buzan, B., Jones, C. and Little, R. (1993) *The Logic of Anarchy: Neorealism to Structural Realism*, New York: Columbia University Press.

Byman, D.L. (2002) *Keeping the Peace: Lasting Solutions to Ethnic Conflict*, Baltimore: Johns Hopkins University Press.

Campbell, D. (1998a) 'MetaBosnia: narratives of the Bosnian War', *Review of International Studies* 24(2): 261–281.

—— (1998b) *National Deconstruction, Violence, Identity, and Justice in Bosnia*, Minnesota: University Press.

—— (1998c) 'Why fight: humanitarianism, principles, and post-structuralism', *Millennium: Journal of International Studies* 27(3): 497–521.

—— (1993) *Politics Without Principles. Sovereignty, Ethics and the Narrative of the Gulf War*, Boulder, Colorado: Lynne Rienner.

—— (1992) *Writing security: United States Foreign Policy and the Politics of Identity*, Minneapolis: University of Minnesota Press.

Chanaa, J. (2002) *Security Sector Reform: Issues, Challenges and Prospects*. Adelphi Paper 344, Oxford: Oxford University Press for the International Institute for Strategic Studies.

Chandler, D. (2004) 'The responsibility to protect? Imposing the "liberal peace"', *International Peace-Keeping* 11(1): 59–81.

—— (1999) *Bosnia: Faking Democracy after Dayton*, London: Pluto Press.

Chatterjee, S. (2002) *Society and Politics in Tajikistan: In the Aftermath of the Civil War*, London: Greenwich Millennium Press.

—— (1995) *Regional Rivalries in Tajik Politics: the Current Scene*, Azad Institute Paper 3, Azad Institute: Calcutta.

Chvyr, L. (1993) 'Central Asia's Tajiks: self-identification and ethnic identity', in Naumkin, V. (ed.) *State, Religion and Society in Central Asia: A Post Soviet Critique*, Reading: Ithaca Press: 245–261.

Clark, I. (2005) *Legitimacy in International Society*, Oxford: Oxford University Press.

Collier, P. (2000) 'Doing well out of war: an economic perspective', in Berdal, M. and Malone, D.M. (eds) *Greed and Grievance: Economic Agendas in Civil War*, Ottawa: International Development Research Centre: 91–111.

Collier, P. and Sambanis, N. (2005) *Understanding Civil Wars: Evidence and Analysis: Europe, Central Asia, and Other Regions* v. 2.

Collier, P. *et al.* (2003) *Breaking the Conflict Trap: Civil War and Development Policy*, World Bank Policy Research Reports, Washington, DC: Oxford University Press/World Bank.

Collins, K. (2003) 'Tajikistan: bad peace agreements and prolonged civil conflict', in Sriram, C.L. and Wermester, K. (eds) *From Promise to Practice: Strengthening UN Capacities for the Prevention of Violent Conflict*, London: Lynne Rienner: 267–306.

—— (2002) 'Clans, pacts and politics in Central Asia', *Journal of Democracy* 13(3): 137–152.

—— (2001) 'Clans, pacts and politics: understanding regime transition', unpublished PhD thesis, Stanford University.

Collins, K.A. and Wohlforth, W.C. (2003) 'Central Asia: defying "Great Game" expectations', in Ellings, R.J. and Friedberg, A.L. (eds) *Strategic Asia 2003–04: Fragility and Crisis*, Seattle, Washington: National Bureau of Asian Research: 291–317.

Connolly, W. (ed.) (1984) *Legitimacy and the State*, New York: New York University Press.

Conrad, B. (1999) *Small Arms Transfers and Disarmament: a Security Leitmotif for Tajikistan in the late 1990s?* London: Conflict Studies Research Centre, K 26, September 1999.

Crocker, C., Hampson, F.O. and Aall, P. (eds) (2001) *Turbulent Peace: The Challenges of Managing International Conflict*, Washington, DC: The United States Institute of Peace.

—— (1999) *Herding Cats: Multiparty Mediation in a Complex World*, Washington, DC: United States Institute of Peace Press.

Crosston, M. (2007) *Fostering Fundamentalism: Terrorism, Democracy and American Engagement in Central Asia*, Aldershot: Ashgate.

Cummings, S.N. (ed.) (2001a) *Power and Change in Central Asia*, London: Routledge.

—— (2001b) 'Introduction: power and change in Central Asia', in Cummings, S. (ed.) *Power and Change in Central Asia*, London: Routledge.

Dadmehr, N. (2003) 'Tajikistan: Regionalism and Weakness', in Rotberg, R.I. (ed.) *State Failure and State Weakness in a Time of Terror*, Washington: Brookings Institute Press: 245–262.

David, C-P. (1999) 'Does peacebuilding build peace? Liberal (mis)steps in the peace process', *Security Dialogue* 30(1): 25–41.

Debrix, F. (1999) *Re-Envisioning Peacekeeping: The United Nations and the Mobilisation of Ideology*, Minneapolis: University of Minnesota Press.

De Martino, L. (2004) 'Tajikistan at a crossroad: contradictory forces at the heart of the Tajik political system', in De Martino, L. (ed.) *Tajikistan at a Crossroad: the Politics of Decentralization*, Geneva: CIMERA: 152–159.

Der Derian, J. (2001) *Virtuous War: Mapping the Military–Industrial–Media–Entertainment Network*, Boulder, Colorado: Perseus/Westview Press.

—— (1995) 'The value of security: Hobbes, Marx, Nietzsche, and Baudrillard', in Lipschultz, R.D. (ed.) *On Security*, New York: Columbia: 24–45.

Der Derian, J. and Shapiro, M.D. (eds) (1989) *International/Intertextual Relations: Postmodern Readings of World Politics*, Lexington, Massachusetts: Lexington Books.

Derrida, J. (1994) *Spectres or Marx: the State of the Debt, the Working of the Mourning, and the New International*, New York: Routledge.

DfID. (2007) 'DFID Programmes in Tajikistan: Current Programme Activity', document passed to the author, June.

Dinkayev, T (2005) Interview with the author, Kulob, 31 May.

Dodson, M. (2006) 'Postconflict development and peace building: recent research', *Peace and Change* 31(2): 244–252.

Doyle, M.W. and Sambanis, N. (2006) *Making War and Building Peace: United Nations Peace Operations*, Princeton, NJ: Princeton University Press.

—— (2000) 'International peacebuilding: a theoretical and quantitative analysis', *The American Political Science Review* 94(40): 779–801.

Dudoignan, S.A. (2004) 'From ambivalence to ambiguity? Some paradigms of policy-making in Tajikistan', in *Tajikistan at a Crossroad: The Politics of Decentralisation*, CIMERA. Available from www.cimera.org (accessed 2 August 2004): 119–150.

—— (1998) 'Political parties and forces in Tajikistan, 1989–1993', in M-R. Djalili, Grare,

F. and Akiner, S. (eds) *Tajikistan: the Trials of Independence*, Richmond, England: Curzon Press: 52–85.

Duffield, M. (2002) *Global Governance and the New Wars: the Merging of Development and Security*, London: Zed Books.

Earle, L. (2005) 'Community development, "tradition" and the civil society strengthening agenda in Central Asia', *Central Asian Survey* 24(3): 245–260.

Engvall, J. (2006) 'The state under siege: the drug trade and organized crime in Tajikistan', *Europe-Asia Studies* 58(6), September: 827–854.

Epkenhans, T. (2005) Interview with the author, Bishkek, Kyrgyzstan, 2 February.

European Bank for Reconstruction and Development [EBRD]. (2005) *Strategy for Tajikistan*, as approved by the board of directors in its meeting on 15 November 2005.

European Commission [EC]. (2005) EU Programme Management Office for Central Asia Border management and drug control (BOMCA/CADAP), *Response of the international community to assist the government of Tajikistan on the Tajik–Afghan border*, 15–16 February 2005, meeting minutes.

—— (2004) EU Programme Management Office for Central Asia Border management and drug control (BOMCA/CADAP), *Joint border assessment at the Tajik–Afghan border*, *August 14–26, 2004*, Bishkek, 11 October 2004, report.

Fatoev, S. (2001) *Tadzhikistan: Desyit Lyet Nizavisimosti* [*Tajikistan: Ten Years of Independence*], London: River Editions Ltd.

Fetherstone, A.B. (2000) 'Peacekeeping, conflict resolution and peacebuilding: a reconsideration of theoretical frameworks', *International Peacekeeping* 17(20): 190–217.

Fierke, K.M. and Jorgensen, K.E. (eds) (2001) *Constructing International Relations: The Next Generation*, New York: M.E. Sharpe.

Flick, U. (2002) *An Introduction to Qualitative Research*, London: Sage.

Foucault, M. (2000) 'The subject and power', in Nash, K. (ed.) *Readings in Contemporary Political Sociology*, Blackwell: Oxford: 8–26.

—— (1991) *The Foucault Effect: Studies in Governmentality*, Burchell, G., Gordon, C. and Miller, P. (eds) Chicago: University of Chicago Press: 97–104.

—— (1988) *Power/Knowledge: Selected Interviews and Other Writings, 1972–1977*, Brighton: Harvester Press.

—— (1974 [1969]) *The Archaeology of Knowledge*, London: Tavistock.

Freizer, S. (2004) 'Tajikistan local self-governance: a potential bridge between government and civil society?' in De Martino (ed.) *Tajikistan at a Crossroad: the Politics of Decentralization*, Geneva: CIMERA: 16–24.

Fukuyama, F. (2004) *State-Building: Governance and World Order in the 21st Century*, Ithaca, NY: Cornell University Press.

—— (1992) *The End of History and the Last Man*, New York: Free Press.

Gaffurov, A. (2005) Interview with the author, Dushanbe, 5 August.

Galtung, J. (1990) 'Cultural Violence', *Journal of Peace Research* 27(3): 291–305.

—— (1975) 'Three approaches to peace: peacekeeping, peace-making and peace-building', in *Peace, War and Defence – Essays in Peace Research* 2, Copenhagen: Christian Ejlers: 282–304.

—— (1969) 'Violence, peace and peace research', *Journal of Peace Research* 6(3): 67–191.

Gawerc, M.I. (2006) 'Peace-building: theoretical and concrete perspectives', *Peace and Change* 31(4): 435–478.

Gebauer, G. and Wulf, C. (1995) *Mimesis: Culture, Art, Society*, Berkeley, California: University of California Press.

Geiss, P.G. (2003) *Pre-Tsarist and Tsarist Central Asia: Communal Commitment and Political Order in Change*, Routledge: London.

George, J. (1994) *Discourses of Global Politics: a Critical (Re)introduction to International Relations*, Boulder, Colorado: Lynne Rienner.

Ghafforzoda, H. (2005) Interview with the author, Garm, Tajikistan, 11 August.

Ghani, A., Lockhart, C. and Carnahan, M. (2005) *Closing the Sovereignty Gap: An Approach to State-Building*, Overseas Development Institute, Working Paper 253, London, September.

Ghani, R. (2001) 'Presidential elections – How country's fortune was decided', *Asia-Plus Blitz* 210(872), 2 November.

Giffen, J. and Earle, L. (2005) *The Development of Civil Society in Central Asia*, London: INTRAC.

Gill, S. (1995) 'Globalization, market civilization and disciplinary neo-liberalism', *Millennium* 24(3): 399–423.

Giragosian, R. (2006) 'The strategic Central Asian arena', *China and Eurasia Forum Quarterly* 4(1): 133–153.

Gomart, E. (2003) 'Between civil war and land reform: among the poorest of the poor in Tajikistan', in Dudwick, N., Gomart, E. and Marc, A. (eds) *When Things Fall Apart: Qualitative Studies of Poverty in the Former Soviet Union*, Washington, DC: World Bank.

Goodhand, J. (2000) 'Research in conflict zones: ethics and accountability', *Forced Migration Review* No. 8, August 2000.

Goryayev, V. (2001) 'Architecture of international involvement in the Tajik peace process', in Abdullaev, K. and Barnes, C. (eds) *Politics of Compromise: the Tajikistan Peace Process*, Conciliation Resources: Accord: An International Review of Peace Initiatives, Issue 10. Available online at: www.c-r.org/our-ork/accord/tajikistan/contents.php (accessed 23 October 2003).

Greenfield, L. and Martin, M. (1998) *Center: Ideas and Institutions*, Chicago: University of Chicago Press.

Gretsky, S. (1994) 'Profile: Qazi Akbar Turajonzoda', *Central Asian Monitor* (1): 16–24.

Gulomov, R. (2004) 'Another fall from grace', 16 August. Available online at: www.tol.cz (accessed 1 September 2004).

Haarr, R. (2005) 'Violence and exploitation of children in Tajikistan', *Central Asian Survey* 24(2): 131–149.

Hakimov, S. (2005) Interview with the author, Dushanbe, 4 August.

Hall, M. (2002) 'Tajikistan: the mirage of stability', *Perspectives* 13(2), November–December.

Hammer, M. (1998) 'Perestroika as seen by some Tajik historians', in M.R. Djalili, Grare, F. and Akiner, S. (eds) *Tajikistan: the Trials of Independence*, Richmond, England: Curzon Press: 45–51.

Hansen, F.S. [F.S. Hansen]. (2005) 'A grand strategy for Central Asia', *Problems of Post-Communism* 52(2): 45–54.

Hansen, L. [Hansen]. (2006) *Security as Practice: Discourse Analysis and the Bosnian War*, London: Routledge.

Harris, C. (2006) *Muslim Youth: Tensions in Transition*, Oxford: Westview Press.

—— (2004) *Control and Subversion: Gender Relations in Tajikistan*, London: Pluto Press.

—— (1998) 'Coping with daily life in post-Soviet Tajikistan: the Gharmi villages of Khatlon province', *Central Asian Survey* 17(4): 655–671.

Hay, E.R. (2001) 'Methodology of the inter-Tajik negotiation process', in Abdullaev, K. and Barnes, C. (eds) *Politics of Compromise: the Tajikistan Peace Process*, Conciliation Resources: Accord: An International Review of Peace Initiatives, Issue 10. Available online at: www.c-r.org/our-ork/accord/tajikistan/contents.php (accessed 23 October 2003).

Heathershaw, J. (2008a) 'Unpacking the liberal peace: the merging and dividing of peace-building discourse', *Millennium: Journal of International Studies* 36(3): 597–622.

—— (2008b) 'Seeing like the international community: how peacebuilding failed (and survived) in Tajikistan', *Journal of Intervention and Statebuilding* 2(3), forthcoming.

—— (2007a) 'Peacebuilding as practice: discourses from post-conflict Tajikistan', *International Peacekeeping* 14(2): 219–236.

—— (2007b) 'New Great Game or same old ideas? Neo-Sovietism and the international politics of imagining "Central Asia"', in Dusseault, D. (ed.) *The CIS: Form or Substance?* Helsinki: Kikimora: 236–268.

—— (2005a) 'The paradox of peacebuilding: peril, promise and small arms in Tajikistan', *Central Asian Survey* 24(1): 21–38.

—— (2005b) 'The village of Kizil Ketmen on an upward trend: a case study of one CAIP community', in Appendix C, Mercy Corps Uzbekistan, *Final Evaluation of the Community Action Investment Program*. Tashkent, Uzbekistan: Mercy Corps, 29 July.

—— (2005c) *Mercy Corps' Peaceful Communities Initiative: Mini-Evaluation of Baseline*, Khujand, Tajikistan: Mercy Corps, July.

—— (2005d) *Water Management, Local Governance and Conflict*, Dushanbe, Tajikistan: GTZ, September.

Heathershaw, J. and Mullojanov, P. (2007) 'Tajikistan after peacebuilding: a study of drivers of change', unpublished report for the Department for International Development, UK.

Heathershaw, J., Juraev, E., von Tangen-Page, M. and Zimina, L. (2004) *Small Arms in Central Asia*, Eurasia Studies Series. Available online at: www.international-alert.org/pdf/pubsec/MISAC_eurasia_4.pdf (accessed: 2 February 2006).

Helsinki Watch. (1994) *Tajik Presidential Election Conducted in a Climate of Fear and Fraud*, Helsinki Watch briefing, November.

Herzog, D. (1989) *Happy Slaves: a Critique of Consent Theory*, Chicago: University of Chicago Press.

Hill, F. (2002) 'The United States and Russia in Central Asia: Uzbekistan, Tajikistan, Afghanistan, Pakistan, and Iran', *The Aspen Institute Congressional Program*, August 15.

Hillier, B. and Julienne H. (1984) *The Social Logic of Space.* Cambridge: Cambridge University Press.

Himmatzoda, M. (2003a) 'Vopros o svetskoi sushnosti gosudarstva' ['The question of the secular nature of the state'], in Seifert, A.C. and Kraikemayer, A. (eds) *O Sovmestimosti Politicheskovo Islama I Beszopasnosti v Prostrantsve OBSE*, Sharki Ozod: Dushanbe: 89–99.

—— (2003b) 'Faktori sposobstvuyushei predotrvrasheniyu vneshnovo vliyaniya religios-novo ektremizma' ['Factors enabling the prevention of the external influences of religious extremism'], in Seifert, A.C. and Kraikemayer, A. (eds) *O Sovmestimosti Politicheskovo Islama I Beszopasnosti v Prostrantsve OBSE* [*On the Compatibility of Political Islam and Security in the Space of the OSCE*], Sharki Ozod: Dushanbe: 201–210.

Hiro, D. (1994) *Between Marx and Mohammed*, London: Harper Collins.

Hoffman, S. (1995) 'The crisis of liberal internationalism', *Foreign Policy* 98, Spring: 159–177.

Hofmann, E. and Buckley, C. (2007) *The Value of Remittances: Effects of Labor Migration on Families in Tajikistan*, draft paper presented to ASN convention, New York, 12–14 April.

Horisova, M. (2005) Interview with the author, Khujand, 24 June.

Horsman, S. (2005) 'Themes in official discourses on terrorism in Central Asia', *Third World Quarterly* 26(1): 199–213.

—— (1999) 'Uzbekistan's involvement in the Tajik civil war 1992–97: domestic considerations', *Central Asian Survey* 18(1): 37–48.

Hughes, J. and Sasse, G. (eds) (2001) *Ethnicity and Territory in the Former Soviet Union: Regions in Conflict*, London: Frank Cass.

Human Rights Watch. (2004) *Human Rights Overview*. Tajikistan. Available online at: www.hrw.org/english/docs/2003/12/31/Tajiki7011.htm (accessed 10 February 2004).

Humphrey, C. (2002) *The Unmaking of Soviet Life: Everyday Economies After Socialism*, Ithaca: Cornell University Press.

—— (1998) *Marx went Away – But Karl Stayed Behind*, Ann Arbor: The University of Michigan Press.

Humphrey, C. and Mandel, R. (2002) *Markets and Moralities: Ethnographies of Postsocialism*, Oxford: Berg.

Huntington, S.P. (1991) *The Third Wave: Democratization in the Late Twentieth Century*, Norman: University of Oklahoma Press.

—— (1968) *Political Order in Changing Societies*, New Haven: Yale University Press.

Iji, T. (2005) 'Cooperation, coordination, complementarity in international peacemaking: the Tajikistan experience', *International Peacekeeping* 12(3), Summer.

Ilolov, M. and Khudoiyev, M. (2002) 'Chapter 11: local government in Tajikistan', in *Developing New Rules in the Old Environment*, Budapest: Local Government and Public Reform Initiative, Open Society Institute, December 2002. Available online at: http://lgi.osi.hu/publications/2001/84/Ch11-Tadjikistan.pdf (accessed 11 October 2005).

International Bank for Reconstruction and Development [World Bank]. (1992) *Statistical Handbook: States of the Former USSR*, Washington, DC: World Bank.

International Commission on Intervention and State Sovereignty [ICISS]. (2001) *The Responsibility to Protect, the report of the International Commission on Intervention and State Sovereignty*, Ottawa, Canada: International Development Research Centre.

International Crisis Group [ICG]. (2005) *The Curse of Cotton: Central Asia's Destructive Monoculture*, Asia Report 93, Osh/Brussels, 28 February.

—— (2004) *Tajikistan's Politics: Confrontation or Consolidation?*, Osh/Brussels, 19 May.

—— (2003) *Tajikistan: A Roadmap for Development*, Osh/Brussels, 24 April.

—— (2001a) *Tajikistan: An Uncertain Peace*, Osh/Brussels, 24 December.

—— (2001b) *Central Asia: Drugs and Conflict*, Asia Report 25, Osh/Brussels, 26 November.

Isamova, L. (2001) 'Armed groups neutralised, but questions remained', *Asia-Plus Blitz* 132 (794), 13 July.

Jabri, V. (1996) *Discourses on Violence: Conflict Analysis*, New York: Manchester University Press.

Jawad, N. and Tadjbaksh, S. (1995) *Tajikistan: A Forgotten Civil War*, London: Minority Rights Group, January.

Jeong, H-W. (2005) *Peacebuilding in Postconflict Societies: Strategy and Process*, Boulder, Colorado: Lynne Rienner.

Johnson's Russia List. (2006) *Oxford Analytica and Ambassador's Response* [re: Tajikistan], 17 March. Available online at: www.cdi.org/russia/johnson/2006–67–18.cfm (accessed 18 July 2006).

Jones-Luong, P. (ed.) (2004) *The Transformation of Central Asia: States and Societies from Soviet Rule to Independence*, London: Cornell University Press.

—— (2002) *Institutional Change and Political Continuity in Post-Soviet Central Asia: Power, Perceptions, and Pacts*, Cambridge: Cambridge University Press.

Jonson, L. (2006) *Tajikistan in the New Central Asia: Geopolitics, Great Power Rivalry and Radical Islam*, London: I.B.Tauris.

Junne, G. and Verkoren, W. (eds) (2005). *Post-Conflict Development: Meeting New Challenges*, Boulder, Colorado: Lynne Rienner Publishers.

Jutila, M., Pehlonen, S. and Vayrynen, T. (2008) 'Resuscitating a discipline: an agenda for critical peace research', *Millennium: Journal of International Studies* 36(3): 623–640.

Kabiri, M. (2003a) 'PIVT i Hizb-ut-Tahrir: sovmestimost I razlichiya' ['IRPT and Hizb-ut-Tahrir: compatibility and difference'], in Seifert, A.C. and Kraikemayer, A. (eds) *O Sovmestimosti Politicheskovo Islama I Beszopasnosti v Prostrantsve OBSE*, Dushanbe: Sharki Ozod: 211–223.

—— (2003b) 'Vozhmozhnosti I predeli integratsiya Islamskikh organizatsiya v evro-aziatskoye prostranstvo' ['Possibilities and limits for the integration of Islamic organizations in the Eurasian space'], in Seifert, A.C. and Kraikemayer, A. (eds) *O Sovmestimosti Politicheskovo Islama I Beszopasnosti v Prostrantsve OBSE*, Dushanbe: Sharki Ozod: 257–275.

Kaiser, M. (2003) 'Forms of transsociation as counter-processes to nation building in Central Asia', *Central Asia Survey* 22(2/3): 315–331.

Kalyvas, S. (2006) *The Logic of Violence in Civil Wars*, Cambridge: Cambridge University Press.

—— (2001) 'Old and new civil wars: a valid distinction?', *World Politics* 54(1): 99–118.

Kamollidinov, P. (2005) Interview with the author, Dushanbe, 17 August.

Kandiyoti, D. (2002) 'How far do analyses of postsocialism travel? The case of Central Asia', in Hann, C. (ed.) *Postsocialism: Ideals, Ideologies and Practices in Eurasia*, Routledge: London: 238–257.

Kangas, R. (1995) 'State building and civil society in Central Asia', in Tismaneanu, V. (ed.) *Political Culture and Civil Society in Russia and the New States of Eurasia*, New York: M.E. Sharpe: 271–291.

Karagiannis, E. (2006) 'The challenge of radical Islam in Tajikistan: Hizb ut-Tahrir al-Islami', *Nationalities Paper* 34(1): 1–20.

Karagulova, A. and Megoran, N. (2006) 'Gothic Kyrgyzstan and the "war on terror": discourses of danger and the collapse of the Akaev regime', paper presented at Central Eurasian Studies Society annual conference, University of Michigan, Ann Arbor, 30 September.

Katzman, K. (2002) 'Tajikistan', in Arminini, A.J. (ed.) *Politics and Economics of Central Asia*, New York: Novinka.

Keen, D. (2000a) 'War and peace: what's the difference?' *International Peacekeeping* 7(4): 1–22.

—— (2000b) 'Incentives and disincentives for violence', in Berdal, M. and Malone, D. (eds) *Greed and Grievance: Economic Agendas in Civil Wars*, Boulder, Colorado: Lynne Rienner Publishers: 19–41.

—— (1998) *The Economic Functions of Violence in Civil Wars*, Adelphi Paper 320, London: Oxford University Press.

Khodjibaeva, M. (1999) 'Television and the Tajik conflict', *Central Asia Monitor* No. 1: 11–16.

Kimmage, D. (2005) 'The Failure of managed democracy in Kyrgyzstan', *RFE/RL Central Asia Report* 5(13).

Kosachi, G.(1995) 'Tajikistan: political parties in an inchoate national space', in Ro'i, Y. (ed.) *Muslim Eurasia: Conflicting Legacies*, Ilford: Frank Cass: 123–142.

Krasner, S. (1992) 'Realism, imperialism and democracy', *Political Theory* 20(1): 38–52.

Krause, K. and Williams, M.C. (eds) (1997) *Critical Security Studies: Concepts and Cases*, London: Routledge.

Kurbonkhojayev, Y. (2005) Interview with the author, Hujond, 22 June.

Lavrakas, T.A. ed. (2004) *Tajikistan: A Guide to the 2005 Parliamentary Elections*, Geneva: CIMERA, December 2004.

Lederach, J.P. (2005) *The Moral Imagination: The Art and Soul of Building Peace*, New York: Oxford University Press.

—— (1997) *Building Peace: Sustainable Reconciliation in Divided Societies*, Washington, DC: United States Institute of Peace Press.

Lezhnev, S. (2005) *Crafting Peace: Strategies to Deal with Warlords in Collapsing States*, Lanham, MD: Lexington Books.

Linz, J., Diamond, L. and Lipsett, S.M. (eds) (1988) *Democracy in Developing Countries: Asia*, London: Lynne Rienner.

Lipschultz, R.D. (1995) 'Negotiating the boundaries of difference and security at millennium's end', in Lipschultz, R.D (ed.) *On Security*, New York: Columbia: 212–228.

Lipset, S.M. (1963) *Political Man: The Social Bases of Politics*, New York: Doubleday.

Liu, M.Y. (2005) 'Hierarchies of place, hierarchies of empowerment: geographies of talk about postsocialist change in Uzbekistan', *Nationalities Papers* 33(3) September: 423–438.

—— (2003) 'Detours from Utopia on the Silk Road: ethical dilemmas of neoliberal triumphalism', *Central Eurasian Studies Review* 2(2): 2–10.

—— (2002) 'Recognising the Khan: Authority, Space and Political Imagination Among Uzbek Men in Post-Soviet Osh, Kyrgyzstan', unpublished PhD dissertation, University of Michigan.

Lovelace, D. (2004) 'Foreword', in Wishnick, E. (ed.) *Strategic Consequences of the Iraq War: US Security Interests in Central Asia Reassessed*, US Army War College: SSI, p. iii.

Lukes, S. (2nd edn 2005) *Power: A Radical View*, Basingstoke: Palgrave.

Lund, M. (2003) *What Kind of Peace is Being Built? Taking Stock of Post-Conflict Peace-building and Charting Future Directions*, a paper for the International Development Research Centre, Ottawa, Canada, January.

Lynch, D. (2004) *Engaging Eurasia's Separatist States: Unresolved Conflicts and* de facto *States*, Washington, DC: United States Institute of Peace Press.

—— (2001) 'The Tajik civil war and peace process', *Civil Wars* 4(4).

—— (1999) *Russian Peacekeeping Strategies in the CIS: the cases of Moldova, Georgia and Tajikistan*, London: RIIA.

MacGinty, R. (2006) *No War, No Peace*, Basingstoke: Palgrave-Macmillan.

McDermott, R.N. (2002) 'Border security in Tajikistan: countering the narcotics trade?' London: Conflict Studies Research Centre, paper K36, October.

MacFarlane, N. (2004) 'The United States and regionalism in Central Asia', *International Affairs* 80(3): 447–461.

MacFarlane, N. and Torjesen, S. (2005) 'Distortions in the discourse of danger: The case of small arms proliferation in Kyrgyzstan', *Central Asian Survey* 24(1): 21–38.

MacKinlay, J. and Cross, P. (eds) (2003) *Regional Peacekeepers: the Paradox of Russian Peacekeeping*, Tokyo: United Nations University Press.

McMann, K. (2004) 'The civic realm in Kyrgyzstan: Soviet economic legacies and activists' expectations', in Jones-Luong, P. (ed.) *The Transformation of Central Asia: States and Societies from Soviet Rule to Independence*, London: Cornell University Press.

Makhamov, M. (1994) 'Islam and the political development of Tajikistan after 1985', in Malik, H (ed.) *Central Asia: Its Strategic Importance and Future Prospects*, New York: St. Martin Press: 195–210.

Malekzade, J. (2005) Interview with the author, 10 May.

Mann, M. (1988) *States, War, and Capitalism*, Oxford: Basil Blackwell.

Marat, E. (2006) 'Impact of drug trade and organised crime on state functioning in Kyrgyzstan and Tajikistan', *China and Eurasia Forum Quarterly* 4(1): 93–111.

March, A. (2003) 'State ideology and the legitimation of authoritarianism: the case of post-Soviet Uzbekistan', *Journal of Political Ideologies* 8(2).

Markowitz, L.P. (2005) 'Collapsed and Prebendal states in post-Soviet Eurasia: cross-regional determinants of state formation in Tajikistan and Uzbekistan', unpublished PhD dissertation, University of Wisconsin-Madison.

Martin, S. (2000) 'What are 'free and fair elections?'' RFE/RL, 28 February. Available online at: www.eurasianet.org/resource/tajikistan/hypermail/200002/0030.html (accessed 12 December 2004).

Matveeva, A. (2007) 'Tajikistan: peace secured, but is this the state of our dreams?' in Lund, M. and Wolpe, H. (eds) *Catalytic Engagement: Leadership Networks for Transforming Intra-state Conflicts*, A project of Woodrow Wilson International Center 'Preventing and Rebuilding Failed States'.

—— (2006) *Central Asia: A Strategic Framework for Peacebuilding*, London: International Alert.

—— (2005) 'Tajikistan: evolution of the security sector and the war on terror', in Ebnöther, A., Felberbauer, E.M. and Malek, M. (eds) *Facing the Terrorist Challenge – Central Asia's Role in Regional and International Co-operation*, Vienna and Geneva. Available online at: www.dcaf.ch/publications/epublications/CentralAsia_terror/Ch.5.pdf (accessed: 17 May 2006).

—— (1999) 'Democratization, legitimacy and political change in Central Asia', *International Affairs* 75, January: 23–44.

Megoran, N. (2005a) 'Preventing conflict by building civil society: post-development theory and a Central Asian – UK policy success story', *Central Asian Survey* 24(1): 83–96.

—— (2005b) 'The critical geopolitics of danger in Uzbekistan and Kyrgyzstan', Environment and Planning D: *Society and Space* 23(4): 555–580.

—— (2004) 'The critical geopolitics of the Uzbekistan–Kyrgyzstan Ferghana Valley boundary dispute, 1999–2000', *Political Geography* 23: 731–764.

—— (2002) 'The Borders of Eternal Friendship: The Politics and Pain of Nationalism and Identity Along the Uzbekistan–Kyrgyzstan Ferghana Valley Boundary, 1999–2000', unpublished PhD dissertation, Sidney Sussex College, Cambridge, September.

Mercy Corps Central Asia Region [MCCAR]. (2005) Final Report for the Community Action Investment Program (CAIP), August.

Mercy Corps Tajikistan [MCT]. (2005) 'Troubled waters contained in Jailghan', CAIP Success Story, received in Tajikistan, April.

Mercy Corps Uzbekistan [MCU]. (2005) Final Evaluation of the Community Action Investment Program (CAIP), Tashkent, 29 July.

Miall, H., Ramsbotham, O. and Woodhouse, T. (eds) (1999) *Contemporary Conflict Resolution: The Prevention, Management and Transformation of Deadly Conflicts*, Cambridge: Polity Press.

Migdal, J.S. (2001) *State in Society: Studying how States and Societies Transform and Constitute one Another*, Cambridge: Cambridge University Press.

—— (1994) 'The state in society: an approach to struggles for domination', in Migdal, J.S., Kohli, A. and Shue, V. (eds) *State Power and Social Forces: Domination and Transformation in the Third World*, Cambridge: Cambridge University Press: 7–34.

Mihalka, M. (2006) 'Counterinsurgency, counterterrorism, state-building and security cooperation in Central Asia', *China and Eurasia Forum Quarterly* 4(1): 131–151.

Milliken, J. (1999) 'The study of discourse in international relations: a critique of research and methods', *European Journal of International Relations* 5(2): 225–254.

Mitchell, T. (1990) 'Everyday metaphors of power', *Theory and Society* 19: 545–577.

Mountain Societies Development Support Programme (MSDSP). (2001) Project of the Aga Khan Foundation, VO Charter 2001, Khorog, February.

Mullojanov, P. (2001a) 'Civil society and peacebuilding', in Abdullaev, K. and Barnes, C. (eds) *Politics of Compromise: the Tajikistan Peace Process*, Conciliation Resources: Accord: An International Review of Peace Initiatives, Issue 10. Available online at: www.c-r.org/our-ork/accord/tajikistan/contents.php (accessed 23 October 2003).

—— (2001b) 'The Islamic clergy in Tajikistan since the end of the Soviet period', in Dudoignon, S.A. and Hisao, K. (eds) *Islam in Politics in Russia and Central Asia: Early Eighteenth to Late Twentieth Centuries*, London: Kegan Paul: 221–250.

Myer, W. (2002) *Islam and Colonialism: Western Perspectives on Soviet Asia*, London: Routledge.

Myers, T. (2003) *Slavoj Žižek*, London: Routledge.

Nabiev, M. (2005) Interview with the author, Kulob, 1 June.

Nakaya, S. (2008) 'Post-war exclusion and violence: impact of aid on transition from war economies to oligarchy', paper presented at the 2008 Annual Convention of the International Studies Association, San Francisco, 28 March.

Naumkin, V.V. (2005) *Radical Islam in Central Asia: Between Pen and Rifle*, Lanham, MD: Rowman and Littlefield: 234–235.

Narziev, M. (2005) Interview with the author, Dushanbe, 5 August.

Nazriev, D. and Sattorov, I. (2005) *Respublika Tadzhikistan: Istoriya Nezavisimosti. Khronika sobytii* [*The Republic of Tajikistan: History of Independence, Chronicle of Events*] vol. 2: *1992*, Dushanbe.

Nematova, G. (2005) Interview with the author, Kulob, 31 May.

Niyazi, A. (1999) 'Islam and Tajikistan's human and ecological crisis', in Ruffin, H. and Waugh, D. (eds) *Civil Society in Central Asia*, Seattle: University of Washington Press: 183–214.

—— (1998) 'Tajikistan I: the regional dimension of the conflict', in Walker, M., Coppieters, B. and Malashenko, A. (eds) *Conflicting Loyalties and the State in Post-Soviet Russia and Eurasia*, London: Frank Cass: 144–170.

—— (1993) 'The year of tumult: Tajikistan after February 1990', in Naumkin, V. (ed.) *State, Religion and Society in Central Asia: A Post Soviet Critique*, Reading: Ithaca Press: 262–289.

Nordstrom, C. (2004) *Shadows of War: Violence, Power, and International Profiteering in the Twenty-first Century*, Berkeley, University of California Press.

Nourzhanov, K. (2005) 'Saviours of the nation or robber barons? Warlord politics in Tajikistan', *Central Asian Survey* 24(2): 109–130.

—— (2001) 'The politics of history in Tajikistan: reinventing the Samanids', V(1) Winter 2001. Available online at: www.asiaquarterly.com/content/view/92/40/ (accessed 16 April 2006).

O'Donnell, G. and Schmitter, P.C. (1986) *Transitions from Authoritarian Rule: Tentative Conclusions about Uncertain Democracies*, Baltimore: Johns Hopkins University Press.

Odyssey Migration Control. (2005) *Assessment of Border Management in Tajikistan*. A technical assessment report prepared for the International Organisation for Migration [IOM], 31 July 2002: acquired August 2005.

Olcott, M.B. (2005) *Central Asia's Second Chance*, Washington, DC: Carnegie Endowment.

Olimov, K. (2003) 'Uroki mezhtadzhikskovo konflikta I perspektivi dlya mirnovo processa v Tadzhikistane' ['Lessons of the inter-Tajik conflict and perspectives for the peace process in Tajikistan'], in Seifert, A.C. and Kraikemayer, A. (eds) *O Sovmestimosti Politicheskovo Islama I Beszopasnosti v Prostrantsve OBSE*, Sharki Ozod: Dushanbe: 118–128.

Olimova, S. (2004) 'Opposition in Tajikistan: pro et contra', in Ro'i, Y. (ed.) *Democracy and Pluralism in Muslim Eurasia*, London: Frank Cass.

—— (2003a) 'Ob obshestvennom vospriyatii umerennovo i radikalnovo Islama' ['On the societal perceptions of moderate and racial Islam'], in Seifert, A.C. and Kraikemayer, A. (eds) *O Sovmestimosti Politicheskovo Islama I Beszopasnosti v Prostrantsve OBSE*, Sharki Ozod: Dushanbe: 55–67.

—— (2003b) 'Politicheski Islam v Obshestve i gosudarstve: dialog ili konfrontatsiya?' ['Political Islam in society and state: dialogue or confrontation'], in Seifert, A.C. and Kraikemayer, A. (eds) *O Sovmestimosti Politicheskovo Islama I Beszopasnosti v Prostrantsve OBSE*, Sharki Ozod: Dushanbe: 26–44.

Olimova, S. and Bosc, I. (2003) *Labour Migration from Tajikistan*, Dushanbe: IOM/Sharq Scientific Research Center, July.

Olimova, S. and Bowyer, A. (2002) *Political Parties in Tajikistan*, International Foundation for Electoral Systems, Washington: IFES, November.

Olimova, S. and Olimov, M. (2001) 'The Islamic Renaissance Party', in Abdullaev, K. and Barnes, C. (eds) *Politics of Compromise: the Tajikistan Peace Process*, Conciliation Resources: Accord: An International Review of Peace Initiatives, Issue 10. Available online at: www.c-r.org/our-ork/accord/tajikistan/contents.php (accessed 23 October 2003).

Ong, A. (2006) *Neoliberalism as Exception: Mutations in Citizenship and Sovereignty*, Durham, N.C.: Duke University Press.

Open Society Institute. (2001) *Tajikistan: Refugee Reintegration and Conflict Prevention*. Forced Migration Project. Available online at: www.soros.org (accessed 19 November 2001).

—— (1999) *Building Open Societies: Soros Foundation Network 1999 Report*, New York: OSI.

Orr, M. (1996) *The Russian Army and the War in Tajikistan*, London: Conflict Studies Research Centre, February.

OSCE. (2005a) 'Interim Report #1', Office for Democratic Institutions and Human Rights, Election Observation Mission to Tajikistan, Parliamentary Elections 2005, 24 January – 7 February 2005, ODIHR.GAL/10/05, 9 February 2005.

—— (2005b) *OSCE/ODIHR Election Observation Mission Tajikistan 2005: Long-Term Observor Team 5, Second Weekly Report*, 11 February 2005, received 3 March 2005.

—— (2005c) 'Interim Report 2', Office for Democratic Institutions and Human Rights, Election Observation Mission to Tajikistan, Parliamentary Elections 2005, 8–13 February 2005, ODIHR.GAL May 2005, 17 February 2005.

—— (2005d) *OSCE/ODIHR Election Observation Mission Tajikistan 2005: Long-Term Observor Team 5, Third Weekly Report*, 18 February 2005, received 3 March 2005.

—— (2005e) *Republic of Tajikistan Parliamentary Elections – First Round 27 February 2005, OSCE/ODIHR Election Observation Mission, Statement of Preliminary Findings and Conclusions*, 2 March 2005, received 3 March 2005.

—— (2005f) *OSCE/ODIHR Election Observation Mission Tajikistan 2005: Long-Term Observor Team 5, Final Report*, 2 March 2005, received 3 March 2005.

—— (2005g) *Republic of Tajikistan Parliamentary Elections, 27 February and 13 March 2005, OSCE/ODIHR Election Observation Mission Final Report*, Warsaw: 31 May 2005.

—— (2004) *Republic of Tajikistan Parliamentary Elections*, 27 February, OSCE/ODIHR Needs Assessment Mission Report 6–10 December 2004, Warsaw: 4 January 2005.

—— (2000) *The Republic of Tajikistan: Elections to the Parliament*, 27 February 2000, Warsaw: 17 May 2000.

Ó Tuathail, G. (1996) *Critical Geopolitics: the Politics of Writing Global Space*, Minneapolis: University of Minnesota Press.

Oxford Analytica [OA]: (2006) 'State weakness may mean renewed violence', 7 March. Available at: Johnson's Russia List, 'Oxford Analytica and Ambassador's Response [re: Tajikistan]'. Available online at: www.cdi.org/russia/johnson/2006–67–18.cfm (accessed 18 July 2006).

Pannier, B. (2004) 'Tajikistan: President dismisses government loyalists, opposition figures', *Eurasia Insight*, 31 January 2004.

Paris, R. (2004) *At War's End: Building Peace After Civil Conflict*, Cambridge: Cambridge University Press.

—— (2002) 'International peacebuilding and the "mission civilisatrice"', *Review of International Studies* 28(4): 637–656.

—— (2001) 'Wilson's ghost: the faulty assumptions of postconflict peacebuilding', in Crocker, C., Hampson, F.O. and Aall, P. (eds) *Turbulent Peace: The Challenges of Managing International Conflict*, Washington: USIP: 765–784.

—— (1997) 'Peacebuilding and the limits of liberal internationalism', *International Security* 22(2): 54–89.

Patomäki, H. (2001) 'The challenge of critical theories: peace research at the start of a new century', *Journal of Peace Research* 38(6): 723–737.

Plater-Zyberk, H. (2004) 'Tajikistan: waiting for a storm?' *Central Asia Series* 4(13), May, London: Conflict Studies Research Centre.

Pochoyev, J. (2005) Interview with the author, Kulob, Tajikistan, 31 May.

Porteous, O. (2003) *Land Reforms in Tajikistan: from the Capital to the Cotton Fields*, A report for Action Against Hunger, Dushanbe, September.

Pouligny, B. (2000) 'Promoting democratic institutions in post-conflict societies: giving diversity a chance', *International Peacekeeping* 7(3): 17–35.

Prazaukas, A. (1997) 'Ethno-political issues and the emergence of nation-states in Central Asia', in Zhang, Y. and Azizian, R. (eds) *Ethnic Challenges Beyond Borders: Chinese and Russian Perspectives of the Central Asian Conundrum*, Basingstoke: St. Martin's Press: 54–89.

Przeworski, A. (1991) *Democracy and the Market: Political and Economic Reforms in Eastern Europe and Latin America*, Cambridge: Cambridge University Press.

Pugh, M. (2006) 'Peace operations and the missing fortunes of war', Draft paper presented to the International Studies Association annual meeting, San Diego, 22–25 March.

—— (2004) 'Peacekeeping and critical theory', *International Peacekeeping* 11(1): 39–58.

—— (2003) 'Peacekeeping and IR theory: phantom of the opera?' *International Peacekeeping* 10(4): 104–112.

Pugh, M. and Cooper, N (with Goodhand, J.) (2004) *War Economies in a Regional Context: Challenges of Transformation*, London: Lynne Reinner Publishers.

Putnam, R. (1993) *Making Democracy Work: Civic Traditions in Modern Italy*, Princeton, NJ: Princeton University Press.

Rahmon, E. (2001) *The Tajiks in the Mirror of History, vol. 1: From the Aryans to the Samanids*, Guernsey: London River Editions.

—— (1999) 'A thousand years in one life' (*tisachi let v odnu zhizn*), *Nizavisimaya Gazetta*, 31 August.

Rahmonova, L. (2005) Interview with the author, Kulob, 2 June.

Rakowska-Harmstone, T. (1970) *Russia and Nationalism in Central Asia: the Case of Tadzhikistan*, London: Johns Hopkins.

Ramböll Management. (2006) 'SIDA Support to Local Government in Tajikistan', unpublished report to SIDA, Dushanbe, Tajikistan, October.

Rashid, A. (2002) *Jihad: The Rise of Militant Islam in Central Asia*, New Haven: Yale University Press.

—— (1994) *The Resurgence of Central Asia: Islam or Nationalism?* London: Zed.

Reeves, M. (2006) 'States of improvisation: border-making as social practice in the Ferghana Valley', paper presented to the annual meeting of the Central Eurasian Studies Society, 29 September.

—— (2005) 'Locating danger: konfliktologiia and the search for fixity in the Ferghana valley borderlands', *Central Asian Survey* 24(1): 67–81.

Reno, W. (1998) *Warlord Politics and African States*, Boulder, Colorado: Lynne Rienner Publishers.

Richards, P. (ed.) (2005) *No Peace, Now War. An Anthropology of Contemporary Armed Conflicts*, Oxford: James Curry.

Richmond, O. (2006) 'The problem of peace: understanding the "liberal peace"', *Conflict, Security and Development* 6(3): 292–314.

—— (2005) *The Transformation of Peace*, Basingstoke: Palgrave.

Richmond, O. and Franks, J. (2007) 'Liberal hubris? Virtual peace in Cambodia', *Security Dialogue* 38(1): 27–48.

Robben, A.C.G.M. and Nordstrom, C. (eds) (1995) 'Introduction; the anthropology and ethnography of violence and sociopolitical conflict', in *Fieldwork under Fire: Contemporary Studies of Violence and Survival*, Berkley: University of California Press: 1–23.

Roy, O. (2002) 'Soviet legacies and western aid imperatives in the new Central Asia', in Sajoo, A.B. (ed.) *Civil Society in the Muslim World: Contemporary Perspectives*, London: I.B. Tauris Publishers, in association with the Institute of Ismaili Studies: 123–148.

—— (2001) 'The inter-regional dynamics of war', in Abdullaev, K. and Barnes, C. (eds) *Politics of Compromise: the Tajikistan Peace Process*, Conciliation Resources Accord: An International Review of Peace Initiatives. Issue 10. Available online at www.c-r.org/our-work/accord/tajikistan/contents.php (accessed 23 October 2003).

—— (2000) *The New Central Asia: The Creation of Nations*, London: I.B. Tauris Publishers.

—— (1999) 'Kolkhoz and civil society in the independent states of Central Asia', in Ruffin, H. and Waugh, D. (eds) *Civil Society in Central Asia*, The Center for Civil Society International, in association with University of Washington Press, Seattle: 109–121.

—— (1998) 'Is the conflict in Tajikistan a model for conflicts throughout Central Asia?' in M-R. Djalili, Grare, F. and Akiner, S. (eds) *Tajikistan: The Trials of Independence*, Richmond, Surrey: Curzon: 132–150.

Rubenstein, R.A. (2005) 'Interventions and culture: an anthropological approach to peace operations', *Security Dialogue* 36(4), December.

Rubin, B.R. (1998) 'Russian hegemony and state breakdown in the periphery', in Rubin, B.R. and Snyder, J (eds) *Post-Soviet Political Order; Conflict and State Building*, New York: Routledge: 128–161.

—— (1994) 'Tajikistan: from Soviet Republic to Russian-Uzbek protectorate', in Michael M. (ed.) *Central Asia and the World: Kazakhstan, Uzbekistan, Tajikistan, Kyrgyzstan, and Turkmenistan*, New York: Council on Foreign Relations: 207–224.

—— (1993) 'The fragmentation of Tajikistan', *Survival* 35(4): 71–91.

Ruffin, H. and Waugh, D. (1999) *Civil Society in Central Asia*, The Center for Civil Society International, in association with University of Washington Press, Seattle.

Rumer, B. (2002) *Central Asia: A Gathering Storm?* New York: M.E. Sharpe.

Safarov, S. (2003) 'Vzglyad Narodnovo-Demokraticheskoi Partii Tadzhikistan na problemu svetsko-Islamskikh sotnoshenie v hode mirnovo protcessa' ['The view of the Peoples Democratic Party of Tajikistan on the problem of secular-Islamic coordination in the course of the peace process'], in Seifert, A.C. and Kraikemayer, A. (eds) *O Sovmestimosti Politicheskovo Islama I Beszopasnosti v Prostrantsve OBSE*, Dushanbe: Sharki Ozod.

Safarova, M. (2005) Interview with the author, Hujond, 21 June.

Said, E. (1994) *Culture and Imperialism*, London: Vintage.

Saifullozoda, H. (2005) Interview with the author, Dushanbe, 17 August.

Sajoo, A.B. (ed.) (2002) *Civil Society in the Muslim World: Contemporary Perspectives*, London: I.B. Tauris Publishers, in association with the Institute of Ismaili Studies.

Sakwa, R. (2004) *Putin: Russia's Choice*, London: Routledge.

—— (2nd edn 1998) *Soviet Politics in Perspective*, London: Routledge.

Salla, M.E. (1998) 'Integral Peace and Power: A Foucauldian Perspective', *Peace and Change* 23(3): 312–332.

Samadova, D. (2005) Interview with the author, Khujand, 21 June.

Sambanis, N. (2005) 'Conclusion: using case studies to refine and expand the theory of civil war', in Collier, P. and Sambanis, N., *Understanding Civil Wars: Evidence and Analysis: Europe, Central Asia, and Other Regions*, Vol. 2, Washington, DC: World Bank.

Saunders, H. (1999) *A Public Peace Process: Sustained Dialogue to Transform Racial and Ethnic Conflicts*, New York: St. Martins Press.

—— (1998) 'The multilevel peace process in Tajikistan', Unpublished paper.

Schatz, E. (2006a) 'Access by accident: legitimacy claims and democracy promotion in authoritarian Central Asia', *International Political Science Review* 27(3): 263–284.

—— (2006b) *Soft Authoritarian Rule and Agenda-Setting Power in Kazakhstan and Kyrgyzstan*, paper prepared for the Central Eurasian Studies Society meeting, Ann Arbor, Michigan, 30 September.

Schmitt. C. (1996 [1932]) *The Concept of the Political*, London: University of Chicago Press.

Schoeberlein, J. (2002) 'Regional introduction: a host of preventable conflicts', in van Tongeren, P., van de Veen, H. and Verhoeven, J. (eds) *Searching for Peace in Europe and Eurasia: an Overview of Conflict Prevention and Peacebuilding Activities*, Boulder, Colorado: Lynne Rienner Publishers: 489–515.

Schwarz, R. (2005) 'Post-conflict peace-building: the challenges of security, welfare and representation', *Security Dialogue* 36(4), December.

Scott, J.C. (1998) *Seeing Like a State: How Certain Schemes to Improve the Human Condition Have Failed*, New Haven: Yale University Press.

—— (1990) *Domination and the Arts of Resistance: Hidden Transcripts*, New Haven: Yale.

—— (1976) *The Moral Economy of the Peasant: Rebellion and Subsistence in Southeast Asia*, New Haven: Yale University Press.

Seifert, A.C. and Kraikemayer, A. (eds) (2003). *O Sovmestimosti Politicheskovo Islama I Beszopasnosti v Prostrantsve OBSE [On the Compatibility of Political Islam and Security in the Space of the OSCE]*, Dushanbe: Sharki Ozod.

Shapiro, M.J. (1997) *Violent Cartographies: Mapping Cultures of War*, London: University of Minnesota Press.

Shapiro, M.J., Bonham, G.M. and Heradstveit, D. (1988) 'A discursive practices approach to collective decision-making', *International Studies Quarterly* 32(4): 397–419.

Shirazi, H.A. (1997) 'Political forces and their structures in Tajikistan', *Central Asian Survey* 16(4): 611–622.

Shoyev, S. (2005) Interview with the author, Khujand, 31 May.

Shozimov, P. (2005) 'Tajikistan's "Year of Aryan Civilisation" and the competition of ideologies', *Central Asia – Caucasus Analyst*, 5 October. Available online at: www.cacianalyst.org/view_article.php?artcileid=3699 (accessed 10 October 2005).

SIDA. (2007) *Making Pro-Poor Growth Sustainable in Tajikistan: An Integrated Economic Analysis*, Country Economic Report, May.

Sisk, T. (2001) 'Democratisation and peacebuilding: perils and promises', in Crocker, C., Hampson, F.O. and Aall, P. (eds) *Turbulent Peace: The Challenges of Managing International Conflict*, Washington: USIP: 785–800.

Slim, R. and Saunders, H. (2001) 'The inter-Tajik dialogue: from civil war towards civil society', in Abdullaev, K. and Barnes, C. (eds) *Politics of Compromise: the Tajikistan Peace Process*, Conciliation Resources: Accord: An International Review of Peace Initiatives, Issue 10. Available online at: www.c-r.org/our-ork/accord/tajikistan/contents.php (accessed 23 October 2003).

Smith-Serrano, A. (2003) 'CIS peacekeeping in Tajikistan', in MacKinlay, J. and Cross, P. (eds) *Regional Peacekeepers; the Paradox of Russian Peacekeeping*, New York: UN University Press.

Smith, G. (1999a) *The Post-Soviet States: Mapping the Politics of Transition*, London: Arnold.

—— (1999b) 'The masks of Proteus: Russia, geopolitical shift and the new Eurasianism', *Transactions of the Institute of British Geographers* 24(4): 481–494.

Smith, G., Law, V., Wilson, A., Bohr, A. and Allworth, E. (1998) *Nation-building in the Post-Soviet Borderlands*, Cambridge: Cambridge University Press.

Smith, R.G. (1999) 'The rocky road to peace', *Central Asian Survey* 18(2): 243–247.

Solnick, S.L. (1998) *Stealing the State: Control and Collapse in Soviet Institutions*, Cambridge, Mass.: Harvard University Press.

Sotirov, V. (2004) 'Introductory word', in *Factors Menacing the Peace, record of the symposium*, record of proceeding, Dushanbe, 14 November 2003. Dushanbe: UNTOP.

Soucek, S. (2000) *A History of Inner Asia*, Cambridge: Cambridge University Press.

Starr, F. (1999) *Civil Society in Central Asia*, Seattle: University of Washington Press.

—— (1996) 'Making Eurasia stable', *Foreign Affairs* 75(1): 80–92.

Stedman, S.J. (1997) 'Spoiler problems in peace processes', *International Security*, 22(2) January.

Stedman, S.J., Rothchild, D. and Cousens, E. (eds) (2002) *Ending Civil Wars: The Implementation of Peace Agreements. A project of the International Peace Academy and the Center for International Security and Cooperation*, Boulder, Colorado: Lynne Rienner Publishers.

Steffek, J. (2004) 'Why IR needs legitimacy: a rejoinder', *European Journal of International Relations* 10(3): 485–490.

—— (2003) 'The legitimation of international governance: a discourse approach', *European Journal of International Relations* 9(2): 249–275.

Strathern, M. (2000) *Audit Cultures: Anthropological Studies in Accountability, Ethics and the Academy*, London: Routledge.

Tabyshalieva, A. (2002) 'Policy recommendations: some strategies for stability', in van Tongeren, P., van de Veen, H. and Verhoeven, J. (eds) *Searching for Peace in Europe and Eurasia: an Overview of Conflict Prevention and Peacebuilding Activities*, Boulder, Colorado: Lynne Rienner Publishers.

Tadjbakhsh, S. (1993) 'The Tajik spring of 1992', *Central Asia Monitor* 2(2), April.

Tetlay, K. (2001) MSDSP, *VO Charter 2001*, Khorog, February.

Thompson, C. and Heathershaw, J. (2005) 'Introduction: discourses of danger in Central Asia', *Central Asian Survey*, special issue, 24(1): 1–4.

Tilly, C. (1991) 'Domination, resistance, compliance … discourse', *Sociological Forum* 6(3): 593–602.

—— (1975) 'Reflections on the history of European state making', in *The Formation of National States in Western Europe*, Princeton, NJ: Princeton University Press.

Torjesen, S. and MacFarlane, S.N. (2007) 'R Before D: the case of post conflict reintegration in Tajikistan', *Journal of Conflict, Security and Development* 7(2): 311–332.

Torjesen, S., Wille, C. and MacFarlane, S.N. (2005) *Tajikistan's Road to Stability: Reduction in Small Arms Proliferation and Remaining Challenges*, Geneva: Small Arms Survey, November.

Tsing, A.L. (1993) *In the Realm of the Diamond Queen: Marginality in an Out-Of-The-Way Place*, Princeton, NJ: Princeton University Press.

Ubaidulloyev, M. (2003) 'Ukrepleniye Grazhdanskovo Obshestva v Tadzhikistane' ['The strengthening of civil society in Tajikistan'], in *The Political Discussion Club*, United Nations Tajikistan Office of Peacebuilding/National Association of Political Scientists of Tajikistan, [UNTOP/NAPST], Dushanbe.

United Nations [UN] (2004) *A More Secure World: Our Shared Responsibility*, Report of the Secretary-General's High-Level Panel on Threats, Challenges and Change, UN: New York. Available online at: www.un.org/secureworld/brochure.pdf (accessed 5 January 2005).

—— (2000) The Report of the Panel on United Nations Peace Operations ['The Brahimi Report']. Available online at: www.un.org/peace/reports/peace-operations/ (accessed 14 June 2004).

United Nations Department of Political Affairs (Electoral Assistance Division) [UNDPA]. (2004) *Electoral Needs Assessment Mission to Tajikistan, 15–25 April 2004: Summary Report*, New York, United Nations, April.

United Nations Development Program [UNDP]. (2005a) *BOMCA*. Powerpoint presentation, created: 11 March 2004, last modified 19 February 2005 (acquired 4 March 2005).

—— (2005b) *Central Asia Human Development Report 2005*. Available online at: www.cagateway.org/cahdr/downloads/Annexes.pdf (accessed 20 September 2006).

—— (2005c) Official transcript of conference, 'Response of the international community to assist the Government of Tajikistan on the Tajik–Afghan Border', 15–16 February, acquired 4 March 2005.

—— (2004) 'Summary of the Community-Linked Development Workshop', Varzob, 21–22 May 2004. Available online at: www.untj.org (accessed 25 July 2004).

—— (2003) 'Tapping the potential: improving water management in Tajikistan', National Human Development Report 2003. Available online at: www.undp.tj/publications/nhdr2003/ (accessed 23 August 2004).

United Nations General Assembly [UNGA]. (2006) 'Estimates in respect of special political missions, good offices and other political initiatives authorized by the General Assembly and/or the Security Council', Report of the Secretary-General, Doc. A/61/525/Add.3, 28 November.

—— (2003) 'Estimates in respect of special political missions, good offices and other political initiatives authorized by the General Assembly and/or the Security Council', Report of the Secretary-General, Doc. A/C.5/58/20, 1 December.

—— (2002) 'Estimates in respect of matters of which the Security Council is seized: United Nations Tajikistan Office of Peace-building', Report of the Secretary-General, Doc. A/C.5/56/25/Add.5, 22 May.

United Nations Office for the Coordination of Humanitarian Affairs (OCHA). (2001) 'United Nations Consolidated Inter-Agency Appeal for Southeastern Europe 2001', 8 November. Available online at: www.reliefweb.int/w/rwb.nsf. (accessed 3 February 2003).

—— (2001) 'United Nations Consolidated Inter-Agency Appeal for Tajikistan 2001', 2 November. Available online at: www.reliefweb.int/w/rwb.nsf. (accessed 3 February 2003).

United Nations Office for Drugs and Crime [UNODC]. (2005) 'Border Control in Tajikistan', April 2004, powerpoint presentation, created 1 December 1999, last modified 7 October 2004 (acquired 4 March 2005).

—— (2003) *The Opium Economy in Afghanistan: An International Problem*, New York: United Nations.

United Nations Security Council [UNSC]. (2000) Press Release SC/6860 4141st Meeting (Night) 12 May 2000. Available online at: www.un.org/News/Press/docs/2000/20000512.sc6860.doc.html (accessed 22 May 2004).

—— (1994) Resolution 968 on establishment of a UN Mission of Observers in Tajikistan and process of national reconciliation. Available online at: www.un.org/docs/scres/1994/scres94.htm (accessed 22 May 2004).

United Nations Tajikistan Office of Peacebuilding [UNTOP]. (2004) 'Summary of Election Assistance to Tajikistan for Parliamentary Elections 2005', Excel spreadsheet, created 23 July 2004, received 5 August 2005.

United Nations Tajikistan Office of Peacebuilding/National Association of Political Scientists of Tajikistan, [UNTOP/NAPST]. (2003) *The Political Discussion Club*.

—— (2002a) *The Political Discussion Club*, no. 1.

—— (2002b) *The Political Discussion Club*, no. 2.

—— (2002c) *The Political Discussion Club*, no. 3.

—— (2002d) *The Political Discussion Club*, no. 4.

—— (2001a) *The Political Discussion Club*, no. 1.

—— (2001b) *The Political Discussion Club*, no. 2.

United States of America, *The National Security Strategy of the United States of America.* (2002). Available online at: www.whitehouse.gov/nsc/nss.html (accessed 11 November 2005).

Urban Institute. (2003) 'Local self-government in Tajikistan viewed through the basic characteristics of the European Charter' March 2003, USAID: Tajikistan Local Government Initiative II.

Usmon, D. (2004) 'Tadzhiski Konflikt I Meri Doveriya' ['The Tajik conflict and measures of trust'] in Bitter, J.N., Guerin, F., Seifert, A.C. and Rahmonova-Schwarz, D. (eds) *Postroennie Doveriya Mezhdu Islamistami I Sekularistami – Tadzhikski Eksperiment* [Building Trust between Islamists and Secularists: the Tajik Experiment], Dushanbe: Devashtich.

—— (2003) 'Samoponimanie, zadachi i tseli Islamiskoi politiki v Tadzhikistane I Srednei Azii' ['The self-understandings, tasks and aims of Political Islam in Tajikistan and Middle Asia'], in Seifert, A.C. and Kraikemayer, A. (eds) *O Sovmestimosti Politicheskovo Islama I Beszopasnosti v Prostrantsve OBSE*, Dushanbe: Sharki Ozod: 45–54.

Usmonov, I. (2005a) interview with the author, Dushanbe, 18 August.

—— (2005b) *Treatise on the State*, Sharki Ozod: Dushanbe.

—— (2003a) 'Process nationalnovo primerenniya v Tajikistane' ['The process of national reconciliation in Tajikistan'], in *O Sovmestimosti Politicheskovo Islama I Beszopasnosti v Prostrantsve OBSE*, edited by Arne C. Seifert and Anne Kraikemaye, Dushanbe: Sharki Ozod: 100–117.

—— (2003b) 'Opasnosti dlya vnutrennei stabilnosti Tadzhikistana' ['Dangers to internatl stability in Tajikistan'], in Seifert, A.C. and Kraikemayer, A. (eds) *O Sovmestimosti Politicheskovo Islama I Beszopasnosti v Prostrantsve OBSE*, Dushanbe: Sharki Ozod: 187–200.

Valiev, R. (2005) Interview with the author, Dushanbe, 4 August.

Vasiliev, A. (ed.) (2001) *Central Asia: Political and Economic Challenges in the Post-Soviet Era*, London: Saqi.

Verdery, K. (1996) 'Nationalism, postsocialism, and space in Eastern Europe', *Social Research* 63(1): 77–96.

Walker, R.B.J. (1997) 'The subject of security', in Krause, K. and Williams, M.C. (eds) *Critical Security Studies: Concepts and Cases*, Minneapolis: University of Minnesota Press: 61–82.

—— (1995) 'International relations and the possibility of the political', in Booth, K. and Smith, S. (eds) *International Relations Theory Today*, Cambridge: Polity: 306–327.

—— (1993) *Inside/Outside: International Relations as Political Theory*, Cambridge: Cambridge University Press.

—— (1990) 'Security, sovereignty and the challenge of world politics', *Alternatives* 15: 3–27.

Wæver, O. (1995) 'Securitisation and desecuritisation', in Lipschultz, R.D. (ed.) *On Security*, New York; Columbia: 46–86.

Weber, C. (1995) *Simulating Sovereignty: Intervention, the State and Symbolic Exchange*, Cambridge: Cambridge University Press.

Weber, M. (2004) 'Politics as a vocation', in Owen, D. and Strong, T.B. (eds) *The Vocation Lectures*, Hackett: Indiana.

Weigman, G. (2004) *The Role of Local Institutions in the Statehood-Building Process in*

Tajikistan, paper given to conference Dynamics of Transformation in Central Asia – Perspectives from the Field, Rome, 5–6 November 2004.

Wennberg, F. (2001) 'The configuration of the other in Tajik political discourse: a research note', *Central Asia Monitor* 3: 5–9.

Whitbeck, J. (2005) Interview with the author, Mercy Corps, May.

Whitlock, M. (2002) *Beyond the Oxus: The Central Asian*, London: John Murray.

Williams, J. (1998) *Legitimacy in International Relations and the Rise and Fall of Yugoslavia*, Basingstoke: Macmillan.

Williams, M.C. (2003) 'Words, images, enemies: securitisation and international politics', *International Studies Quarterly* 47: 511–531.

Wishnick, E. (2004) *Strategic Consequences of the Iraq War: US Security Interests in Central Asia Reassessed*, US Army War College: SSI.

World Bank. (1992) *Statistical Handbook: States of the Former USSR*, Washington, DC: World Bank.

Žižek, S. (2000) *The Fragile Absolute*, London: Verso.

—— (1989) *The Sublime Object of Ideology*, London: Verso.

Zoirov, R. (2003) 'Strategiya pvedeniya po otnesheniyu k Hizb-ut-Tahrir' ['Strategies of conduct in relation to Hizb-ut-Tahrir'], in Seifert, A.C. and Kraikemayer, A. (eds) *O Sovmestimosti Politicheskovo Islama I Beszopasnosti v Prostrantsve OBSE*, Dushanbe: Sharki Ozod: 224–245.

Zürcher, C. (2004) *Analysis of Peace and Conflict Potential in Rasht Valley*, Shuraobad District and GBAO, Berlin: Analysis Research Consulting, March.

Index

Abdullaev, Kamoluddin 35, 184n12; and international peacebuilding discourse 45–7, 87, 146–7; scepticism of 175
Abdullo, Mullo 39, 120–1
Abdullo, Rashid ix, 32, 34, 66
Abdullojonov, Abdulmalik 32, 34
'administrative resources' 97, 171
Adolatkhoh (Party of Justice) 91, 187n10
Afghanistan 27, 178; in comparison with Tajikistan 31, 51–2, 128; as influence on opposition 27, 32, 72, 189n17; as perceived threat to Tajikistan 32–3, 130–1, 133; as priority for international community 127–8; as refuge during Tajikistan civil war 29–30, 32–3, 105, 120
Agrarian Party 90, 186n1
Aini, Saidriddin 70
Akiner, Shirin 24, 74, 183n2, 190n60
aksakal: and community development 149, 153, 155, 166; definition of 181; historical context of 68; subject role of 61
Asht district 73, 145, *146*, 155, 163–4, 183n4
Asozoda, Muso 66–7, 111, 130–1
Atkin, Muriel 26, 62, 115, 172, 183n2, 184n7–8, n10
authority: as attributed to leaders 65–9, 150, 153–4; de-centring of 111–13; definition of 60–1; and dialogue 105; during war 28–30; and elections 92–103; fungibility of 87; gender dimensions of 75–8, 84, 164; of international peacebuilders 3–5; national elite discourse of 16, 61–2, 65–9; and opposition 106–9; as property of peace 12–13, 17, 109; recentring of 19, 109–11, 114; regional elite discourse of 133–4; resignation to 81–3, 101–3; and

security 118–19, 121, 127; shifting popular perceptions of 155, 158–9; *see also* consent; legitimacy; state, authority of
avlod 74, 168–9, 181

Baudrillard, Jean 139, 141–3
Beetham, David 7–8, 170, 176, 183n4
Beshkent district 78–9, *146*; *see also* Kizil Ketmen village
Border *see* state border
Border Management in Central Asia (BOMCA) programme 130, 139–40, 189n32–3
Bourdieu, Pierre 1

Central Asia 133–5; difficulties of defining 133–4; elite discourses of 71, 111, 132–5; international perceptions of ix, 43–7, 128–30, 178; international support for civil society in 47, 50, 147, 171; international support for governments in 49–52, 127, 129–30; legitimacy in 7–8, 74; neo-Sovietism in 63–4; as region community 126, 133–4; regional organisations of 32, 134; the state in 81, 142; trafficking in 137, 190n70
Central Committee on Elections and Referenda (CCER) 94, 95, 97; District Election Committees (DEC) of 88, 97–9; as interlocutor with international community 103, 187n20
Chandler, David 55, 171, 177
civil society 47, 148
civil society peacebuilding 4, 36, 41, 43–4, 45, 47–9, 51, 146–8; criticisms of 53, 55
civil war in Tajikistan: course and events of 24–30, 97; elite historiography of 1,

border as 'frontier' of 127–30;
Tajikistan as member of 140; *see also*
international peacebuilding; UN
International Crisis Group (ICG) 2, 44, 46,
51–2, 93
International Foundational for Electoral
Systems (IFES) 92, 94, 96, 103, 187n20
International Monetary Fund (IMF) 80
international peacebuilding, discourse of
3–5, 35–6, 183n2; alternative
conceptions of 12; criticism of 4–5,
174–5; discourse of civil society
peacebuilding, liberal discourse of 3–4,
93–4, 103; discourse of statebuilding,
effects of 113–15; future of 177, 9;
general theories of 4; hidden practices of
53–5; neo-liberal practices of 55–7, 58;
political economy analyses of 4–5; post-
structuralist analyses of 4–5, 57–8;
properties and processes of 12–13; *see
also* civil society peacebuilding;
statebuilding; UNTOP
International Research and Exchanges
Board (IREX) 48, 94, 96, 187n20
inter-textuality *see* discourse analysis
Iskandarov, Mahmudruzi 38, 91, 105, 124
Islam 23–5; dialogue with secularism 103,
105; official clergy in Tajikistan 25,
122; as pacifying social force 83;
perceived association with terrorism of
43, 83, 121, 129–31, 175, 186n28; Shia
Ismaili 21; unofficial clergy in
Tajikistan 25, 183n5
Islamic Movement of Uzbekistan (IMU)
38–9, 54, 133, 191n76
Islamic Revival Party (IRP) 90–1; during
civil war 25, 28; formation of 25, 183n5;
as Islamic Movement of Rebirth 30–2;
militia of 27; as 'only legal Islamic
party' 93, 113, 130; post-conflict
discourses of 105–6; and post-conflict
elections 34, 89–90, 92, 97, 100, 186n3,
187n21, 188n46

Jamoat 68, 96, 165, 191n10
Jamoat Resource Centre (JRC) 49, 51; as
Jamoat Development Committee (JDC)
148, 191n11
Jirgital district 124, 145, *146*, 149–50
Jonson, Lena 2

Kabiri, Muhiddin 91, 106
Kabodiyon district *146*

Kazakhstan 31, 134, 137, 144
Kenjayev, Safarali 26–7, 91
Khatlon province 21, 90, 191n3; author's
fieldwork in *15*, 73, 142, 145, *146*; *see
also* Kulob, Sharituz
Khudoiberdiyev, Mahmud 33–4
Khudonazarov, Davlat 26, 184n7
Khujand (Leninabad) 22, 48, 67, 78, 107,
108, 184n4
Khujandi (Leninabadi) factions 22, 26, 68;
during civil war 22, 28–30; after civil
war 32–3, 35, 91; during Soviet era 22
khukumat 181; involvement in elections of
97–9; as permission giver 94, 96, 114,
148; raisi (heads) of 68, 90; tensions
with 75, 108
kishlak: as community 68, 74, 150, 181,
191n5
Kizil Ketmen village x, 160–1
kolkhozes and kolkhoz system 18, 21–2,
181; and civil war 24, 75; as enduring
institutions 81–2, 167
Kosimov, Suhrob 34, 120, 122
Kulob region 13, 19, 96, 184n4, 191n3
Kulobi faction 21–2; during the civil war
28–9, 32, 75, 123, 184n10; after the
civil war 53, 71, 89–90; *see also*
Danghara faction; Mirzoyev, Ghaffor;
Rahmon, Emomoli; Ubaidulloyev,
Mahmadsaid
Kyrgyzstan 31, 39, 133, 135, 141; CAIP in
191n7, 192n14, 192n36; in comparison
with Tajikistan 49, 69, 78, 101, 131,
184n7; 'Tulip Revolution' in ix, 44, 111

labour migration *see* seasonal labour
migration
legitimacy, concept of; and authority 7, 11,
109; in Central Asian studies 7; equation
with acceptance 7; and livelihoods 170;
objectivist conception of 6–7;
subjectivist conception of 7–8; and
peace 6; Weberian and Weber's
understanding of 7n4; *see also* Beetham,
David
legitimate order 1, 7–8, 174, 176–8, *178*;
authority and 109; discursive
constitution of 8, 11, 33; form of 115;
livelihoods and 164, 169, 170; and
normative concerns 178–9; processes of
85, 114, 117, 141, 169; sovereignty and
127, 135, 141; *see also* emergence;
peace

220   *Index*

eBooks – at www.eBookstore.tandf.co.uk

A library at your fingertips!

eBooks are electronic versions of printed books. You can store them on your PC/laptop or browse them online.

They have advantages for anyone needing rapid access to a wide variety of published, copyright information.

eBooks can help your research by enabling you to bookmark chapters, annotate text and use instant searches to find specific words or phrases. Several eBook files would fit on even a small laptop or PDA.

NEW: Save money by eSubscribing: cheap, online access to any eBook for as long as you need it.

Annual subscription packages

We now offer special low-cost bulk subscriptions to packages of eBooks in certain subject areas. These are available to libraries or to individuals.

For more information please contact webmaster.ebooks@tandf.co.uk

We're continually developing the eBook concept, so keep up to date by visiting the website.

www.eBookstore.tandf.co.uk